THE TEARS BEHIND THE DREAM

BAHIA K.

First paperback edition (2024)

Book design by Bahia K. / Publishing Push

ISBNs
Paperback: 978-1-80541-351-6
eBook: 978-1-80541-352-3

THE TEARS BEHIND THE DREAM

THE TRUE STORY OF A BRITISH EXPATRIATE IN LIBYA

FROM BLISS TO WAR TO RAPE TO FORGIVENESS

BAHIA K.

This book is dedicated to each and every one of my female Libyan friends whose pleas to not give up my fight for justice kept me going during the tough times, and to all the women around the world struggling to be heard.

To all those who will read this book, thank you for hearing my voice and making my journey worthwhile.

MEDITERRANEAN SEA

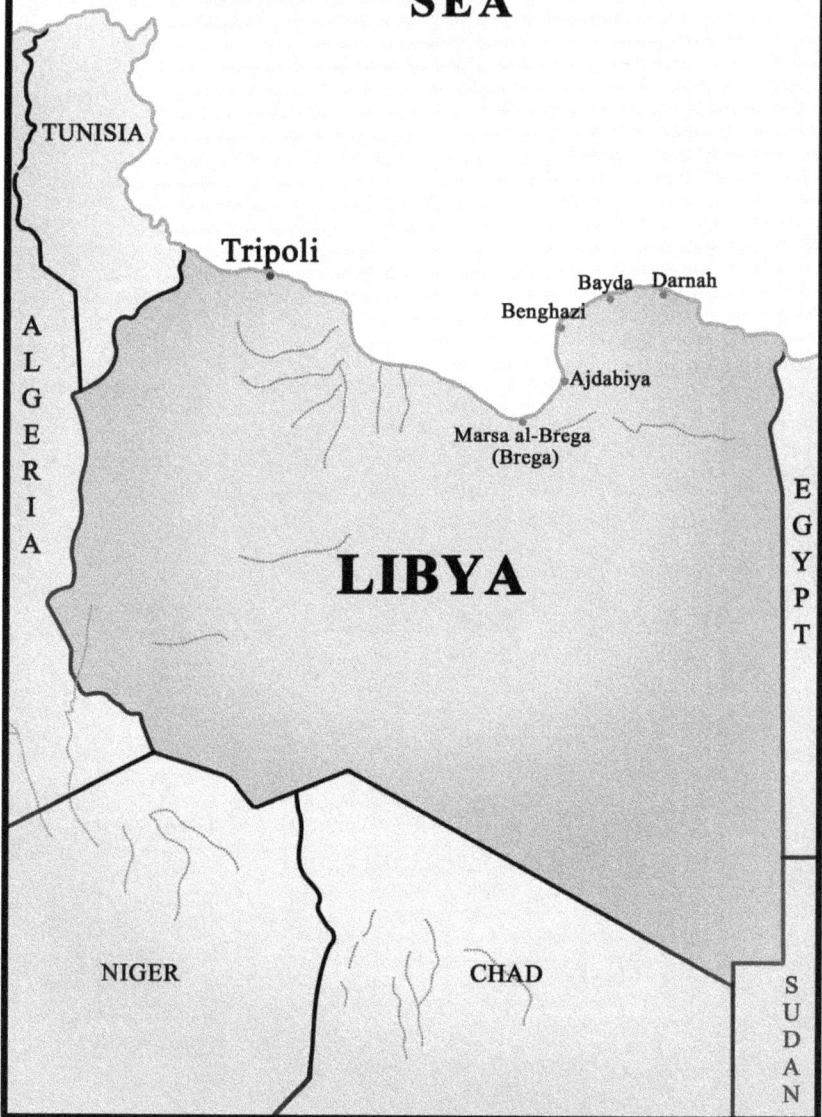

TUNISIA

Tripoli

Bayda   Darnah

Benghazi

Ajdabiya

Marsa al-Brega
(Brega)

A
L
G
E
R
I
A

LIBYA

E
G
Y
P
T

NIGER

CHAD

S
U
D
A
N

CONTENTS

FOREWORD

Tired of my humdrum life in London, I decided, in the spring of 2002, to dive into uncharted territory by accepting a job offer with a major oil company in Libya. Only too eager to embark on what I perceived to be a once-in-a-lifetime opportunity, I resigned from my employment in London without batting an eyelid. For nearly a decade, I lived inside my employer's highly secured residential compound and grew to love my host country so much that it soon became my home away from home. That was until early 2011 when the Arab Spring reared its head in the region and a coalition of western nations took it upon themselves to 'liberate' Libya by demanding regime change. The shocking demise of Colonel Gaddafi, the country's long-standing leader, in late 2011, opened the door to mounting unrest replacing the tight security that had prevailed throughout his leadership. With the war officially over, I was recalled to work by my employer, and excitedly returned to the country I loved and considered my second home.

Life inside the compound resumed painstakingly, but full of hope for the future. Until Friday, 7 June 2013. This date will remain etched in my soul forever—like an ugly, indelible scar. That day, a man scaled the garden wall of my house inside the residential compound and raped me at knifepoint. Besides the traumatic ordeal of the rape, its aftermath proved to be equally as traumatic.

As the victim of a serious crime, I hadn't expected the struggles I encountered on the long, arduous road towards an elusive justice, nor the gross, calculated perversion of power from some of the parties in authority I expected assistance from.

My desperation for redress intensified with each setback, and so did my deep resentment at the appalling treatment I received from the very institutions I'd naively expected support from: my employer, the Libyan authorities, the British Embassy in Tripoli, the British government ministers... No one seemed remotely interested in my plight. Gradually, my pent-up frustrations turned into a steely determination that, despite the wall of apathy erected around me, I'd find a way to stand and be counted.

The idea of telling my story in a book was born after years of desperately striving for justice. While I never had any aspirations or ambitions to put pen to paper before, I had no options left to scream my helplessness at a world unwilling to listen. With this book, I am also honouring the promise I made to my female Libyan colleagues not to give up my quest for justice, and that my fight would also be theirs.

Besides immortalising my story on paper, my ultimate hope is that it will raise questions about the treatment of rape victims in cross-border cases such as mine, inside a system paying only lip service to the fight against sexual violence, but conveniently turning a blind eye when the pursuit of justice is deemed too sensitive to the political status quo between governments. If my story could inspire the lifting of the taboo surrounding the issue of sexual violence crimes in countries like Libya so that victims could freely denounce that abhorrent violation of a woman's whole being, then my ordeal wouldn't have been in vain and I really could live with that. The following is by no means a thesis on Libya or its workings—it's simply my story.

APRIL 2000

Lying on a beach in Tunisia on a hot afternoon with my friend Janet, I lazily perused an English newspaper when an advertisement for senior British secretaries to work in Libya caught my eye. Janet and I were on a week's holiday from our hectic lives in London.

'Jan, listen to this!' I said as I sat up to read the advertisement aloud, 'Major Libyan oil company seeking senior British secretaries. Excellent salary and benefits. Free accommodation and return flights home. Interviews to be held at our London agency.'

It all sounded too good to be true, and the perfect opportunity of working abroad that I'd been dreaming of for so long, but not expecting to ever materialise.

'Yep, it sounds good, but... in Libya? Really?' she said, raising quizzical eyebrows in my direction. 'And where's Libya anyway?'

'Over there, on your right.' I grinned, pointing to the horizon.

'OK... and what do you know about Libya?' she insisted, the deep frown on her face betraying her disquiet at the destination.

'Not much,' I had to admit. I only knew the bare facts— that it was located over the Tunisian border and that Colonel Gaddafi was its alleged despotic leader, so much so that the country had been labelled a pariah state by the west for as long as I could remember. Not an enticing invitation to visit, but my interest was piqued, and I was tempted enough to resolve to find out more about the job and Libya once I returned home.

From the moment I laid eyes on that job advertisement, it fixated in my mind as something I had to see through to the end. I decided to follow my instincts and to apply for the job as soon as I arrived home. *Work... Eat... Sleep...* For years, my life in London had been reduced to a mind-numbing rat race, with the future looking like more of the same, and I desperately yearned for a radical change that only a move abroad could satisfy. This job advertisement presented me with the perfect opportunity to transform my monotonous life, and I simply had to grab this chance with both hands. But while I'd dreamt of this fresh start for what seemed like an eternity, I couldn't ignore the apprehension that stirred inside me each time I thought of uprooting myself away from London to embark on such a drastic move at the age of forty-eight. It was both daunting and exhilarating at the same time.

I suspected that remnants of an adventurous spirit of bygone days still lived inside me—that same spirit which landed me at London's Heathrow Airport on Christmas Eve 1974, at the age of twenty-one, with one suitcase and barely enough cash or English vocabulary to sustain me, but spurred on by a heart overflowing with the fearlessness and boldness of youth.

Throughout my adolescent years in a small town in eastern France, I developed such an all-consuming passion for all things British that I dreamt of making a life in England— anywhere in England! And I did so contentedly for over thirty years, happily living and working in London until I thought of myself as just another Londoner. I'd fulfilled my teenage dream. The slow process of slotting into a different culture, learning its language and discovering its quintessential characteristics was massively challenging at times, but always incredibly fascinating.

But as I became increasingly dissatisfied with my humdrum life in London, I soon recognised the signs of those itchy feet as they once again burnt with a desire for foreign shores. But much time had passed since I'd settled in London, and the free-spirited teenager of yesterday had long morphed into a mature adult with grown-up responsibilities. For a while, I reasoned that dreaming of yet another life abroad was rather juvenile at my advancing age, that I'd already had my dream come true once and that once in a lifetime was surely enough. I stifled my longing for new horizons by relegating it to the farthest corners of my mind, and continued with my predictable life in London. Until that hot afternoon on a beach in Tunisia. As soon as I laid eyes on that advertisement, my suppressed desire for a life abroad resurfaced with a vengeance. Only this time, I had an overwhelming sense that fate was stepping in, and that life had caught up with me at the least expected moment on that Tunisian beach.

This potential change fitted perfectly well with the way I perceived life as a succession of stages that might steer me at any moment towards other new, unexplored parts. I sensed instinctively when one stage was ending and time fast-approaching for the next one to begin. I was not only receptive to that notion, but welcomed it; it made life that much more exciting and surprising. Something deep inside told me that another life chapter was edging itself on my horizon, which made me supremely confident that the job would inevitably be mine once I was called for an interview.

At that time, I owned my home in London, and had been working for a reputable international investment company in Central London for over a decade. Even though I was ecstatic at my potential move to Libya, I couldn't silence a tiny, nagging voice in my head warning that I might be in the midst of a mid-life crisis and about to throw away a perfectly safe future at an age when I should, realistically, be planning for retirement instead. I heeded the warning, seriously questioning whether this change, at my age, in a country like Libya, might prove to be misguided at best or, at worst, full of pitfalls—or both.

Libya was remembered mainly for the 1984 incident at its embassy in London, which resulted in the fatal shooting of a British police woman. I started researching the country in more depth, but despite my best efforts, could find no favourable or encouraging reports on it—a 'dictatorship' and a 'pariah state' seemed to be its principal characteristics.

Oh my God, I wondered, *how safe will this place be for a lone woman?* I told myself that nearly twenty years had passed since the embassy incident and tried hard to banish from my mind any negative thoughts that might shatter my dream of moving abroad. I convinced myself that the scale of the change I planned would be scary under the best of circumstances, and that the nagging voice in my head was merely ensuring that I remained objective enough to curb my unbridled enthusiasm and prevent me from jumping into a potentially dangerous situation so far from home. I appreciated that tiny voice in my head looking out for my best interests, but I trusted my instincts and, this time, they fully embraced this opportunity, screaming for me to grab it with open arms and run with it. A die-hard optimist by nature, I cast any lingering doubts aside as my determination to uproot myself grew stronger by the day. I turned off that tiny voice in my head, and was ready to take a leap of faith and follow my destiny wherever it took me.

As it happened, the job was put on hold for nearly a year, giving me another chance to reconsider my plans and assess the impact this change would have on my life. When the time came to attend the first round of interviews, I had no hesitation whatsoever that I was doing the right thing. I was further reassured at a second interview with the company's personnel manager, Mr Ahmed Mubarak.

'Libya's had a bad image in the west for a long time, but it's really not as bad as it's reported,' he said with a soft smile and a shrug. 'I promise you that you'll be perfectly safe, both in the country and inside our residential compound. I've no doubt that you'll enjoy living and working with us.'

I didn't need any more convincing. I accepted on the spot the position of senior secretary at Sirte Oil Company for the Manufacture and Distribution of Oil and Gas (SOC), one of the largest international oil companies in Libya. A start date in early April 2002 was agreed when I would travel to the small town of Marsa al-Brega, in the east of the country, where the company was located.

The major oil company I'd be working for recruited all its expatriate personnel through its own agency in London's St. John's Wood, and was a subsidiary of the state-owned National Oil Corporation of Libya, which controlled the entire oil industry in the country. These facts sealed my move with an 'above board' stamp of approval. I was euphoric that my dream of a new life abroad was taking shape and about to come true after all.

I spent my remaining time in London floating on the proverbial cloud nine, and, from that moment on, had no misgivings about my imminent departure for Libya or my new start on foreign land. But in spite of my exhilaration, I couldn't help feeling a knot in my stomach each time I thought of breaking the news to my family and friends that I was about to move to a country shunned by the rest of the world. I expected a barrage of questions and plenty of concern for my safety as a lone woman in an allegedly high risk country, and their reactions were exactly as I'd anticipated.

'Libya? You can't be serious!' said my sister Jameela, her furrowed brow reflecting her astonishment at my destination choice. 'Libya as in the embassy incident?'

'Yeah, *that* Libya.' I nodded. 'The incident happened in 1984, a long time ago... Things have changed a lot since...'

'Oh, have they really?' she shot back sarcastically. 'And how would you know that?'

'There must be safer places for you to go to, especially on your own,' chimed in Adam, her husband, the look on his face mirroring Jameela's bewilderment. 'How much do you know about Libya?'

The questions kept coming quick and fast whilst my brain scrambled to come up with reassuring facts about a country I still had to read anything positive about.

'Well... I've been reading about it a lot, and it's *not* as terrible as it's made out to be,' I said confidently in an attempt to raise the country's appeal levels to them. 'Besides, as an expat, the company will be responsible for *everything*, including my safety. I'll be fully taken care of. But most importantly, I'll never get another opportunity like this at my age so I'm taking it. My mind is made up!'

'We want to be happy for you, but we're not sure Libya's the right place to go to... especially alone,' added Adam, his initial look of concern still all over his face.

'I'm worried about your safety there... Promise to keep in touch and to get back at the first sign of trouble,' said Jameela, the sombre tone in her voice hinting at her deep concern at my decision.

My friends, however, pointed out in more brutal terms their perceived madness of moving to 'those parts of the world'.

'*Wow*... You've gotta be joking! Libya?'

'Don't you think the country's blacklisted for a good reason?'

'How can you think it wise for even a second to go live there?'

'You're all welcome to visit at any time' became my automatic reply to their unsettling questions whilst I fought to ignore the uneasiness they raised inside me each time they expressed their disbelief at my Libyan plan.

Of course, I understood my friends' calls for caution, but once I realised that most couldn't even locate Libya on a map and that their negative perception of the country was based solely on the embassy incident of twenty years earlier, I simply refused to let the less palatable aspects of Libya dampen my enthusiasm. Instead, I resolved to focus solely on my dream of foreign shores soon becoming a reality. I was determined to let my spirit of adventure take over and to allow nothing to stop me from embarking on this once-in-a-lifetime experience.

While I could locate Libya on a map, I still knew very little about it at the time. I promised to educate myself further about the country before my arrival there. Being of North African origins, I already had the immense advantage of sharing the same Arab culture with the Libyan people, and could speak enough Arabic to get by in the country. This job opportunity was, therefore, also a chance of going back to my roots and experiencing first-hand the cultural bonds that connected me with the Libyan people. It was going to be a journey of discovery, but I had to admit that, had the job location been in any other country around the world, I'd have dived in with the same enthusiasm; Libya just happened to be the country on offer during my longing for change, and I was totally up to the exhilarating challenge of exploring its way of life.

Even though Libya sounded like it was located on the other side of the world, it was in fact less than a three-hour flight from London—the time it could take to get into work in Central London on a bad travel day. The job provided an all-expenses-paid opportunity towards a more financially secure future, with a decent salary and free housing and utilities inside the company's own residential compound.

I resigned from my London position without a second thought, and arranged with a real estate agency to lease my home. It seemed that even the stars were aligning to facilitate all the practicalities of my move, filling me with an overwhelming sense that this new chapter in uncharted territory was going to be an experience that would change my life forever. I feverishly packed my suitcases, and began counting the days until I left London en route to Libya. I buzzed with jubilation, blissfully unaware that I'd just made a choice that would one day turn my whole life upside down. Little did I know then that crushing pain would be the final destination, and that many years down the line, I'd experience the most harrowing time I ever lived through.

LIBYA

Located at the centre of the North African coastline, on the edge of the Mediterranean Sea, Libya is bordered by Tunisia to the north-west, Algeria to the west and Egypt to the east. About ninety percent of the country lies in the Sahara Desert, with most of its six-million population concentrated along its fertile coast strip. Its idyllic climate of mild winters and long, hot summers is only exacerbated by the dry, sand-bearing *ghibli* wind blowing from the desert in the spring and early summer to turn the air into a stifling, blurry red dust shroud.

Libya is home to a magnificent architectural heritage yet to be fully explored: hidden gems like the ancient city of Leptis Magna, a UNESCO World Heritage site boasting of some of the world's finest remains of Roman architecture; the Greco-Roman colony of Cyrene, in the Jabal al-Akhdar mountains, home to the sanctuary of Apollo; the Roman site of Apollonia (Soussa), with its acropolis and temples to Zeus and Apollo, or the oasis city of Ghadames, a labyrinth of tunnels and houses built below ground as protection from the scorching heat of the Sahara Desert…

For most of its history, Libya was subjected to foreign domination by the Phoenicians, Greeks, Romans, Ottoman Empire and, more recently, through the Italian colonisation from 1911 to 1943. Libya was declared an Italian colony in 1912, becoming by the 1930s the new 'America' for hundreds of thousands of Italian emigrants. The country was conquered from Italy by the Allied forces in 1943, but, by the end of 1945, was under occupation again by the British and French forces.

Libya gained its independence from Allied occupation in 1951 with the creation of the 'United Kingdom of Libya' under the leadership of the British-backed King Idris Senussi I, who ruled the country until 1969 when a bloodless military coup led by a young army officer named Muammar Muhammed Gaddafi brought about the overthrow of the monarchy and the establishment of the 'Libyan Arab Republic'. One of Gaddafi's first measures on seizing power was the expulsion of the Italian community, and the closure of all western military bases on Libyan soil. Thus began Gaddafi's forty-year iron-fist rule over Libya and its people, which would end in bloody circumstances decades later.

Libya, severely restricted by its unforgiving desert habitat, had no natural resources and was heavily reliant on foreign aid and imports to bolster its economy. But the discovery of oil in the late 1950s dramatically changed the country's bleak economic landscape. Gaddafi's rise to power brought significant social reforms to improve the quality of life of his countrymen: salaries were increased twofold whilst a welfare state was put in place to provide free medical care and education to all Libyans. Gaddafi abolished the post-1951 Libyan constitution, and defined his own political philosophy in his 'Green Book'. He nationalised both the banking system and the oil industry, effectively removing the American oil companies from the country, which, undoubtedly, set the tone for the future perpetually strained relations between the US and Libya.

Libya is, by tradition, a tribal society, with a majority of its population being affiliated with a tribe. The tribal system is an unknown concept in the western world, but an extremely powerful, traditional force in countries like

Libya where it plays a major societal role. A tribal society is structured around the identification with a particular family, community or even town, and an individual's last name often reflects the tribe he or she belongs to. Loyalty to other tribe members being key, affiliation with a tribe is a potent medium to obtain a wide-range of privileges ranging from securing employment or housing to administrative favours. Tribes are especially involved in solving family disputes and bringing solutions during times of discord, and, in many aspects, they are a strong force for good. The actions of each individual tribe member carry a huge impact on the reputation of the entire tribe, and any improper conduct would bring disgrace to the individual's family and, by extension, the whole tribe. The good or bad reputation of a family and, therefore, that of the tribe, is of such significance that it influences the lives of individual members on a social, political and economic level. But even though tribal identity is extremely important to a majority of Libyans, they don't let it interfere with their sense of patriotism—they might belong to different tribes, but, as a nation, they are one.

As a collective, tribe members provide each other with valuable support, but, most of all, unfailing loyalty at all times. This system not only defines its members' identity and rules over their decisions, but it also ensures their welfare and protection at times of conflict, as seen during the 2011 armed conflict. Many years later, I'd experience, to my own detriment, the extent and consequences of this unfailing loyalty.

Libya is a deeply religious, patriarchal society in which men and women hold clearly defined roles. I had an inkling as to what to expect due to my own similar cultural origins.

There exists no ambiguities about the primary role of each gender—men are perceived as the providers and protectors of their families whilst women as homemakers first and foremost. This is a notion considered rather outdated in the progressive western world I'd lived in most of my life, and I was curious at what changes I'd discover on that front. It's often left unsaid that Gaddafi's takeover of Libya opened up society to women as he affirmed their rights inside Libyan society. A quote from his Green Book states that: 'Women, just like men, are human beings. This is an incontestable truth. Therefore, as humans, it is a fact that women are equal to men and to discriminate between them is a glaring inexcusable injustice.'

In order to free the Libyan women from the strict social restrictions previously imposed on them, he founded the Revolutionary Women's Formation to pave the way for reform. A law was introduced in 1970 which affirmed equality of the sexes and wage parity. Another, in 1972, criminalised the marriage of girls under the age of sixteen, and made consent a prerequisite for marriage. Like their male counterparts, Libyan women are able to vote, access higher education, work, drive, and are represented in many professional fields governed by an equal pay for equal work policy.

At the time of my arrival in Libya in April 2002, the country had been under US economic sanctions since 1981 as the result of an incident in which two Libyan jets allegedly fired on a US aircraft taking part in a naval exercise over international waters claimed by Libya. In 1992, the UN imposed its own sanctions after Libya was blamed for blowing up Pan-Am flight 103 over Lockerbie, Scotland, killing two hundred and fifty-nine people on board. The UN and US sanctions were lifted in 2003 and 2004 respectively, leading to a normalisation of relations between Libya and the US.

Marsa al-Brega (Brega Sea Port)

The town, often referred to simply as 'Brega', lies some eight hundred kilometres to the east of the capital, Tripoli, and was initially just a small fishing village on the edge of the Mediterranean Sea, which was destroyed during World War II. But the remaining landmine-infested area was selected as the terminal for Libya's first oil pipeline, and a new town and port were built in the early 1960s to transform the old fishing village into a bustling port and major export hub for Libyan oil and gas. Large scale oil production began with the first shipment in 1961, launching the new town on its way to being the country's first petro-chemical centre and one of five major oil terminals in eastern Libya. Transportation links between Benghazi and Tripoli to the west, and the Egyptian capital, Cairo, to the east, are facilitated by a coastal highway passing through Brega. The nearest town, Ajdabiya, is located some eighty kilometres to the east of Brega.

Sirte Oil Company (SOC)

The company, often referred to simply as 'SOC', is a subsidiary of the state-owned National Oil Corporation of Libya (NOC), which controls the whole of Libya's oil industry. During the 1960s and 1970s, SOC was known as Esso Libya and ran in partnership with the American oil giant, Esso, until the latter ceased its Libyan operations in the mid-1980s, passing full control to Esso Libya and leading to the creation of SOC.

Besides SOC owning and running the largest oil refinery in Libya, the company also owns and manages the whole of Brega: the port, the single-runway airport for the operations of its own aircraft, the processing plants, the natural gas fields, the administrative buildings, the residential compound, the schools, the medical and shopping facilities... The landmine-littered fishing village that Brega once was had become a hugely productive, massively expansive, successful venture, and a vital economic asset to Libya.

SOC Residential Compound

The company's residential compound in Brega, fully owned and controlled by SOC, had been designed to provide housing, office accommodation, medical, educational and shopping facilities to all its employees and their families. Made up of a handful of settlements a few kilometres apart, it was home to over ten thousand Libyan employees and their families, as well as expatriate workers. The compound, a vast enclosure delimited by security fencing, was divided into three distinct areas.

Area 1 housed Libyan families and female expatriate employees, and was the site of the management office building, training centre and other administrative facilities. It was also the location of SOC's own bank, largest guesthouse, primary and nursery schools, medical centre, supermarket, dining hall and gymnasium.

Area 2 provided accommodation for mainly single Libyan employees, and basic facilities such as a small supermarket, administrative offices and a technical training centre.

Area 3 was home to Libyan families, and boasted a larger supermarket than those in the other two areas, as well as a number of small, modern boutiques. On its outskirts stood the Bright Star University of Technology, founded in 1981.

All the houses inside the compound were bungalow-type properties with gardens, tucked behind high, orange-painted boundary walls. The wide, clean streets all led to Brega's stunning white sandy beaches.

Due to the nature of the company's business, the most stringent security measures were implemented inside the compound. Taking photographs of the installations was strictly prohibited, whilst checkpoints manned by armed guards stood not only at the entrances to the compound, but also inside it at the boundary lines between each of the three areas. Employees carried identification badges to be presented at checkpoints, while no outsiders were allowed access inside the compound without prior approval from SOC management, rendering the SOC compound an impenetrable fortress to non-residents and unauthorised people.

MY ARRIVAL IN LIBYA

I left my house in South London for Gatwick Airport on a grey morning in early April 2002. I'd hardly slept a wink the night before as a stubborn mix of excitement and apprehension swirled around in my head to keep sleep at bay. Threatening rain clouds loomed over the city, and I smiled smugly at the prospect of landing in the Libyan sunshine in a few hours' time. As I carried my bags to the waiting taxi, it dawned on me that there was no turning back from the leap into the unknown I was making. Heart jumping wildly in my chest, I slammed the door shut behind me, hoping with all my might that the airline ticket to Tripoli inside my handbag would be my pass to a better tomorrow. But in spite of my excitedness, I couldn't ignore the nervous, fluttering sensation in the pit of my stomach that I felt throughout the flight.

Thankfully, by the time the aircraft landed at Tripoli's international airport, any misgivings had melted away. I exited the plane into the bright sunlight and felt as though I'd stepped into a baking oven. The air was so hot I started sweating profusely while my light raincoat looked grotesquely out of place. In no time, I'd been transported into an exotic world where a brazen sun shone boldly, and where a different language was spoken all around me by men and women strolling leisurely in long, flowing robes. Smiling broadly, some would exclaim, 'Marhaba! Welcome to Libya!' each time they came across a foreigner. I felt immediately at ease in this alien, yet somehow familiar, environment.

I took my place in line at the end of a long queue of foreign businessmen at an immigration desk, and quietly surveyed my surroundings. Within seconds, an officer waved me out of the line to approach his desk, ahead of dozens of waiting men.

'Sorry, everyone, just following orders,' I said, rather embarrassed at this uncivil queue-jumping.

I learnt later that it was considered unbecoming for men to stand in line in front of women. I was then ushered into a waiting area until SOC's private aircraft was ready to fly me on the last leg of my journey to Brega. I took a seat by the largest air-cooling machine in the room, and chatted with a group of Filipino workers who happened to be returning to the compound from leave.

During the flight to Brega, I was struck by the jolly ambience inside the aircraft and the relaxed familiarity between the passengers who all seemed to know one another. An hour later, the aircraft started its descent towards Brega's tiny airport. I stared out of the window, my heart bursting with uncontained delight. No highways, no built-up areas, no towering buildings in sight. Nothing but sea, sand, a handful of dwellings scattered here and there, and a single landing strip on which the plane touched down safely. I'd finally arrived at my new home!

As soon as I exited the aircraft into the hot air, large sweat beads began forming on my forehead again. I followed the flow of passengers into the small arrival hall, unsure as to what to expect next. There was laughter and chatter all around whilst I stood out awkwardly like a sore thumb for a brief instant before a small group of women approached me.

'Bahia?' asked a tall, blonde-haired woman.

I smiled and nodded.

'Welcome to Brega!' she said.

'*Marhaba*! Welcome!' said another in a pale blue headscarf and dark sunglasses.

'Thank you. *Shukran*. I'm so happy to be here,' I replied, flashing my broadest smile and wiping dripping sweat off my forehead.

The women took turns to introduce themselves then helped me retrieve my bags. The blonde woman was Julie. She was British and the dental hygienist at the compound's medical clinic; Farah, in the light blue scarf and dark glasses, was Libyan and she and I would be working for the same manager; Hiba, the pretty, petite, dark-haired secretary was from Syria; Annie, the oldest of the group, was a secretary from Scotland; and Sandy, a nurse from the Philippines. I was excited that, except for Farah, I'd be living on the same street as all these women. Work colleagues being next-door neighbours was a novelty, but I was looking forward to the experience. I felt at home from the moment I'd set foot in Tripoli earlier that day, but the women's friendly welcome only served to deepen the feeling until any shred of nervousness I might have had about my future in a 'high risk' country vanished altogether.

Outside the airport, an SOC chauffeur patiently waited to drive us to the beach restaurant where a reservation had been made in honour of my arrival. In all my working life, I'd never been greeted so warmly on my first day anywhere. The short drive to the restaurant gave me my first glimpse of the compound. The streets were deserted and reassuringly uneventful. There wasn't one grey building in sight to spoil the pristine skyline, no traffic jams with their annoying honking of horns, and no crowds of worn-out people scurrying for buses or trains. Nothing but bright sunshine, soothing tranquillity, and towering palm trees all around. The clean, wide roads were lined with flowery shrubs bursting with white and pink blooms, and I could barely make out the large bungalows standing behind their high, orange-painted garden walls. In the background, the magnificent expanse of the blue sea revealed itself in breathtaking simplicity. My spirits soared as I took in the natural beauty around me and imagined my life in such an idyllic setting. *Wow... This is so beautiful and so peaceful*, I thought, utterly mesmerised by it all.

'But where's everybody?' I asked, smiling broadly.

'Well, this is as busy as it gets in Brega,' said Julie. 'You'll get used to it in no time. We love it and you will too.'

'I already do,' I laughed. And I meant it.

True to its name, the restaurant sat right on the beach, on the first floor of a small two-storey building. I stepped out of the bus into the warm, invigorating sea air, closed my eyes and breathed in deeply. The huge floor-to-ceiling windows inside the restaurant gave unobstructed stunning views of the Mediterranean Sea as it reached out as far as the eye could see to meet a cloudless sky. I couldn't believe that the picture-postcard scenery before me was going to be part of my daily surroundings. The dazzling sun, the sandy beach, the shimmering blue sea, the palm trees, the relaxed atmosphere—there was a cosy holiday feel to the compound that I was more than ready to call home. I was in a dream I never wanted to wake up from, but the unmistakable aroma of hot flatbread drifting from the kitchen quickly brought me to my senses; it was so thick as it spread across the whole dining room that I could almost taste it, and I felt suddenly ravenous. Over a delicious meal of traditional Libyan soup, grilled chicken and roasted vegetables, the women filled me in on life inside SOC's residential compound.

'It will be nothing like London, that's for sure,' said Julie, 'And always remember that people here don't rush for *anything...*'

The rest of the women giggled and nodded in agreement.

'You know what's the best perk of the job?' chimed in Hiba. 'The beach on our doorstep! You didn't have one in London, did you?' she teased.

The beach on my doorstep was a humongous cherry on the cake, and I hadn't even asked for that much in my dreams.

'It all sounds too wonderful to be true, so where's the catch?' I asked jokingly. 'And don't hold back, I can take it!'

'OK, where shall I begin?' said Annie with a feigned, downcast look on her face. 'The office hours for a start... You'll have to be at your desk by seven thirty every morning.' She paused for a brief moment for effect before adding, 'But don't worry, a company driver will drive you to and from work each day.'

'Wow... A driver? Really?' I'd already figured out that Annie was the joker of the group, and I wasn't quite sure whether she was pulling my leg or not.

A snap of my daily laborious bus and train journeys into Central London flashed before my eyes. But company driver or not, nothing could possibly dampen my enthusiasm at that point. And Annie wasn't kidding—a bus driver would, indeed, pick me up from outside my home each morning. I was over the moon that my Libyan adventure was going to be so unlike anything I'd experienced before. The new setting for my hopes and dreams seemed perfect, but I was too immersed in this dream come true to realise that the most perfect picture could conceal a dark, evil facet within it. I'd only had a tiny insight into my new life in the compound, but I felt so incredibly privileged to have been given the opportunity to experience it that I gave up trying to contain the persistent smile etched on my face since I left London that morning.

By the time I left the restaurant, a friendly bond had formed between these women and I, and I felt instinctively at peace inside the laid-back environment of the compound. I was then driven to the house allocated to me by SOC, which would be my home in Libya.

House 1518 in Area 1 of the compound stood in a small cul-de-sac known as 'Secretary Street' for the simple reason that the majority of SOC's expatriate female employees were housed there, in spite of the majority being medical personnel. The street comprised two rows of about twenty dwellings with gardens tucked behind high, orange-painted walls. All but a couple had been designed for single occupancy, and many were empty as they were in need of maintenance. My neighbours hailed from different parts of the world—Britain, the Philippines, Syria, Bulgaria, Serbia… The street's cosmopolitan feel was the only similarity with London.

I approached house 1518 with visible delight at the stunning sight of the majestic palm tree and mimosa branches cascading over the garden wall in an explosion of golden blooms. These magnificent trees in my garden were another cherry on the cake I hadn't asked for. I pushed the gate into the courtyard and came face to face with the cute bungalow that was going to be my home. It looked like a doll's house. It had three windows fitted with exterior, horizontal steel shutters. Inside, it was a self-contained, basically furnished one-bedroomed dwelling, freshly painted throughout in pure white. The strong smell of paint still lingered in every room.

It was clean, unfussy but functional, and I couldn't have asked for more.

However, regardless of my housing conditions or the beauty of my surroundings, my priority living alone in a 'high risk' country was for my safety. I'd lived in London for decades, and had grown steadily concerned at its increasingly violent environment. Like countless other Londoners, my property had been burgled and my car broken into. Such occurrences were part of life for large-city dwellers, but they'd made me quasi-paranoid over my personal security. I was tremendously relieved that all the windows of the houses on Secretary Street had steel shutters that could only be operated from the inside, and that security grilles were fitted to outside doors, but also intrigued as to the reason behind all these security measures if the compound was as safe as the women had told me at the restaurant.

To reinforce the security of its expatriate women employees further, it was company policy that no male employees— other than SOC's own maintenance workers—were allowed onto Secretary Street. In addition, SOC security guards made regular rounds in their patrol cars, adding to the strong sense of safety not only on Secretary Street, but around the entire compound. SOC was responsible for the protection of all its employees inside the compound, and it was reassuring that the company took its responsibility extremely seriously.

In time, I came to realise that there was no crime to speak of in the compound and that everything about Brega made it an unlikely setting for criminal activity. Gradually, I began to free myself of that omnipresent threat to my personal safety that I'd lived under in London, and of the fear of being either mugged, or having my house or car broken into.

I was housed in Area 1 of the compound, but my office was located in Area 2, some ten kilometres away. Indeed, just as Annie had mentioned, a company bus driver picked women employees up from outside their houses just after seven o'clock in the morning, and dropped them off outside their office buildings. As Annie and I would be working in the same building, the driver picked us up together from Secretary Street. I was glad for her company on my first day, and she promised to introduce me around to break me in gently into the company's office protocol. Annie had worked for SOC for over twenty years, and was well-liked by the locals. Whilst waiting for the company driver on that first morning, she shared her first massively hilarious piece of advice.

'When your boss leaves the office, don't ever think of asking where he's going,' she said. 'Just let him go… Ask *no* questions!'

I looked at her, slightly confused. As a personal assistant, organising my boss' schedule and being aware of his whereabouts during working hours had always been an essential part of my duties.

'OK, let me explain,' she continued. 'One day, soon after I started, I did just that… I asked my boss where he was going. He looked at me with utter surprise, grinning at my perceived audacity and said, "Even my wife doesn't ask me where I'm going, so I'm certainly not going to tell *you!*" Needless to say, I never asked again!'

Machismo Libyan style! I couldn't help but giggle as I imagined the scene in my head, and promised myself to tread carefully to avoid hurting any sensitivities my new boss might be harbouring on his freedom of movement during work hours. It looked like it was going to be a different work experience altogether, but I had to admit that this unusual office protocol could only make my duties a lot easier.

'Oh… and there's another thing,' she said. 'Do you know what *wasta* means?'

I shook my head. 'Never even heard the word before,' I replied.

'Well, I dare say that you'll find out soon enough,' she said. 'If you need anything done in the compound, and I do mean *anything*, you'd better know someone who can help you… or someone who knows someone who can. That's *wasta*… Without it, you'll get nowhere.'

It was a little intriguing, but it was a fact that an influential person in anyone's life could make the impossible happen so I wasn't overly concerned by this *wasta* thing. It was true anywhere and just the way the world operated. I expected to come across interesting, even bizarre, cultural practices, and was ready to adapt and deal with any challenges, including the quirkiest ones.

Just after seven in the morning on my first day at the company, Annie and I were picked up from Secretary Street by Hameed, the SOC driver, and set off towards our office building in Area 2. There were about a dozen Libyan women employees inside the bus.

'*Salem*,' they said with subdued smiles.

Too early for any chit-chatting, the rest of the journey took place in silence. As the bus left the residential area and proceeded on the road towards Area 2, the tall structures of Brega's sprawling industrial installations came into view, spewing out dark plumes of polluting smoke into the clean morning air. The thick smoke spiralled up and spread across the sky. Suddenly, the acrid, rotten-egg-like stench of chemicals seeped inside the bus, and made me gag. I looked around, but no one else seemed disturbed by it.

'You'll soon get used to it,' said Annie.

Each employee was dropped off outside her office building, and it took about fifteen minutes to arrive at mine. It was a large, beige structure which had been originally designed as a hotel. Inside, natural sunlight flooded in through an exceptionally high glass roof and illuminated the whiteness of the marble flooring. The building comprised four floors arranged around a sizable reception area with inviting sofas and tall green plants. *So far so good!* I thought.

My first day at anything always made me a little nervous, and I wished I could fast forward by a couple of weeks, but I really had nothing to fret about. My first day at SOC as senior secretary to the transportation manager, Mr Adam Bayda, couldn't have been more pleasant. Annie had already filled me in on what a charismatic character Mr Bayda was, but there was another cherry on the cake in the office too— the huge space with all mod cons all to myself! Large windows along the whole length of one wall framed spectacular views of a vast grassy area opposite the building on which a herd of camels lazily trudged under the palm trees all day long. And beyond this stunning scenery, the deep blue sea melted into the cloudless sky, adding the perfect backdrop to a dreamy landscape. I was dazzled by the beauty of it all. I was a million miles from the crowded, open-plan London office space I'd squeezed into with over one hundred other employees. Each morning as I walked into my new office to be greeted by this jaw-dropping scenery, I felt as though I was stepping into a dream, and gave thanks for the opportunity of this experience.

Mr Bayda, a man in his mid-sixties, was an older Libyan version of the American actor Marlon Brando—a grey-haired, golden-skinned, larger than life character. One could sense his powerful aura just by looking at his towering, formidable figure.

'*Marhaba*! Welcome to Brega!' he said in a cheery voice, a big smile and a firm handshake all at once. 'You're pleased with your house? If you need anything at all, in the office or at home, just let me know...'

Indeed, I'd soon learn that Mr Bayda made many things possible for many people, in or out of the office. Although I didn't know it at the time, he was going to become my own *wasta*, and I couldn't have imagined better support.

Mr Bayda had lived in the United States for several years, which accounted for his perfect command of the English language. Each morning, his powerful voice could be heard down the corridor long before his towering frame burst into the office. His commanding manner could be quite intimidating at times, but he was a warm and pleasant man whose bursts of laughter were as loud as his fortunately rare anger outbursts. His relaxed, jovial disposition put me at ease from day one and, before long, an easy working relationship formed between us. Mr Bayda managed SOC's transportation department with a firm hand and didn't hesitate to raise his forceful voice to hammer a point. A no-nonsense manager with an exacting manner, he expected the highest standards from his staff, and didn't suffer fools gladly, a trait often reflected in his tendency to be rather blunt at times when frustrated. But despite the pressures of his workload, Mr Bayda never failed to make himself available to anyone in need of his assistance, whether work-related or not.

As SOC employees, the majority of the Libyan residents had lived and worked in the compound most of their lives, which created, over time, an extremely tight-knit community. It was, therefore, inevitable that the residents' personal life would encroach upon their professional one. Mr Bayda had undeniable clout and was a powerhouse in every sense of the word, and was treated with reverence by those around him, who viewed him as their much-needed *wasta* at times of need. Every single day, a line of callers would form outside his office, patiently waiting for the help he generously gave. I'll forever hold fond memories of the endless discussions he and I had on various subjects from politics to life in general. Mr Bayda's retirement a few years later heralded the end of a unique office experience and, had he still been around, many of the tragic events that occurred all those years later wouldn't have happened or, at the very least, would've been dealt with with the fairness and efficiency that were so typically his.

Farah, who'd been part of the group of women meeting me at the airport the day before, had an office next door to mine. She was Mr Bayda's Arabic-speaking assistant, a sharp-minded, inquisitive young woman who fussed over him like a mother hen. She saw him as a father figure and didn't shy away from seeking his advice on personal issues. And she wasn't the only one as other women employees also turned to him for counsel. To all the residents in the compound, Mr Bayda was a tower of strength who could make their troubles disappear, which he unfailingly did with his humble manner and spirit of generosity.

Weekends in Libya fell on Fridays and Saturdays and, for a while, I found starting the working week on a Sunday altogether bizarre. The early rising for the seven o'clock bus pickup took a little getting used to at first, but very soon, the mere thought of the glorious weather ahead, the beach nearby and the compound's laid-back holiday vibe were all the motivation needed to spring out of bed at dawn. The early start filled me with a buzzing energy that lasted well into the day. In no time, I came to rely on the faint light of dawn filtering through the tiny gaps in the steel shutters and the first call to prayer from the nearby mosque to gently awaken me each morning.

The white sandy beach, a mere five-minute walk from my house, was the most amazing perk to my job. Not surprisingly, it played an intrinsic part of life for all the compound's residents, with picnics, ball games on the sand, swimming in the inviting warm waters, or simply relaxing under the cloudless sky, being daily activities for all. I'd often meet up there after work with either Sandy or Annie to queue up at the beach restaurant for spicy burgers and chips before sitting on the warm sand, feet in the water, and chatting away until the sun went down in a blaze of fiery reds over the glistening blue sea. This picture of blissful serenity was nothing short of magical, and one I shall keep in my heart forever.

Some weekends, Sandy and I would set off for the beach at the break of dawn for an invigorating yoga session. Even at that early hour, I always felt safe. A few people would be out jogging, and they'd wave with a cheerful '*Salem*'. After leisurely stretching into various yoga poses on the edge of the water, Sandy and I would lay on the soft sand until mid-morning, chatting and basking in the warm glow of the rising sun as it cast its first rays over the still sleepy compound, before slowly making our way back home for breakfast.

Despite no longer enjoying the materialistic choices London had offered, I was delighted to be in such a harmonious, safe environment, and felt a profound sense of contentment that I'd never experienced before. I still walked around with that smile of pure bliss permanently etched on my face since my arrival in Libya, and which I no longer tried to repress. My whole being seemed to be glowing and dancing with joy. Indeed, these were peaceful, happy days, and I hugely appreciated how fortunate I'd been for that job opportunity coming my way when I'd least expected it.

Most of the older Libyan employees had lived inside the compound all of their lives. Working for SOC and living inside its residential compound offered substantial advantages to them. They were allocated large, fully-furnished family houses with gardens, with no rent or other expenses to pay for, whilst any repairs were carried out, free of charge, by the company's services department. The employees' children attended the schools run by SOC inside the compound until they reached college age, when the company arranged for their daily commute to and from a college in larger towns outside Brega. Later on, they could be sent abroad to further their education, then, upon graduation, be employed by the company. Free daily transportation to and from Ajdabiya, Benghazi or Tripoli on SOC's coaches or aircraft was available to all employees. A job within SOC offered significant benefits for the local employees and their families, but also guaranteed the education and professional future of their children. Most Libyan workers owned their own homes in cities outside of Brega to which they'd return at weekends or upon retirement. Working for SOC and living at its residential compound was a win–win situation for Libyans.

There were about one thousand five hundred expatriate employees in the compound while I was there—from various countries in Europe, North Africa, the Middle East, North America and Asia. It was company policy for expatriate employees to report any problems they experienced inside the compound to their immediate managers whose duty it was to resolve. Expatriates' salaries were paid directly into their bank accounts abroad, with no possibility of access until each returned on leave to his or her country. Female expatriate employees were paid a monthly allowance of one hundred Libyan dinars—approximately twenty British pounds—to cover food expenses, whilst their male counterparts took all their meals, free of charge, at the compound's dining halls. As all accommodation, utilities and travel expenses were provided free of charge, I found it unbelievably liberating not to think of bills to be paid while in the compound.

English was the language spoken between Libyan and expatriate employees, and I was often impressed that many Libyans spoke good English, bearing in mind that some had never travelled outside of Libya. They'd learnt basic English at school or at the compound's language centre, but most were keen on improving their skills by interacting with the foreign employees. This thirst for learning was not limited to the English language, but to knowledge in general, and was prevalent amongst the majority of young Libyan employees I came across. Bearing in mind that half of the population was under the age of thirty, it could only bode well for the future of Libya. I often reflected on how much the Libyan people would have achieved had sanctions not been inflicted upon them to block their advancement, and had they been allowed the same opportunities that their peers abroad benefitted from as a basic human right.

Every month, a priest from a church in Benghazi was invited to hold Mass inside the Area 1 primary school for the Christian expatriates. In every aspect, SOC provided an efficiently run home to all its residents in which the most minute, practical details of life inside an enclosed, highly secured area of several thousand people had been thoroughly thought out to cater for all their needs. It seemed that everything had been designed in such a way as to make the life of all its employees—Libyan and expatriate alike—as smooth and trouble-free as possible.

I became close friends with four women on Secretary Street: Sandy, Hiba, Annie and Mary, a nurse from Bulgaria. Living on the same street and working for the same employer seemed rather strange at first, but it certainly was conducive to making friends quickly. Foreign women were advised to keep themselves appropriately covered up at all times, not because of any potential trouble with the locals, but merely out of respect for their customs. The sight of expatriate women in swimwear on the beach wasn't unheard of, and, although it wasn't openly commented upon by the locals, it was certainly quietly frowned upon. Politics was a subject best to avoid discussing with Libyans, and, in time, I came to experience that, indeed, the majority were reluctant about engaging in any political exchange. SOC being a subsidiary of a governmental corporation, many Libyan employees believed that there were undercover agents working within the company, ready to report to the state authorities. As would be expected anywhere in the world, there were real sensitivities and boundaries to be respected if living in Libya was going to be easy and problem-free. I enjoyed working with my Libyan colleagues and appreciated my group of friends on Secretary Street, and was sure that, with time, some would remain friends for life. Sadly, events further down the line would one day bring these friendships to an abrupt end.

As my life in the compound slowly took shape, an easy, stress-free routine emerged, leaving me in no doubt whatsoever that I'd done the right thing by leaving my old London life behind. An irrepressible burst of contentment would surge through me each time I marvelled at my surroundings—the tall, elegant palm trees, the mesmerising beauty of the rising sun, the sugar-white sand or the deep blue of the sea. It was a radical change from the environment I'd left behind, and I never failed to give thanks for the chance to experience it. I enjoyed working with Mr Bayda and Farah so much that going to the office became something to look forward to rather than the mundane occupation that office work usually turned into. I settled into the relaxed holiday camp ambience of my surroundings with unsurprising ease, and watched the days tick by peacefully, a whole world apart from the stressful demands of my past life in London.

Libyan work colleagues were friendly and easy-going, and the majority spoke good English. I couldn't fail to notice a level of respect from the local male employees towards their female counterparts that I hadn't experienced before. I'd worked in large open-plan offices in London, and was accustomed to the good-natured, at times cheeky, banter between employees; I'd even enjoyed it, but this was different. Both men and women seemed to have an innate awareness of what was appropriate to do or say when in close proximity to the other gender. There was a tacit code of conduct in which banter between them didn't include any uninhibited or indiscreet talk, and I found it incredibly refreshing that no inappropriate language would be heard in the office. There was a level of high regard and protectiveness towards women in Libya in general, which might seem stifling to a westerner, but Libyan women expected no less from their men. Life was built around a different order of rules and customs which, at times, appeared a little archaic to the westerner I'd become, but I always recognised their profound wisdom. I learnt to appreciate being invited to jump a long line of male customers in stores or at the airport's immigration desks, purely on the basis of my gender. There was a level of respect towards parents and the elderly that was quasi-unheard of in the western world. Respect and obedience towards parents was an explicit religious commandment that was certainly obeyed to the letter in Libya where elders were invariably held in the highest esteem for their experience and wisdom. The more I delved into Libya's ways and customs, the more I felt at peace with who I was destined to be, but most of all, that I was finally free to express it.

Shortly following my arrival at the compound, Hiba and I visited a shopping area called Crossroads, which was located immediately outside the compound's main security checkpoint in Area 1. It was an arid, dusty area with a small row of shops and nothing around but desert for as far as the eye could see. The compound residents often came to this area in search of some food variety. But the area was so bleak and the shops so cramped that I knew I wouldn't be returning in any hurry. I'd make do with the supermarket near my house and whatever goods it provided. Its label as a 'supermarket' was a grossly exaggerated description of the modest, one-level warehouse-type building which offered only the most basic food supplies due to the economic sanctions Libya was under at the time. It was a far cry from the overflowing shelves of my local Sainsbury's back home, but I was still basking in the novelty of my Libyan experience, and so the materialistic sparsity in the shops didn't concern me one bit.

At some point during my first visit to the supermarket, the store butcher, a white-haired, bespectacled man wearing SOC's dark blue overalls, gestured timidly for me to approach the counter he stood behind.

'*Salem*! Me, Hamza... I go... to Tripoli next week... on the plane?' he asked politely in broken English.

Utterly puzzled by his question, I merely looked at him without a word as my brain raced to figure out any possible link I might have to the local store butcher. Indeed, part of my work entailed arranging SOC's employees' travel, but I couldn't work out for the life of me how a butcher had entered the equation.

'Umm... Let me look into it,' I said. 'I'll come back and tell you tomorrow. *Insha'Allah*.'

The supermarket was located less than one hundred metres from my house, but I exited the store so baffled by my encounter with its butcher that I lost my bearings and had no idea which direction to head towards. I knew I was in very close proximity to my house, but everywhere I looked, I saw palm trees and orange-painted garden walls. Then I noticed a small group of teenagers in colourful Bermuda shorts and flip-flops sitting on the pavement playing cards, and I made my way towards them.

'*Salem. Ayna* Secretary Street?' I asked.

Without hesitation, one of them stood up and offered to walk me there.

'*Salem.* My name is Ameer,' he said in English as he reached out for my shopping bag.

The shopping bag had my purse in it. In a flash, my over-cautious London mentality burst to the fore, and a tiny voice in my head warned that entrusting a teenager with my purse in a 'high risk' country was something I might live to regret imminently. But, out of sheer embarrassment, I resisted the urge to grab my shopping bag back from him, choosing instead to hope for the best.

'You're new in Brega?' he asked.

I nodded, a soft smile on my lips and a hawkish eye fixed firmly on the shopping bag he carried.

'Then welcome!' he said, turning the first corner into Secretary Street and handing me my grocery bag with my purse still safely tucked inside it.

I was relieved Ameer's intentions had been innocent, feeling a twinge of remorse at my initial suspicion. As a token of my appreciation, and to alleviate my guilt, I offered him a tip of a couple of dinars.

'No… No… It was my pleasure. *Salem!*' he said, politely declining my offering and walking away with a friendly wave of the hand.

I watched Ameer turn the corner, feeling foolish that I'd managed to get lost in my own neighbourhood, and uncomfortable at having mistrusted him outright for no reason. After decades of living in London where the norm was to invariably be wary, even suspicious, of one's fellow man, this unexpected kind gesture from a teenager of all people made me even more thankful for living amongst such a decent community. Again, I let that smile of blissful contentment spread uncontained across my face.

The next morning, I recounted to Farah my conversation with the supermarket's butcher. She listened with a wide grin on her face.

'That was my father,' she laughed.

'Your father? And why was your father asking me about his flight to Tripoli?' I asked, still none the wiser.

That was the moment the missing link was revealed and it all fell into place in my head. I learnt that every adult inside the compound either worked for SOC or was an employee's family member—from the road sweepers to the school teachers, to the bank tellers, to the supermarket's butcher in this particular case. The compound was a community of people, who all happened to be employed by one company: SOC. Many had attended the schools run by SOC inside the compound that their children now attended, everyone shopped at the facilities provided by SOC and received medical care at the clinics managed by SOC inside its compound. Living and working under one roof created a natural camaraderie between all the residents and a safe environment in which work colleagues became next-door neighbours and friends. From that moment on, I never felt any confusion when approached—even at the most unlikely places—by anyone enquiring about travel arrangements.

Except for the beach, its restaurant and a gym, there were no other recreational facilities in Area 1 to speak of, but, luckily, the hot climate was conducive to all kinds of outdoor activities. It was uncomplicated living and a drastically simpler way of life from the one I'd been used to. A regular gym user back in London, I was delighted that there was one in the compound close to my house. I scheduled to attend at the weekends, on Friday and Saturday afternoons, during the women's opening hours, and I shall never forget the first time I visited.

The early summer sun beat down on the compound mercilessly while the suffocating heat was far more conducive to the midday nap that residents indulged in than the sweaty gym session I had in mind. The road was deserted as I approached the plain, one-level blue- and white-painted building a stone throw away from the beach. I winced at the blinding whiteness of the sand.

As I got nearer, I noticed an old man sitting with his back against the trunk of an old juniper tree, legs outstretched, lost in the pages of a book on his lap, his white turban and light grey *abaya* a striking contrast to his sun-baked skin. I slowed down my steps to take in the exquisiteness of the scenery before me. I then approached the entrance to the building, and the old man stood up, walking slowly over to me, one hand extended towards mine.

'*Salem. Marhaba. Asmi* Mahmud,' he said with a wide, toothless smile.

Mahmud was the gym janitor and he didn't speak a word of English. He told me that only a handful of women came to the gym in the afternoons due to the intense heat, and that he was delighted he finally had a customer. Inside, the large, no-frills gym was a world apart from the fancy, high-tech type I'd been a member of in London, but it provided all the basic equipment. Mahmud quickly turned on the noisy air conditioning units in the boiling gym before returning to reading his book under the welcome shade of the juniper tree. Unsurprisingly, there were no spa facilities at the gym, but my disappointment was short-lived as I refused to let the scarcity of any material comforts bother me. Each passing day opened my eyes to the sparse simplicity of life in the compound and to the multitude of small luxuries I'd taken for granted in London. But I'd laid the necessary mental groundwork to accept things as I'd find them, and instead embrace the unpretentious way of life I'd chosen. I became a gym user at weekends and enjoyed my weekly fitness sessions there until SOC decided to allocate the women their own gym, right opposite my house.

At the end of my workouts, I'd stroll lazily to the beach and flop down onto the soft, warm sand for a quiet moment of relaxation before making my way home. Sitting in silent contemplation of the timeless, natural beauty before me, I'd breathe in the energising sea air deep into my lungs, and let the healing power of the sun spread gently all over me. These precious, priceless moments were my new luxuries and I hoped to lock in each minute detail of my surroundings deep inside me to cherish for the rest of my life. Each time I sat on that white sand and marvelled at the limitless expanse of the sea, I had the overwhelming feeling that everything in my life was in sync.

My life in Libya was taking shape in the best possible way. Each morning, I sprang out of bed, full of joy at the prospect of another hot, sunny, stress-free day ahead. Each instant that I spent in these new surroundings reaffirmed to me that the secret to inner fulfilment was to be found in true simplicity and awareness of what really mattered in life; I was supremely grateful for the lesson.

At the time of my arrival in Libya, US economic sanctions were still in force, and I could feel their impact on the day-to-day life of ordinary Libyans. While the food supplies in shops were basic and limited to say the least, the only positive point was that prices were considerably cheaper than in London. But the shortage of goods didn't bother me in the slightest; instead, it made me realise that I could get by on so much less. It opened my eyes to the mountains of food carelessly thrown away daily in affluent countries, whilst the sanctions brought home the immorality of imposing on a nation a limit on the foods its people ate, on the medicines to treat them, on the clothes they wore or on the places they travelled to, all to force it to bend to a political agenda. It was akin to cruelly erecting a ring of steel around a whole people and watching their struggle for survival, or deliberately holding back life-sustaining water from a wilting plant. It was a silent, callous war, but, most of all, supremely counter-productive. Such deliberate, crippling sanctions only led to distress for the people living under them, and long-term animosity and hostility towards those imposing them. Despite the unfairness of it all, and the daily hardship these measures inflicted on the locals, they displayed nothing but the most stoic acceptance of their reality. I had no doubt that their strong religious beliefs and sense of family and community played a major part in their tolerance of the harsh difficulties imposed on them. The whole population endured this de facto collective punishment patiently, living through it to the end, a humbling experience for the pampered, over-indulged foreigner that I was.

Even in these less than ideal circumstances, I encountered nothing but kindness and generosity from the Libyan people. The compound might have offered only the most basic necessities, but the warmth of both the climate and its residents, the safety of my surroundings, the sandy beach on my doorstep and the friends I was making, all more than compensated for the materialistic niceties I was doing without. I was going to live in glorious simplicity, and was more than ready for the privilege.

In many ways, this was the perfect opportunity to assess what really mattered in my life. It was a form of training of mind, body and soul to reach a deeper awareness of the true meaning of life, with its inevitable mix of trials and blessings. I learnt to relish my modest living conditions, feeling enormously fortunate at being able to find beauty and true contentment in the very things that money couldn't buy. Watching the golden sun set on the beach was a magical, spiritual moment that I sought daily, and I felt a strong sense of belonging amongst this warm, welcoming community. I found abundance despite the sparsity, and learnt to rejoice in the smallest things instead. My thirty years in busy London had made me crave a more uncomplicated and spiritual way of life, and I found it in a workers' compound, in a far-away land between the desert and the sea. The country's shortage of material goods was inconsequential to me. The endless hours spent back home on a mindless hunt for a fashionable item of clothing, bag or shoes in crowded shopping malls were replaced by soothing relaxation and meditation on a secluded Libyan beach. My thirsty soul was being quenched at last, and I wasn't prepared to trade this new-found serenity for the world. During these early days in Libya, on this side of heaven, I couldn't have asked for anything more.

The more I discovered about Libya and its values, the more I felt comfortable. I appreciated the Libyan people's innate hospitality, their unpretentious ways, and admired them for adhering to their strong ethics. A work colleague, Amin, once confided that, 'No one would ever go hungry in Libya because we all look out for one another.' This statement summed up the core of the Libyan people. It was this spirit of generosity and compassion towards one another that instantly captured my heart, making me feel so at home in Libya.

Surprisingly, the modern, westernised woman I considered myself to be found it immensely liberating that there existed no pressures on women to conform to certain fashion diktats so prevalent in other societies. There was no emphasis on looking a certain way, no trendy dress code to obey and no incitements to jump on that shallow, fast-changing fashion bandwagon. It was incredibly empowering to be within a society that didn't objectify women, knowing there would be no bikini-clad beauties sitting on cars to attract buyers. People seemed to look beyond the physical appearance and, in true east-meets-west style, they dressed in either traditional or western attire, the dress code simply demanding a decent appearance in public. Local women in Brega wore the traditional *abaya*, that loose overgarment covering the whole body, which had never been part of my wardrobe or even on my mind as an alternative choice of clothing, especially in the hot Libyan climate. Not until I came across a 1980s scientific study carried out in the Negev Desert by researchers at Harvard and Tel Aviv Universities, which showed that loose clothing over the entire body was the best suited to keep cool in hot climates and protect from the extreme heat of the desert sun. I hadn't expected that, and decided to test the veracity of this research by donning an *abaya* for a whole day. By the end of that day, I was hugely impressed by the many advantages I'd found in wearing one.

As a start, it was easy to throw over leggings and a vest top, adding a freedom of movement non-existent when wearing tight-fitting clothing, and it was no more constricting or heat-retaining than any other garment. But, most of all, it would make getting ready for work in the mornings significantly stress-free, the perfect solution to that tiresome indecision about what to wear that I, like most women, experienced most days. I was soon won over and, for a while, colourful, loose, flowing *abayas* became garments of choice in my Libyan summer wardrobe.

Although I'd researched basic facts about Libya before I set foot in the country, I was often caught short over my expectations. Totally ignorant that Libya was a cash only society across the board, I'd arrived with only my bank debit card and little cash. But there were no ATMs anywhere at the time I was there, and certainly none inside the compound. A day or two after my arrival at the compound, I asked Annie the location of the nearest ATM.

'The nearest? Umm… let me see,' she said slowly. 'I'd say somewhere on the other side of the Med. Malta? Italy? Take your pick!' she added before bursting into laughter.

The lack of ATMs proved to be hugely problematic during my first year in the compound. SOC paid its expatriates' salaries directly into their bank accounts in their home countries, and with no ATMs available in the country, cash withdrawals were not possible. With the Tripoli immigration department detaining my passport for nearly a year upon my initial arrival, it had been impossible for me to return to London for not only a break, but for some much-needed cash. I lived on the modest monthly allowance of one hundred dinars I received towards my food expenses, but reflected that if I was prepared to live a less pampered life, then the opportunity had just presented itself to rise to the challenge and prove it. For nearly a year, I kept to a strict budget, counting Libyan pennies, at times too broke to afford the barest food essentials provided by a country under economic sanctions. But I was buoyed by the invaluable spiritual riches of a carefree life in the sun, amongst a friendly community so I simply tightened my belt and hoped for an imminent release of my passport. After that first year, I made sure to bring back enough cash from my London breaks to never have to count Libyan pennies ever again.

It was company policy to forward its foreign recruits' passports to the immigration authorities in Tripoli for the necessary registration process. The passports would then be returned within weeks to their owners. I'd initially applied for the job under my identity as a French citizen, but received my first British passport just before the job interview process was completed, and decided to use my British passport to work in Libya. I didn't think for a second that this change in formalities would raise suspicions with the Libyan authorities, but it certainly did. It took nearly a year before my British passport was released by the immigration department—not before a lengthy investigation into my being a potential spy was carried out.

'A spy?' I spluttered at a grinning Mr Bayda as he handed me my passport.

'No, of course I didn't believe you were a spy,' he said nonchalantly. 'But the immigration people have to do their job…'

Suddenly, a surreal scene played out in my head in which undercover Libyan secret service agents in dark glasses and long robes stood on desert dunes, their binoculars tracking my every move across the compound, or lurking behind bushes, long-lens cameras at the ready to capture incriminating evidence of espionage activities on my part. And all the while, without a single care in the world other than settling into my new life in the sun, I'd been blissfully clueless of the goings-on behind the scenes at the immigration department.

Once my initial shock subsided, Mr Bayda revealed that the notion of a person being a citizen of two countries simultaneously was alien to Libyans, and was the reason behind the Department of Immigration's investigation. At that moment, I thanked my lucky stars that I'd always lived a law-abiding life, devoid of any illegal activities that might have qualified me in the eyes of the Libyan authorities as an undesirable alien to be swiftly deported from the country—or worse. I was delighted at regaining possession of my passport and looked forward to a long overdue break to London after nearly a year's absence, and bringing back some much-needed cash.

Many of the unoccupied houses on Secretary Street were in need of maintenance, and were left in a state of quasi-dilapidation behind their garden walls. After a few months at house 1518, serious plumbing issues forced me to relocate to another on the opposite side of the road. A year later, structural problems caused me to move to yet another house on the same street. This third house, number 1551, had been originally designed for a family, and was, therefore, larger than most of the properties on the street. It was a corner property with three palm trees in the garden. I was over the moon at the unexpected upgrade, and threw myself wholeheartedly into transforming this house into an Arabian

Nights inspired haven. After a few trips back and forth to London, I managed to move all my clothes and personal items to my home inside the compound, and felt totally settled in my Arabian sanctuary. My happiest days in Libya were spent in house 1551, in blissful ignorance that my safe haven would become the nightmare setting of my rape many years later.

House 1551 stood on a corner, and I soon noticed that young kids had the unfortunate habit of throwing stones at its windows each time they walked by. The impact of the stones hitting the windows' steel shutters was massively irritating. After putting up with the nuisance for a few days, I reported the issue to Mr Bayda who calmly responded that he'd sort it out.

I was at my desk one afternoon a couple of days later, when my neighbour, Sandy, called.

'Why is there a security guard sitting on a chair outside your house?' she asked. 'He's been there for hours.'

I didn't know the answer. I was as puzzled as Sandy was, and couldn't imagine why on earth a guard would be sitting outside my house. I walked straight into Mr Bayda's office in case he knew any more than Sandy and I did.

'Of course I do!' he said with a mischievous wink. 'Trust me… It will soon stop the kids throwing stones at your windows.'

When I told Mr Bayda about the incidents, he made no comment as to how he proposed dealing with the matter. But, given his no-nonsense manner, I should have known that he wouldn't hesitate to implement the most draconian measures. He'd ordered a guard to be posted outside my house to catch the stone-throwing culprits in action, and send a clear message that no anti-social behaviour would be tolerated against the female residents on Secretary Street. I was beginning to grasp the meaning of *wasta*, and appreciated its necessity to bring effective results. I certainly was grateful to have someone as powerful as Mr Bayda as my own *wasta*, especially in a part of the world where, I'd been warned, nothing happened without it.

After a couple of days of conspicuous surveillance, the security guard deemed his mission accomplished and left. It was a drastic measure against a minor issue, but the message was heeded loud and clear, and there was no more stone-throwing at my windows after that. I was in good hands under Mr Bayda's protection, and trusted that he'd solve any problems I might encounter swiftly and decisively. Safe in this cocoon-like environment, I sat back and watched the years roll by leisurely and uncomplicatedly.

Every few months, as a break from the somewhat uneventful atmosphere of the compound, I'd spend the weekend in Benghazi with either Sandy or Hiba. SOC had an office and guesthouse in the city which we were allowed to use for our weekend breaks. We'd catch the company bus after work on a Thursday afternoon and return on Saturday afternoon, after an exciting couple of days in the lively city.

Benghazi, located some two hundred and fifty kilometres from Brega, is the second largest city in Libya, and one of the country's major economic centres. In Benghazi, unlike the prevalent desert habitat of the rest of Libya, desert sands gave way to lush green hills and white sandy beaches. Excursions to the ruins of Cyrene, to Jabal al-Akhdar (the Green Mountains) or further south into the desert would be a tourist's dream and a testament to the richness of the country's unspoilt natural beauty and untapped tourism potential. The influence on the city's architecture by its Arab, Ottoman and Italian past rulers was reflected in magnificent structures such as the al-Berka Palace, the largest architectural Ottoman construction, the Bait-al Medina al-Thaqafi Museum or the Benghazi Cathedral in Maydan al-Catedraeya (Cathedral Square).

The majority of the Benghazi residents believed that throughout his rule Gaddafi held a mistrust and resentment towards them, which was evidenced by the deliberate neglect of the city's infrastructure by the authorities in Tripoli. This disregard was perceived as payback for the population's historical dissent towards central rule being transferred from Benghazi to Tripoli following Gaddafi's takeover. This snub of the city by the central authorities would later be one of the reasons for the 2011 uprising of the Benghazi population against the Libyan leader.

Whenever my friends and I visited the city, we were invariably greeted with warmth and courtesy from its people with their cheery 'Marhaba! Welcome to Libya!'—a testament to their friendly disposition towards foreigners. A city where east and west merged harmoniously, it was modern, sophisticated in some parts, and uniquely traditional in others. Many hours were spent leisurely exploring the city's trendy boutiques on Shari' Dubai (Dubai Street) or strolling through the fragrant *souks* in search of yet another trinket to take home. I'd excitedly penned a long list of sites to visit in the city during my time in Libya, unaware that my time was counted and that my plans would never materialise.

In 2009, my work department in Area 2 moved to Area 1, into a smaller, brand-new, one-level building, in which I still had a large office to myself. I now lived and worked in the same area, with my new office a mere ten minutes' walk from my house. I stopped getting on the company bus each day, and enjoyed the daily walk to and from work, with my favourite music plugged to my ears and not a care in the world. Although Mr Bayda had retired a few months previously and I thoroughly missed his reassuring presence in the office, it was still a blissful time when everything in my life seemed to fall conveniently into place.

My new manager, Mr Amir Fahmi, was a man in his mid-fifties, an ebullient, talkative character, whose eyes twinkled each time he narrated stories about his past foreign travels. He too had perfect command of the English language, and although I didn't develop with him the same rapport I had with Mr Bayda, the office continued being a pleasant and relaxed place to be in.

Twice a year, I returned to London on breaks, and looked forward to catching up with family and friends, as well as stocking up on jars of Marmite and English marmalade to take back to Brega like some priceless commodities from another world. It was always hugely exciting going back to London, but throughout my time there, I couldn't help counting down the days until my return to Libya. The more I got used to the sheltered Brega environment, the more I felt like a fish out of water when in London. I missed the slow pace of Libyan life and the stress-free ambience of the compound. There was no sign at that time that a storm was slowly brewing in that region that would forever change life in Brega as I knew it.

THE ARAB SPRING

Protests first erupted in Tunisia at the end of 2010, following the self-immolation of a street trader stopped from selling his ware by the police. This tragic event led to unrest spreading across the whole country in what came to be known as the 'Jasmine Revolution', and to the overthrow of President Ben Ali and his government in January 2011, after twenty-three years in power. The tides of discontent then expanded to various parts of the Middle East and North Africa against autocratic regimes and the perpetually ailing economies that were the lot for their long-suffering populations. Within weeks, it was Egypt's turn to face violent clashes between government forces and demonstrators, leading to the Egyptian president Hosni Mubarak's resignation in February 2011 after thirty years in power.

While these uprisings spread across those regions like wildfire and appeared to be spontaneous reactions to specific events, they were, in reality, the unavoidable result of the inevitable awakening of the Arab street which had been simmering under the surface for far too long. Over the past two centuries, after enduring the brutal colonisation of their countries by foreign powers, these societies have had to suffer more brutality at the hands of autocratic leaders in power for decades. The widespread social discontent, the entrenched political corruption, the never-ending economic decline, and the joblessness of educated youths no longer prepared to accept the status quo were legitimate catalysts for these revolts. At an age where social media was part of everyday life, the Arab street was waking up and reacting to the stark reality that it'd been cheated for far too long by its leaders. The youths were ready to revendicate their legitimate rights to the kind of dignified life any citizen across the world was entitled to—no more, no less.

Despite the rebellions expanding to other countries in the region, Libyans were confident that their country, under the iron-fist control of Gaddafi, would remain safe from such social upheavals. In reality, the storm looming across the whole region was a long time coming to Libya too, and timid rumblings for change had already begun in some parts of the country, with protests taking place since mid-January 2011. Unsurprisingly, they started in Benghazi and other cities in the east of the country, ushering in the '17 February Revolution', and culminating in the tragic demise of Gaddafi, the country's long-standing, all-powerful leader, in October 2011.

Initially, the protests in Benghazi were the consequence of yet more delays in the completion of social housing being built there; they then spiralled out of control, leading to government offices being attacked. In view of the recent events in Tunisia and Egypt, and to prevent the same outcome, the government swiftly injected vast sums of money into the delayed housing projects, but it was too late to appease the population. As confrontations continued into February 2011, the police responded with increasingly lethal force, firing live ammunition into demonstrators. This was the precursor to the 'Day of Rage' on 17 February, which erupted into deadly clashes and violent protests throughout the east of the country.

Safety tucked inside the remoteness and isolation of the compound, I didn't immediately measure the extent or seriousness of the events unfolding around the country. There was a news blackout on state television, and my Libyan work colleagues, despite their uneasiness at what was going on in their country, didn't express anything other than their hope that all would soon be back to normal. Since no one inside the compound appeared unduly worried, I went along with the prevailing mood, believing I was still perfectly safe inside the compound.

My first inkling that trouble was brewing close to Brega came one morning in early February 2011. I was part of a group of about a dozen expatriate employees travelling to Ajdabiya for the yearly medical check-up required to renew our work visas. Once the check-ups were completed, we congregated at our agreed meeting point, and waited for Mabrouk, the SOC chauffeur, to drive us back to the compound.

All of a sudden, a crowd of hundreds of people emerged from around the corner, chanting and punching the air with clenched fists. I couldn't make out what they were saying, but judging by their demeanour, it appeared to be quite ominous. A palpable uneasiness descended upon our group just as Mabrouk pulled up in the company bus, frantically gesturing for us to get on board.

'*Yallah, yallah*! Let's go! Quick!' he cried out.

He didn't have to say it twice. We scrambled onto the bus and he sped off towards the safety of the compound, one hour's drive away. In those few short minutes as I watched the angry protesters, I'd had a brief glimpse into the early stages of the catastrophic events that would engulf Libya for many years to come. Although still an unspoken threat that everyone seemed either determined to ignore or too fearful to articulate, it was now inescapable that trouble was edging closer to Brega, and no one knew whether the unfolding events would lead to the dramatic outcome seen in neighbouring Tunisia and Egypt. But the compound, with its enclosed, tightly secured, fortress-like environment, seemed totally unaffected by the stirrings going on in other parts of the country. Its residents continued with their uneventful day-to-day life for a few more weeks before Brega was dragged into the country's tumultuous new reality.

One early evening at the end of February 2011, Hiba and I set off on our regular one-hour stroll towards the compound's tiny airport. She'd usually park her car at the start of our route before we walked to the airport and back. The route was in the middle of nowhere, providing the ideal setting to unwind before bedtime. That particular evening, on our way back towards the car, the faint brouhaha of raised voices stopped us in our tracks. Hiba and I looked at one another apprehensively.

'What's that?' she asked.

It was too dark to see anything other than a mass of shadowy figures marching in the distance.

'Let's hurry back to the car,' I said, remembering the protest in Ajdabiya just a couple of weeks earlier.

We sprinted back to the car and, as we approached it, the voices grew distinctly louder and the shadowy figures clearer. It was hard to believe, but sure enough, a protest was underway inside our peaceful compound, where strict security and order had always been the rule. Hiba drove the short distance to Secretary Street as we speculated whether the unrest outside of Brega had managed to slip past the tight security of the compound. I was uneasy at what I'd just witnessed, and greatly concerned at the implications for the compound and its residents in the coming days.

I went to bed that night hoping against hope that Hiba and I had misread the situation, and that all would be well again. The next morning, as I set out on my way to work, I noticed trash scattered along the usually spotless route to the office: charred debris, torn book pages, loose papers, broken bottles, loudspeakers...

Unsettled by the chaotic scene before my eyes, I hurried towards my office building. I just had time to step inside the reception hall before my mouth fell open. A soldier in full army uniform and Kalashnikov rifle rushed past me, straight into my manager's office. At that very instant, any lingering hopes I had that the compound was still safe, evaporated into thin air. The dreaded threat of a full-scale armed conflict in Libya was now a reality on my doorstep. I sat at my desk, anxiously waiting for the soldier to leave my manager's office before I flew inside. The telephone on Mr Fahmi's desk rang off the hook. He looked up at me wearily, and let it ring. His face was sombre, devoid of any trace of his usual joviality.

'*Salem.* What's going on?' I blurted out. 'Why was that—'

I stopped dead in my tracks. *What the hell's happened here?* I thought. His office walls were bare. Every single portrait of Gaddafi—and there were many—had been taken down. This had to be a hugely significant move. There had been at least ten large portraits of the country's stony faced leader adorning Mr Fahmi's office walls. They'd hung supremely on his walls ever since the department relocated to this building, but, most importantly, they were still hanging there the day before. They'd been hurriedly taken down and gathered into a large pile on the floor, waiting to be removed from his office at the earliest opportunity.

'There's no problem at all,' he said unconvincingly. 'None at all...'

The telephone stopped ringing, and he looked relieved. I recounted to him the protest of the previous evening during my stroll to the airport with Hiba, and the trash on my way to the office that morning. I didn't dare ask about the Gaddafi portraits piled up against the wall. It was the cliched big elephant in the room, but I instinctively felt the issue too sensitive to mention, although it spoke volumes by itself.

'Really, everything's fine... We'll be placing cannons around the compound by the weekend, just to be sure...' he added.

Cannons around the compound? Just to be sure? Of what exactly? My anxiety increased tenfold at the thought of deadly military artillery positioned around the compound while I was still inside it. The previous evening's protest, the timely removal of the portraits of the all-powerful Gaddafi, and now the prospect of cannons around the compound within days were more than enough signs that Brega was, indeed, under a serious, imminent threat. Was SOC—a subsidiary of a government company—expecting an attack by opposition rebels?

I recalled when we moved into this building a few months earlier, and how my manager had excitedly asked for suggestions to hang his collection of Gaddafi's portraits for maximum effect. His office being a rather large space, they were hung in several prominent places, and Mr Fahmi was exceedingly proud at this display of allegiance to his leader. Until I suggested the empty wall behind his desk for one portrait.

'What? And turn my back on *him* all day?' he sneered, eyes wide with genuine shock.

His reaction took me aback, and I felt greatly embarrassed at my faux pas. I couldn't understand this fervent adulation towards any leader. Gaddafi's portraits took place of pride all over Libya, in each and every administration building, shop, medical clinic, school or business establishment. They were displayed on every wall of every building throughout the land, the leader's steely eyes drawing his people's gaze onto him in a perpetual reminder of his undisputed authority over them. The bold removal of these portraits in Mr Fahmi's office indicated that a major turning point had been reached, and that all the bubbling unrest that had been taking place outside of the compound was now edging dangerously closer to it.

The cannons that SOC planned on positioning around the compound could only mean one thing—that an armed attack by anti-government fighters was imminent. I stood in Mr Fahmi's office for a moment, feeling utterly helpless, trying to digest the significance of the alarming events that were unfolding. The loud, urgent ringing of the telephone on Mr Fahmi's desk started again. I watched him as he slowly lifted the receiver, and reflected that allegiance and loyalty to a leader were, indeed, fragile values that would crumble like sandcastles as soon as danger and personal safety were at stake. I spent the rest of the day observing the endless streams of anxious employees rushing in and out of his office, in search of reassurance about the disturbing developments that threatened their peaceful life inside the compound.

With each passing day, the threat of impending danger became more tangible as news from Benghazi or nearby Ajdabiya revealed increasingly uninhibited protests. Events had taken a drastic turn for the worse the moment that armed soldier had burst into Mr Fahmi's office a few days previously, and it surely was only a matter of time before something dreadful happened inside the compound. I desperately needed to find out what was going on around Brega, but no one seemed to know any more than I did. My Libyan work colleagues insisted that, 'All will be well very soon, *Insha'Allah*,' and I desperately wanted to believe them. I gathered whatever snippets of information circulated around the office to exchange with my Secretary Street neighbours at the end of the day to shed some light on what might be going on around us.

One afternoon on my way home from the office, I bumped into two of my street neighbours, Mandy and Linda. And they couldn't wait to unburden themselves of their day's events.

'Injured fighters were brought to the clinic this morning,' started Mandy.

'Yeah, some were foreign. We treated them while they had guns pointed at them. It was so scary,' added Linda.

'Oh my God! At our clinic? Fighters? But where's the fighting taking place? Inside the compound?' I asked, my whole being begging for a negative answer.

Linda shrugged. 'Not sure,' she said helplessly.

That SOC nurses carried out their duties at the clinic under war-like conditions was extremely unsettling, and didn't bode well for maintaining the strict security that had existed inside the compound.

As there were no obvious signs yet of any fighting inside the compound, and SOC hadn't issued any official statement about any imminent trouble, I tried to be stoic about the injured fighters at the medical clinic, and desperately clung to lame, futile reassurances as I couldn't handle the thought of being trapped inside an enclosed battlefield. My brain refused to draw or accept the only logical conclusion that fighting must be going on very close-by if injured fighters were brought to the compound's clinic. Within a few days, SOC advised all its employees that due to the fast-deteriorating situation, they were free to leave the compound and return home. And so, the exodus began. Libyan employees evacuated their families to their homes outside of Brega, a safer option than a residential compound about to fall under attack at any time. A number of expatriate employees promptly followed suit and flew out to their home countries. The bleak prospect of an armed conflict in Libya was now firmly on the cards, and no one knew whether the country was heading towards the same *dénouement* Tunisia and Egypt had seen.

It was incredibly dispiriting watching the slow and painful unravelling of the life I'd enjoyed at the compound as neighbours and colleagues said their goodbyes. No one had any idea if they'd be able to return to the compound one day and resume their peaceful life of not so long ago. In the meantime, I could only wish them peace and safety, and plan my own departure. Mary and Sandy had left the compound a few days earlier, but I, for some unfathomable reason, felt strong resistance each time the thought of leaving crossed my mind. In truth, deep inside, I didn't believe that this highly protected, government-linked fortress would ever come under attack from opposition forces or anyone else for that matter. I decided to keep an eye on developments and stay put until the very last, inevitable moment, which I naively expected would never come. I stubbornly pushed the thought of leaving out of my mind despite the events of the past few weeks and the throngs of neighbours and colleagues fast-exiting the compound. I was incredibly relieved when Hiba confided that she'd also decided to stay until it was no longer safe to do so. Hiba and I not only lived opposite each other, but worked in offices within a short walking distance of one another. We believed that last-minute resolutions between the warring factions would put an end to this madness, and, until that moment, we resolved to sit tight, maintain closer contact, and review the situation if it worsened. We didn't have to wait too long.

Wednesday, 2 March 2011 was supposed to start like any other ordinary day in the compound, but it was going to be radically different. Just after six o'clock that morning, a deafening thud startled me awake. It seemed to be coming from right outside my house. I opened my eyes, stretched out lazily, wondering what that noise could have been before remembering that Wednesday was garbage collection day. I blamed the ruckus on noisy garbage collectors and thought nothing more of it. Still groggy, I got out of bed slowly and made my way drowsily towards the bathroom. I'd barely had time to turn on the light when the rapid rat-a-tat of gunfire stopped me in my tracks, jolting me into full consciousness. I'd never been in any proximity to real gunfire before, but its blood-curdling sound was unmistakable.

I instinctively turned the light off, and dropped to the floor, shaking from head to toe. Raw terror engulfed my entire being as I realised that the threat of an armed battle inside the compound was no longer a threat; it had become very real and was happening right on my doorstep. My heart started pounding uncontrollably inside my chest as I struggled to breathe. Paralysed with fear, I crumpled into a cowering heap behind the bathroom door, and thought of my loved ones—my mother, father, brothers, sisters. Would I live through whatever was coming and see them again? I'd never experienced such life-threatening danger so imminently close. Suddenly, my mind flashed back to a decade earlier to recall the warnings from family and friends about working in a country like Libya, and I wondered whether they'd been right all along.

My brain raced with petrifying thoughts and scenarios. Why didn't I leave when I had the chance to? What if I was taken hostage? I was furious with myself for playing down so many signs of fast-approaching chaos. I was so distraught that I thought I'd lose my mind if I didn't speak immediately to someone, anyone. The gunfire was ringing all around my neighbourhood, and I panicked that the telephone line would soon be disabled. I took a deep breath before crawling as fast as I could across the hallway towards the telephone in the living room. I reached out for the receiver and heard the reassuring humming of the line before my trembling fingers frantically dialled the five digits of my manager's home number. A despondent Mr Fahmi confirmed that anti-government rebels were at that very moment fighting against government forces for control of Brega and its oil installations. The most profound sense of dread crept up the back of my neck as he revealed what was unfolding in Brega.

'Don't leave your house under any circumstances! Stay put!' he said. 'I'll call you with more news throughout the day. But I'm sure it'll soon be over.'

He attempted to reassure me, but the agitation in his voice told me to expect the worst. He'd said it would soon be over, but for whom?

Numb with fear, I lay sprawled on the living room floor for a moment, too stunned and fearful at what might come next. I couldn't count on the telephone line remaining operational, and dreaded being trapped inside my house, isolated from anyone. There was no way on earth I could go through such stressful times alone. I berated myself again for foolishly believing I'd be safe in the compound despite all the recent warnings—the growing protests, the injured fighters at the clinic, the cannons around the compound. How could I have been so heedless of them all? The situation had been growing steadily worse right in front of my eyes, but the infuriating optimist in me had stubbornly chosen to hope for the best.

I closed my eyes to calm my agitated mind, but all I could focus on was the sound of the ongoing artillery fire and explosions. I thought of the people around the world whose lives were marred by daily fighting—how did they go about their day when bullets were flying all around them? I crawled towards the television set and switched it on. Aghast, I watched as the BBC World News reported on the fighting in Brega. The situation had become so serious it had made the international news!

Strangely enough, now it was official news outside of Libya, wild, unrestrained panic set in while my whole body shook uncontrollably. The thought of being in mortal danger, far from my family and friends, was something I'd never imagined being in before, not even in my worst nightmares. I dialled my sister Jameela's number, who answered before the phone even had a chance to ring.

'I've been trying to call you, but couldn't get through,' she blurted out. 'Brega's all over the news. I'm so worried! I knew this would happen!'

'I'm OK, really. But there's a lot of gunfire everywhere. It started early this morning… I thought it was the garbage men!' I half joked, trying to steady my quivering voice.

'Will you be able to leave? I'll contact the embassy for you this morning!' she said.

'My boss says it'll be over soon. I'm just going to wait it out,' I said, trying to reassure her. 'I'll keep in touch whenever I can, but don't worry… I'm OK.'

I understood that morning what absolute terror was, but there was no use displaying my fears to Jameela and causing her anxiety in a situation she had no control over. I then dialled my friend Diane's number in London. Diane was an SOC contractor and regularly visited the compound on business. She was still in bed when I informed her that fighting was going on in Brega between government and rebel forces. After a stunned silence, she suggested I speak with a journalist friend of hers at a well-known international news network, and give a live report from the ground as it were. I quickly assessed the risks of such an interview while I was still inside the compound, and declined, too afraid of any consequences on my safety. My last call was to Hiba whose house was right across the road from mine. I didn't have to ask her how she was faring—her trembling voice said it all.

'Put the kettle on,' I said. 'As soon as the gunfire stops a bit, I'm coming over for coffee.'

I crawled back into the bedroom as speedily as my shaky legs would let me, and put on a T-shirt, tracksuit bottoms and running shoes—practical attire just in case a speedy getaway became necessary at any point. I threw a change of clothes into a small bag, then sat curled up on the floor in the dark bedroom. I shut my eyes, breathing deeply to calm the frenetic racing of my heart, and waited for a lull in the gunfire.

After a few moments that felt like an eternity, the firing paused long enough to decide that the time had come for my dash to Hiba's house. I took a deep breath, tried to steady my wobbly legs, and made my way towards the front door. I opened it a crack and cautiously peeked into the garden. It was eerily still. Even the usual chirping of the birds was silent. I shuddered at the thought of being confronted by fighters once I stepped onto the street or, worse still, being fired at. I pushed the numbing thought out of my head and, shaking like a leaf, unlocked the padlock from the garden gate as quietly as I could. I winced as it creaked open, and furtively scanned the street; it was empty and deathly silent. The only sound was the out-of-control thumping of my heart inside my chest. The stillness and sense of foreboding that filled the morning air didn't bode well for the day ahead.

There was no time to waste. I mumbled a little prayer, took another deep breath, threw my bag over my shoulder, yanked the gate fully open, and bolted across the street towards Hiba's house at breakneck speed. The combination of adrenaline and raw terror gave me proverbial wings, and I flew into her garden like some unstoppable supersonic missile. Hiba, pale and shaking, stood by her front door waiting for my high-speed arrival. The relief that I'd made it out of my house safely, and that I wouldn't have to go through this dramatic time alone nearly brought me to tears. My legs buckled and I collapsed on her couch to catch my breath.

'I bet... you... didn't know... I could run... that fast,' I gasped. 'I'm pretty sure... I've broken... a record!'

'Yeah, you're definitely in the wrong job!' she replied with a strained smile.

Our attempt at humour to release the suffocating, unbearable tension we were under was short-lived as the sharp rat-a-tat of machine guns started again to bring us back to our grim reality. At that instant, I vouched for the undeniable truth of safety being found in numbers—even at only two. I felt intense relief at being with a friend, and not having to endure alone a day of battling enemies.

In an effort to keep her house as inconspicuous as possible, Hiba had lowered all the steel shutters. The television was on in the living room, providing the only source of lighting. Slumped on her couch, Hiba and I watched with unbelieving eyes as the fighting between the government and opposition forces dominated the news on all international channels. There we were, inside the compound, watching it being attacked live on television. We spent the morning flicking through channels for updates on the fighting while the sound of sporadic gunfire rang around us. It was a surreal moment, but far too dramatic to start marvelling at the wonders of modern technology.

At times, some of Hiba's friends called for moral support. Everyone was huddled at home, hoping and praying for a swift end to this nightmare. Suddenly, my cell phone rang.

'Hello? My name is Peter Jackson,' said an unfamiliar voice. 'I'm with the Foreign Office.'

My heart quickened at this unexpected ray of hope in the midst of the ongoing turmoil.

'We're aware of what's going on in Brega... We're monitoring developments closely and looking at ways to get you out of the compound, should the situation worsen. In which case, you might have to be airlifted by helicopter…'

My heart missed a beat. Did he just say 'airlifted by helicopter'? My eyes popped out of my head whilst my jaw dropped all the way to the floor at the mind-blowing plan. The situation was getting more surreal by the minute, and with all the madness going on around me, I now had to worry about dangling from a helicopter over the SOC compound!

'We carried out a similar rescue in the desert a few days ago,' he added, 'but it's a risky operation so we're weighing up other options… Please stay strong… We'll get you out!'

I breathed a huge sigh of relief at the mention of 'other options' to the hair-raising helicopter plan. I was incredibly reassured by his decisive tone and firm promise that I'd be rescued, whatever the means. I felt boundless gratitude that the British authorities kept an eye on *little ol' me* at such a dangerous time, and incredibly privileged to be a citizen of a country whose government would go to such lengths to bring them to safety. I only hoped that Hiba's government would also step up with an offer of assistance.

While tremendously relieved that the Foreign Office was figuring out a plan for my rescue, I couldn't help the sense of dread in the pit of my stomach each time I visualised in my mind the daring mission—me and my crippling phobia of heights, holding on to dear life as I helplessly dangled from a helicopter hoisting ladder over the Libyan desert! It wasn't going to be a pretty sight, and certainly not what I'd signed up for all those years ago. The scene seemed far more appropriate for a James Bond movie, and I prayed with all my heart that a more 'down to earth' alternative would be found. But just in case I was destined to swing over the

Libyan desert, I reminded myself that beggars couldn't be choosers and that I had to escape to safety from the fast-deteriorating situation around me regardless of the means of transportation on offer. It just wasn't the time to be fussy. In fact, with the dramatic circumstances enfolding around me, dangling from a helicopter over the Libyan desert was as good a way of returning to safety as any first-class British Airways flight. And it sure would be something different to relate to my family and friends for years to come—if I ever made it out alive.

Over the next couple of days, Mr Jackson called a few more times to enquire about how I was bearing up before I was finally able to leave the compound—thankfully without the need for a helicopter hoisting ladder! Although I never spoke to Mr Jackson again, I shall forever be grateful to him for his support and comforting words at a time I so desperately needed them.

Again, I thought of the people living in war zones, with the threat of death hanging over their day-to-day lives, and no offers of rescue from anyone. I thought of man's unquenchable thirst for war, and his failure to heed any lessons despite history being littered with the horrors and ravages they invariably inflicted on innocent people. A powerful nation could invade a weaker sovereign one under all kinds of false pretexts, and unleash a war on it to replace a head of state deemed hostile, all supported by the astronomical financial profit to be had by keeping the wheels of the war machine turning.

The tragedy was that these amoral wars were triggered by a few on millions of innocent people, like pawns to be sacrificed at the altar of hungry money-making war machines. I pondered, with a heavy heart, the man-made injustices of our world, and the deceptiveness of governments when they ruthlessly prioritised their strategic interests over the lives of their populations. It was deplorable that a significant war industry existed, buoyed by military spending growing at vertiginous speed whilst world peace was certainly not the motivation behind such a high-profit industry. In fact, wars became easier to start thanks to increasingly deadly state-of-the-art technology that removed any direct risk to aggressors using fully autonomous weapons able to launch laser-guided missiles at the touch of a button by an operator sitting safely behind a screen in another continent altogether. And to desensitise the masses to the normalisation of war, these deadly aggressions were cynically turned into entertainment and video games.

To normalise something so inherently evil was immoral, but no doubt the future will reveal the catastrophic consequences of such devilish plans in due course. In the meantime, it didn't bode well for the prospect of peace in our world any time soon. There could never be peace in the world as long as wars are turned into a profit opportunity, and governments continue to be motivated by greed and self-serving interests. There could never be peace in the world as long as private military contractors are available for hire, ready to fight anywhere in the world on behalf of unprincipled governments. There could never be peace in the world as long as we don't value the lives of all citizens around the world equally, and only shed tears for our own, whilst remaining coldly insensitive to the abject misery and injustices meted out to others.

In the early afternoon, still cooped up at Hiba's house searching for yet more television news to the background sound of artillery fire, came a terrifying moment which still makes me shudder. A loud commotion erupted all of a sudden, which seemed to be coming from Secretary Street itself. Hiba turned the television off before we rushed to her living room window to investigate. There was a cacophony of voices quickly followed by the sound of the houses' metal garden gates being kicked forcefully. Hiba and I stood paralysed with fear, looking helplessly at each other. I saw the colour drain from her face, and I felt it drain from mine. Numb with terror, the prospect that armed fighters—regardless of who they were or what cause they were fighting for—were about to storm the house brought me to a state of near collapse. I had flashes of horrifying scenarios if they broke into the house and found two cowering, defenceless foreign women. I'd never known such a state of physical debility as I experienced at that instant.

'Quick! Under the bed!' said Hiba.

We flew to her bedroom in utter panic and dove under her bed in synchronised clumsiness. The bed was low on its legs and, despite our petite frames, we struggled hard to crawl under it. At a different time, the scene would have been hilarious, but the moment was too dramatic to dwell on its comical side. The sound of the gates being kicked grew closer to the house. Hiba began to pray, her recitation faint and laboured, while I breathed heavily in an effort to slow down my frenzied heartbeat. After what seemed like an eternity in our indecorous, claustrophobic position, the telephone on the nightstand suddenly rang. Quick as lightning, Hiba's hand darted out from under the bed and lifted the receiver. She didn't wait to hear who was at the other end and launched into a heart-rending plea for help.

'There's something happening on our street right now! We're alone in the house... Please, help!'

I was terrified that a worse ordeal was making its way towards us, and felt my whole body being sucked inside a deep, dark hole. I closed my eyes and started praying. I had no idea who might be calling in the middle of this crisis, but maybe help was on its way to rescue us from this madness, or a warning that rebels were now controlling the compound and hunting for foreign workers to take hostage. My heart sank in my chest at the spine-chilling thought.

'This is SOC Security! We're on your street! It's over, so feel safe to come out.'

The nightmare had ended, and we were out of harm's way—for now. I took long, deep breaths to calm my overwrought nerves. Hiba and I remained under the bed for a moment, unable to move, before painstakingly crawling out from under it, disoriented, legs like jelly, weighed down by the heavy mental strains we'd been under since the early morning. I felt giddy, my whole body ached, but the relief was so immense I didn't know whether to laugh or cry. Hiba and I finally stepped out from the dark house into the sun-drenched garden, and I winced at the sharp contrast.

We were greeted by the reassuring sight of the company's armed security guards who revealed that the rebel fighters had pushed the government forces into retreat. I was quite sure this wasn't good news bearing in mind the compound was quasi-government property. But at that very moment, I couldn't care less about who'd repelled whom, why or how; I just felt tremendous relief, and a renewed humongous loathing for wars. I rejoiced that the fighting was over for now, but if the government forces had been pushed back from a site that was a vital economic asset, then it didn't take a war strategist to expect their swift return with all the necessary military power to reclaim what was theirs.

The momentary relief gave way to pressing concerns that opened the floodgates for all kinds of terrifying scenarios. How soon would the government forces return? What would happen if the rebels retained control of the compound? What were my chances of leaving now heavy fighting had started inside the compound? As a foreigner, had I become a potential hostage to be exchanged between warring enemies? Suddenly, the thought of dangling from a helicopter hoisting ladder over the Libyan desert never seemed more appealing— and the sooner, the better. At least, I would've been granted the privilege of an escape denied to my Libyan neighbours and colleagues. I'd come to Libya in search of a new life experience, but after a blissful decade, circumstances had radically changed. The danger of my situation dawned on me loud and clear. I might soon be rescued out of this mayhem, but it was heartbreaking that this beautiful, hospitable country was on its way to being forced into a conflict that would have far-reaching repercussions for its people for years to come.

At some point in the afternoon, one of Hiba's close friends, Sumaya, dropped by with her one-year-old baby daughter, Aya. Sumaya lived within walking distance, but I couldn't fathom how she could be out and about with her baby so soon after what had just happened.

'Aya's been crying all day. I had to take her out for a walk to calm her down,' she said as we all sat, still shaken, sipping tea and munching on biscuits in a welcome change from the day's earlier events.

Baby Aya, all soft curls and huge brown eyes, clung to Sumaya's protective arms, her tiny hands clamped tightly onto her mother's *abaya*, unwilling to let go. She remained oblivious to the favourite doll Sumaya waved gently in front of her to coax her out of her fear.

'I hope we don't have to live through more heartache,' said Sumaya. 'I was just a kid, but I still remember the night Benghazi was bombed.'

She then recounted the day, twenty-five years earlier, when the US launched a simultaneous fifteen-minute air assault on both Tripoli and Benghazi. She was seven years old at the time, but the terrifying experience still lived inside her. Twenty-five years later, it was her baby daughter's turn to be traumatised through another man-made conflict. It all seemed so infuriatingly and tragically senseless.

Hiba and I stayed huddled at her house for the rest of the day in fearful anticipation of the return of Gaddafi's troops. Would they be back tonight under cover of darkness? Or tomorrow? Or in a few days? No one knew other than it was another inevitable threat hanging over Brega. As that frightful day drew to an end and night fell, dark and ominous, my anxiety started to rise. Hiba sensed my restlessness.

'I'm taking a sleeping pill tonight,' she said. 'Would you like one too?'

'Yes, please! But only half…'

Unaccustomed to sleeping aids, that half-pill knocked me out cold until the next morning, and made me groggy for part of that day. It was reassuring that no fighting had taken place during the night—either that or the pill had done a great job of rendering me quasi-comatose and I'd missed all the action.

The morning started out like any ordinary morning in Libya—bright and warm under the rays of the sun spreading slowly across the compound. Even the chirping birds had returned, but why was the air still heavy with impending doom?

It later transpired that in the early hours of Wednesday, 2 March 2011, government forces—and not the suspected garbage collectors—entered Brega in a convoy of over one hundred vehicles to retake the town from the rebel forces. In what came to be referred to as 'the First Battle of Brega', rebel forces had gained control of the oil refinery, the port, the airport, and the town's university. The incredibly bizarre news that fighting had been taking place around Brega was shocking to me and to all of my friends on Secretary Street. Sheltered inside the seclusion of the compound, with no evidence of fighting inside it, none of us had had any inkling that rebel forces had controlled the town all along. It had been business as usual for the compound's residents. But on that particular morning, rebel reinforcements had made their way from the nearest town, Ajdabiya, towards Brega for a face-off with the government forces, and succeeded in forcing them into retreat. The next day, government fighter jets bombed the area between the oil refinery and Brega's residential zone.

The situation had worsened beyond my wildest fears, invalidating the pact that Hiba and I had made to remain in the compound until it became too dangerous. My manager, Mr Fahmi, called early the next morning with the news that SOC was making arrangements for the remaining foreign employees to be transported to the Egyptian border from where they could make their way home. Since the grim events of the previous day, all employees, Libyan and foreign alike, rushed to leave the compound en masse. It was heart-wrenching to watch Libyan colleagues endeavouring to evacuate the expatriate workers to safety whilst they remained stuck in a deadly struggle they never asked for. As mere human beings, we all shared the same basic aspirations for a decent, peaceful place in this world, and yet millions were denied the opportunity to realise those aspirations by others' thirst for wars. The reasons for war were invariably branded under the banners of freedom or liberation to conceal their true motives—from militarily weaker regions being coveted for their natural resources, to the ousting of leaders deemed uncooperative by a powerful nation. And the buoyant war industry, whose interests were in direct opposition to global peace, made it all possible as billions were spent on military equipment by many nations whose citizens lived in poverty. Morality and decency had no place in the equation.

The events of the last few days in Brega had given me an insight into the terror inflicted on innocent people by warmongers, and I'd seen quite enough. The country was descending into chaos, and no one knew the extent to which the Libyans would become pawns in a wider political game played from outside of their own borders. I could only hope for a peaceful resolution to be found quickly, and for the Libyan people to remain safe and united.

Early the next morning, with my spirits lifted by the prospect of being en route towards Egypt later that day, I hurried to my house to pack a few clothes for my journey back home to London. With tears welling up in my eyes, I locked my house and padlocked the garden gate, with no idea whether I'd get the chance to return one day. Early that afternoon, Hiba and I said our goodbyes to all those who'd worked so unselfishly for our evacuation before boarding the coach that was to take us through the rebel-held territory in the east, and all the way to the Egyptian border. It was an incredibly bittersweet moment—relieved to be escaping the fighting, but heartbroken, and somewhat embarrassed, that our Libyan colleagues were denied the same opportunity. Would we meet again? Would they survive whatever was about to be unleashed upon them? My heart broke all over again as I recalled baby Aya's terror as she desperately clung to her mother. How many more times would she live through such terrifying moments? After a decade living in Libya, the compound and the country had become my home away from home, and it was unbearably painful to walk away from it all, even at these perilous times.

I lost count of the innumerable hours it took our coach to reach the Egyptian border as the driver kept an agonisingly slow pace through the rebel strongholds of Benghazi, Bayda and Darnah. He made several stops at specific areas to allow other fleeing foreign workers to jump on board. Mentally exhausted by the events of the past couple of days, Hiba and I sat in heavy silence, needing no words to express the emptiness we both felt inside. At regular intervals, the armed rebel fighters manning the checkpoints along the never-ending route would wave at the driver to stop. The first time this happened was a scary, confusing moment. With feline agility, a smiling young man, dressed in the conspicuous brown and beige commando style trousers, shirt and cap, hopped on board, Kalashnikov rifle at the side. In seconds, I felt that familiar sense of dread creep up at the back of my neck.

'Salem!' he said brightly before asking for the passengers' passports. He inspected each document before wishing us all safe travel, adding, 'Libya will soon be freed, and you'll all be welcome to return.'

His demeanour had been so easy-going and polite that I wondered who the bad guys were in this crazy state of affairs.

These interruptions by rebels at checkpoints happened several times along the journey, but they stopped giving rise to alarm as the men were invariably well-mannered. I was shocked at how young they appeared to be, and profoundly saddened that they had no better life choices than standing at the frontline of a deadly conflict. But the last time the coach was waved down at a checkpoint turned out to be a highly nerve-racking moment for Hiba and I. I handed the young rebel my passport, which he examined with particularly close attention. He did the same with Hiba's while still holding on to mine. Then, without a word, he walked away clutching both passports, and hopped off the coach. Hiba and I were the only women on board. Visions of a worse nightmare to come played out in my mind, and my heart started pounding wildly again. Within minutes, the young rebel reappeared and returned our passports with a polite smile. Like all the others before him, he wished all the passengers a safe journey home and, again, I wondered who the bad guys were.

Surprisingly, two Swedish journalists were allowed on board for a brief moment to speak to passengers before the coach was waved through to continue its tortuous journey. I breathed a sigh of relief, and closed my eyes tightly in a futile attempt to seal myself away from the madness of it all.

Finally, just before midnight, the coach arrived at the Egyptian border. It was freezing cold, and I was physically and mentally drained, but tremendously relieved to be out of the Libyan chaos. A handful of Egyptian guards stood by, waiting to lead all the coach passengers into a huge hangar inside which hundreds of men, women and children lay on the floor, huddled under blankets in the icy-cold temperature. My jaw dropped at the overwhelming scene before me. I wondered who these people were, and what other calamity had brought them here. I had no doubt that right in front of my eyes was another consequence of the human devastation that man created. I'd seen such images only on television news reports about some refugee crisis in some far-away part of the world. It was heart-wrenching.

I spent that sleepless night in Egypt sitting on the floor with Hiba and a dozen other SOC employees, our backs against the cold walls, resigned to the ten-hour wait until another coach arrived for our journey to Cairo airport. The coach arrived much later than expected, and we piled into it wearily for the long drive to the Egyptian capital. Shivering, starving and utterly exhausted, I plonked myself wearily on the first seat, and closed my eyes. Hiba did the same in the seat next to mine. Lost in thoughts, I relived in my mind the events of the past couple of days. No one on the coach spoke.

After countless gruelling hours on another endless road, the coach entered the cacophony of Cairo, with its manic honking of car horns and chaotic traffic congestion that made the M25 look like a lonely country lane. At long last, the coach arrived at the city's international airport, and the time came for everyone to go their separate ways. Hiba and I decided to stay overnight at one of the airport hotels for a last meal together and some much-needed sleep before parting ways in the morning. The sense of security and tranquillity at the hotel was a far cry from the recent events in Brega. It was disconcerting watching people go about their normal business whilst just over the border people were being fired at, bombed and killed. My status as a foreigner had granted me the privilege to escape the conflict in Libya, but God only knew what the Libyan people were about to experience. The situation was utterly heartbreaking, and the thought of an impending catastrophe about to hit Libya weighed heavily on my mind. I had no doubt that the distressing events I'd just lived through would change me forever.

Hiba flew out the next morning to Syria, and I to London. We said our tearful goodbyes and, to soften the sad finality of the moment, made plans for a reunion in the near future. Deep inside, I had no idea whether we'd ever meet up again, but, whatever happened, we promised to keep in touch.

EVACUATION TO LONDON

I arrived in London in a blur of shock and disbelief at the events of the last few days in Libya. I felt utterly deflated, with no plans other than making time to recover from the ordeal I'd just experienced. I was indescribably relieved to be on safe soil at last, but my heart wept at the events unfolding in Libya that were bound to impact the Libyan people, and my own life. Again, I watched people go about their business, seemingly oblivious to the horrors that others were going through in a land not too far away.

I found it impossible to concentrate on anything other than the crisis playing out in Libya. Even though my body was safely back home in London, my mind was still firmly in the Brega compound. With the real prospect of a war in the country, my concern for my Libyan friends and colleagues intensified by the minute. My days were spent riveted to the many television debates speculating on the future of Libya. Would events follow those of neighbouring Tunisia and Egypt, and result in the ousting of the Libyan leader? Would civil and political unrest follow as it did in Egypt? A coalition of nations now demanded the departure of the Libyan leader under the guise of liberating the Libyan people from his totalitarian rule. The coalition's endless reference to its war project as a 'liberation' was clearly designed to give its interference a sense of legitimacy, that the inevitable war was for a greater cause. I wasn't fooled. The more I listened to their hypocritical concern for the Libyan people, the more I felt repulsed by the scheming tactics of those in power, and deplored the helplessness of ordinary people at the hands of unscrupulous leaders. I could only pray for a swift end to the crisis in the best interests of the Libyan people alone.

With no idea of how long the conflict would last or whether SOC would recall its expatriate workforce afterwards, I thought it worthwhile to use this enforced time-out to acquire a new business skill. It was principally to occupy my mind with something other than the Libyan crisis, but it was also to prepare for a professional reconversion in case a return to Libya wasn't on the cards. The conflict in Libya was considered by SOC as a *force majeure* and, as such, the company wouldn't pay its expatriates a salary during their time out of the country. I had no idea how long I'd be without a pay check, and had to consider other options, including the dreaded one of rejoining the London rat race again. Each time I recalled how much I'd loved my time in Brega—its hot climate, stress-free holiday-like environment, safety, friendly people, the white sandy beach on my doorstep—I knew I couldn't possibly go back to riding the crowded London buses and trains in the cold and rain. Just thinking about it filled me with deep anxiety.

Working in London had once been part of a teenager's dearest dream, and had been incredibly fascinating, but it was all part of a long-gone period of time to which there was no going back. My laid-back life in Brega had been the exact opposite to my London life. After decades of thriving in the hustle and bustle of a major European city, I'd come to appreciate the away-from-it-all, soothing tranquillity of a secluded environment somewhere on the edge of the Libyan desert. The cocoon-like setting and slow pace of life I'd known for over ten years had changed me to the core. The compound had become an oasis of peace and serenity I couldn't wait to return to after my London breaks. Whatever the outcome in Libya, I decided that my working days in London were definitely over.

With that thought firmly engraved in my mind, I enrolled at a language school in Central London on a six-week course for a qualification to teach English to foreign students. Happy that I'd found a constructive project to occupy my time, I eagerly prepared for my return to the classroom. The experience took me right back to my school days all those many years ago, when raising a hand for permission to speak and going home to piles of homework had been *de rigueur*. And I was about to fully realise how difficult returning to the classroom was going to be at my age. I hadn't expected the course to be so challenging, combining intense study during the day with mountains of homework far into the night—a constraint I didn't take to gladly at first. I came close to dropping out several times during the first two weeks had it not been for the sobering fact that the course had been paid for. There were seven other students in class, all from different professional backgrounds, and all much younger than I was: bubbly Anna, a solicitor; handsome Peter, an architect; and five university graduates, Jill, Maggie, Caroline, Jane and Rosy. My co-students' academic background made me rather apprehensive about my own capabilities not only as a mature student, but as one who hadn't received an English school education in the first place. But it quickly transpired that I had nothing to worry about as my English language classes at my French *lycée* all those years ago stood me in good stead. The hardest part of the course was learning the basics of the… Welsh language!

The purpose of the task was to place the student teachers in the shoes of the foreign pupils to grasp the mental process at play when communicating with someone who couldn't understand the words spoken to him or her. It made every sense, but I could have thought of several other languages ahead of the unfathomable Welsh! Part of the course homework entailed the preparation of a daily forty-five-minute English lesson to present to some of the adult foreign students attending the school, and there was always a steady stream of volunteers for these classes. It was thoroughly nerve-racking standing in front of a group of some twenty people, all with limited English, to teach a lesson whilst being assessed, not only by my other co-students, but also by a tutor sitting conspicuously at the back of the classroom. To my utter astonishment, my performance was consistently evaluated as that of a 'calm, confident teacher, in control of her class'. A statement in total contradiction to the extreme nervousness that gripped me inwardly throughout the lesson. These evaluations taught me just how utterly deceiving impressions and appearances could be!

All my co-students and tutors were a joy to study with, but the enormous amount of daily homework required, and having to function on less than three hours' sleep each night for several weeks made for an extremely demanding and exhausting time. Even though the course deprived me of much-needed sleep, the whole process was undoubtedly worthwhile, even with my difficulties at grasping the basics of the Welsh language. I received my diploma at the end of the course with great pride, confident that it would open doors to working abroad again. I was even grateful for the rigour of it all as it certainly took my mind off the events in Libya for a while.

Once the course was over and I'd caught up on the many hours of lost sleep it had inflicted upon me, my feelings of restlessness resurfaced stronger than ever. I resumed my all-consuming search for the latest updates on events in Libya, and spent hours trying to communicate with Libyan colleagues, often in vain. I spent my days waiting for positive developments to end the ongoing conflict to enable me to return to my happy life inside the compound of not so long ago. The uncertainties of my job and the preoccupation of earning no salary for an unknown period of time, coupled with a mind full of apprehensions about the future in general, began to take their toll on me.

Since my return to London, I'd been obsessively engrossed in the Libyan crisis, and was aware that, for my sanity, I had to find a stable routine, however temporary, to settle into. Although I'd started half-heartedly searching for teaching positions abroad, my prospects didn't look too promising—I was too old for one job at a school in Indonesia, whilst the second was in a tiny rural village in the depths of the Russian countryside, the description of which filled me with sheer horror. In truth, I wasn't overly concerned at being out of work for a little while as I couldn't possibly commit to another job until I had a clearer idea of how long the Libyan crisis would last. The optimist in me believed wholeheartedly that I'd resume my employment in Brega one day and, until then, I wasn't ready to turn the page on the Libyan chapter. Since I was fortunate to have paid off the mortgage on my London house a few years earlier, and had enough savings to keep me afloat for a year, I decided to take a whole year off before seriously looking for another job; a year during which

I hoped that the Libyan crisis would end and I'd be recalled to Brega.

In the meantime, I planned to take my mind off the Libyan crisis by visiting my sister Anissa and her family in Algeria, and looked forward to reconnecting with my birthplace after so many years. I left Algeria as a child, and, consequently, never felt deeply connected to it. Too young to foster any patriotic feelings towards the country of my birth while I lived in another, I grew to consider myself rather a free spirit with no complex identities or loyalties, just a citizen of the world content to adapt and integrate anywhere—happy to be French in Paris, English in London, or European in Madrid, Amsterdam or Brussels. The strong, emotional attachment to a homeland, that spontaneous affinity with people sharing the same cultural bonds, was alien to me, but I was looking forward to reconnecting with my roots.

I travelled to Algeria in late summer of 2011, staying with Anissa and her family for a couple of months during which I delighted at re-immersing myself in a familiar, yet long-forgotten environment, and rediscovering my country of birth, its amazing folks and all their endearingly eccentric idiosyncrasies. Gradually, feelings that had been buried deep inside me began stirring, awaking in me a sense of awareness and pride in belonging to a nation—I'd come home. I'd been on a much-needed journey to take my mind off events in Libya, but, instead, my visit proved to be a long-overdue opportunity to reconnect with myself. It was also the time I became aware, in the most unexpected way, of the impact that my last days in Brega had had on me.

It was just after midnight when I was jolted out of sleep by the thud of loud explosions. I immediately sat up in bed and listened. I had the strongest sense of déjà vu as my mind took me back to the first day of battle inside the compound, when the Gaddafi forces had fought the rebels. These events were still at the forefront of my mind, and they'd made me extra sensitive to any sound remotely resembling gunfire or bombings. And this time, I wasn't about to blame the Algerian garbage collectors! I felt that all too familiar dread creep up at the back of my neck, just like it had on that awful morning in Brega. No, I had no doubt that I'd heard explosions this time too. Had a conflict broken out in Algeria out of the blue? Or was someone attempting a takeover? I jumped out of bed, shaking, driven by the same panic I'd felt in Brega just a few months before. What were the odds of finding myself in another conflict, in a different country, for the second time in a few months? How unfortunate would that be! Quick as a flash, I threw on a dressing gown over my pyjamas, and flew out of the bedroom into the hallway.

'Everybody up! We're being bombed!' I shouted, banging frantically on every bedroom door. Arms flailing above my head, legs unable to stand still, I felt hugely frustrated at the lack of urgency displayed by my still sleeping hosts.

'Everybody downstairs *now*!' I ordered. 'And don't switch on the lights!'

At long last, one door slowly cracked open, and Anissa's face appeared.

'What do you mean, "We're being bombed"?' she asked, rubbing her sleepy eyes and a look of utter bewilderment on her face.

'Don't know who's doing it, but there's bombing going on, that's for sure…' I blurted out impatiently.

Since hearing the explosions a few minutes earlier and while I waited for my hosts to make an appearance, I'd figured out my theory of what might be unfolding: Algeria, located between Tunisia and Libya, had its own potential for political upheaval, and was now likely in the grips of an uprising similar to that which befell its close neighbours. My anxiety skyrocketed at my unbelievable misfortune of finding myself in a second war zone so soon after escaping from one. And this time, there would be no offers of an airlift to safety over the Algerian desert!

One by one, the bedrooms emptied out of their groggy, bemused occupants: Anissa, Malik, her teenage son, and her daughters Malika and Soraya all stood yawning and staring at me in dazed confusion at my growing agitation. With the authority of a drill sergeant, I led everyone into the large living room downstairs, under the strict orders to be silent and not to switch on the lights.

'Umm… today's the first of November,' said Malika timidly, looking expectantly at her mum for support, clearly unsure whether to laugh at my irrational behaviour or worry about my clearly disturbed state of mind.

Anissa switched on the lights before calmly pointing out that the first of November was the anniversary date of the start of the Algerian war of independence from French occupation. Those 'bombs' I'd heard had been the midnight gun salute to commemorate the event.

'No kidding! You're sure?' I asked as a massive wave of indescribable relief swept through me. 'Oh my God, that's just so good to hear!'

But relief quickly mixed with acute embarrassment at my uncalled-for antics. I'd unceremoniously woken up the entire household, and I only hoped that Anissa's neighbours hadn't also been privy to my hysteria. We all had a hearty laugh at my willing expense before going back to bed, no one more relieved or jubilant than I. Five months had passed since those traumatic days in Brega, but I'd just found out that they had implanted lingering fears inside me that were ready to rise at the most unlikely occasions. For a while, even the backfiring of a car would cause me to shake violently; such extreme reactions after being exposed to only two days of artillery fire. I lay in bed, hugely relieved that Algeria was safe from the threat of war, but heavy-hearted at the thought of the innocent people trapped in war zones with no hope of escape, of baby Aya and all the children like her, who experienced mayhem as a start to their young lives.

I returned to London re-energised by my renewed sense of identity, and resumed my daily search on the ongoing crisis in Libya. Unlike the revolts that Tunisia and Egypt had faced, the Libyan war of 'liberation' quickly degenerated into an armed struggle between forces loyal to Gaddafi and rebel forces opposed to him. Brega became the site of numerous clashes between the two groups and, between March and April 2011, the town changed hands half a dozen times until the imposition by the UN of a no fly zone cleared the way for the advance of the rebel forces. At least, there was no ambiguity as to who the western coalition was in support of.

More heavy fighting and bombardment followed until mid-August 2011, when the rebel forces finally took control of the whole of Brega. Much farther west from Brega, the rebel forces gained control of the capital, Tripoli, in August 2011, and overthrew Gaddafi's government. After months of a conflict backed by the military intervention of a western coalition on a mission to overthrow the Libyan leader at all costs, the Gaddafi regime had finally collapsed. On 20 October 2011, the shocking news came that Gaddafi had been captured and killed by rebels in his hometown of Sirte. The gruesome television footage of his final moments circulated on a loop on all news networks, followed by even more appalling footage—the exhibition of his corpse and that of his son, Mutassim, on the bare floor of an empty warehouse in the city of Misrata. Local people lined up to enter the warehouse to take photographs of the two bloody corpses. This ghastly public spectacle was horrifying, and in total contradiction to the religious values held by the Libyan people.

Bab al-Aziziya, Gaddafi's palace in Tripoli, overrun by rebels, stood in ruins, its doors wide open to any reporters willing to rifle through official papers. Much of the palace had been hastily bulldozed by the rebel forces following its takeover in August. The allied coalition's objective had been met, and the regime had not only collapsed, but, most importantly, Gaddafi had been eliminated and, along with him, the urgent threat he represented to some western leaders. It was mission accomplished for the western allies who hastily retreated, seemingly unconcerned at the dangerous political vacuum they were leaving in their trail.

RETURN TO BREGA

Months after the death of Gaddafi in October 2011, which heralded the official end of the Libyan conflict, SOC began recalling its expatriate employees to work. My life—and that of all Libyans—had been suspended for a whole year to accommodate a senseless war, but the madness had ended and Libya now had the chance to rise up from the ashes to rebuild itself for its people. The time I'd prayed for so hard had arrived, and I was beyond elated to be returning to my home inside the compound. I'd seen footage of the destruction the war had inflicted on the country, and was aware that many areas in Brega had been severely impacted. I had no idea quite what to expect, but had high hopes that life would resume as I'd known it inside the secured environment that had become my second home. Libyan employees were slowly returning to their homes in the compound, and I was ecstatic at the thought of soon reuniting with friends and work colleagues.

I flew back to Benghazi exactly a year after I'd fled the country at the start of the conflict. Stepping onto Libyan soil again was both exhilarating and incredibly emotional.

'*Marhaba*! Welcome back to Libya!' someone shouted out as I excitedly made my way through the airport.

As long as the war had ended, then the worst had surely passed, and I was more than ready to make do with what was left, but, for now, I simply wanted to savour the moment of my return to the country. I spotted the familiar logo of an SOC coach waiting outside the airport, and my heart leapt with joy—I was just a few short hours from home! A beaming

Mabrouk, the SOC chauffeur, patiently waited to drive me and other employees to the compound.

'*Salem*! *Marhaba*! The war's over!' he said, grinning from ear to ear.

The mood on the bus for the three-hour journey to the compound was lively and cheerful, but punctuated from time to time by the sobering sight of burnt-out cars and abandoned army tanks along the route as evidence of the recent war. It had all been so senseless, but the hostilities were over and peace would now prevail. It was late in the evening, rainy and dark, when I arrived at the compound's coach station in Area 1, just a stone's throw away from my house. I could feel my heart dancing wildly inside my chest. I could see no sign of any damage to the immediate vicinity. I was met by Nasser, a Libyan colleague charged with driving me to my house.

'*Marhaba*! Welcome back!' he said cheerfully as he shook my hand vigorously. 'How are you?'

I smiled humbly in response to a question which should have been directed at him after the tough year he and his people had endured.

'No, how are *you*?' I asked.

'*Hamdullah*! We've survived!' he replied with a smile that lit up his whole face. 'Your house is in a bad way so I'll take you to another. It's only temporary until yours gets fixed up.'

My heart sank a little as I wondered what his words really meant. I got in his SOC truck and, as he drove the short distance to the temporary house, my eyes feverishly scanned the area for the familiar sites of my neighbourhood—the supermarket, the clinic, the kids' playground… I could see no signs of damage. Nasser told me that the temporary house had once been occupied by one of the SOC pilots and his family. *It must really be huge then,* I thought with some apprehension.

He parked the truck outside the massive property which was just a short walking distance from my own. Nasser got out of the truck and, out of the back, grabbed a colourful blanket and pillow, still in their clear plastic wrap. He pushed the garden gate open, and hurried towards the front door of the house which he merely kicked open with his foot.

'There's no lock...' he said casually as he entered the house.

I stood on the threshold for a brief moment, staring at the gaping hole where the missing lock should have been. I walked into the huge living room, my mind already fully made up that I wouldn't spend a minute inside a house that couldn't be locked.

'I'll get your suitcase...' said Nasser as he dropped the blanket and pillow on a dusty dining room table and rushed back out to his truck.

Before this conflict, many of my neighbours on Secretary Street didn't bother locking their front doors, even at night, the compound being such a safe environment. But a war had just taken place which had, somehow, drastically changed the equation. Nasser returned with my suitcase, and I voiced my concerns to him.

'No, don't worry! Nothing will happen to you!' he said dismissively, making me feel like I was fussing over some exceedingly trivial matter.

For a brief instant, I indeed wondered whether I might be fussing over nothing in the face of what Nasser and his countrymen had just lived through, and decided that I wasn't.

'See you at work tomorrow. *Insha'Allah!*' he said excitedly before dashing out of the house, past the gaping hole of the missing lock in the front door.

I stood in the living room for a moment, feeling suddenly despondent, alone and uncomfortable in this large, unfamiliar house, and wondered what to do next. I hadn't expected this. The only thing I was sure of was that I wouldn't spend the night in this house, but where else could I go? I inspected the spacious kitchen, the bathroom, then the four sizeable bedrooms. The whole house was basically furnished and in need of a thorough clean-up as thick dust covered every surface. As though the missing front door lock wasn't enough, two bedrooms had windows with missing glass panes, and there was no telephone. The more I surveyed the house, the more my determination not to spend a minute there intensified. There was no way that I'd occupy a house with a missing lock on its front door, broken windows and no telephone. I threw a few clothes into a small bag, put my suitcase inside a cupboard in one of the bedrooms, and made my way through the dark rainy evening towards the medical clinic close-by.

Mary, my next-door neighbour on Secretary Street, had returned to the compound the previous week, and was accommodated at the clinic as her own house had also been severely damaged. There were no patients at the clinic as the compound was only just getting back on its feet, and so the beds were made available to the medical staff whose houses had become uninhabitable. I wasn't part of the medical personnel, but this was an emergency, and I was sure there'd be somewhere there I could lay my head, at least for that first night. Before the war, Mary and I had been good friends.

She was someone who spoke her mind, who had no airs and graces about her, and I appreciated those qualities in her. I grew to value her friendship and trust her. We shared many happy moments together—yoga on the beach at the weekends, shopping and long lunches in Ajdabiya, or just sitting in her garden, chatting away while sipping herbal tea. We'd kept in touch throughout the war, and I was delighted to be minutes away from seeing her again—another happy moment in store to follow the recent unhappy times. After a warm and joyful reunion, I let Mary in on my concerns over the condition of my temporary house.

'No problem! Stay with me at the clinic. We've enough spare beds,' she said.

I gratefully accepted her offer then spent the whole evening with her and other nurses in one of the consultation rooms, catching up on our time after leaving Brega at the start of the war. Although I was thankful at not having to spend the night at the temporary house with its missing front door lock, I suffered from chronic white coat syndrome, and wasn't too comfortable with the idea of spending a night on a hospital bed when my health didn't warrant it, with stress-inducing equipment wherever I lay my eyes. Even in these post-war times when any fuss appeared downright indecent, my squeamish disposition about anything medical was too strong to ignore. Luckily, I was exhausted by the long journey to Brega from London, and fell asleep quickly, hoping that the next day would bring a better housing alternative.

The first call to prayer from the golden-domed mosque next door woke me up early the following morning. The joy at hearing it again was indescribable. I stretched out lazily, looked at the empty hospital bed beside mine, and smiled at the unpredictability of the situation. I wondered what could be in store next before reminding myself that now the war was over, things could only get better. After a quick shower, I readied myself for work, eager to escape the queasy ambience of my surroundings. Beaming with glorious anticipation at being moments away from walking into my office and reuniting with my work colleagues, I stepped out of the clinic into the bright morning, and straight into what felt like the light at the end of the dark tunnel that the past year had been.

When I arrived at the compound the previous evening, darkness had already fallen, shrouding any damage, but the bright morning light held no such sensitivities and exposed the full extent of the destruction inflicted on this part of Area 1. The first casualty on my route to the office was the large guesthouse opposite the medical clinic. It had once been the grand location of official company functions, with its lavish interior, spacious rooms, and somewhat garish decor. It had also been a *pied-à-terre* for the Gaddafis as they travelled through Brega. The Gaddafis always arrived unannounced—at least to the compound residents—without any fuss, but plenty of armed soldiers. I recalled how, many years before the war, I'd left my house for work one morning to be met by long lines of soldiers lying in sleeping bags on the pavement leading all the way to the guesthouse, one hundred metres away. The house now stood roofless—almost defiantly so, its smashed walls riddled with bullets, its large windows blown out into a pile of shattered glass and mangled metal on the ground. I walked on, my heart beating faster at what awaited next.

Immediately round the corner were the ruins of a large family house, pulverised into rubble whilst its adjoining houses remained untouched. The destruction along my office route was extensive, with some houses completely obliterated. I'd seen online footage of the bombed-out areas around Brega when I was in London, but to witness the devastation on the ground and remember that people had died was surreal and incredibly painful. SOC had started clearing the debris and rubble away, leaving vast empty areas where spacious family houses had stood not so long ago, tucked behind their orange-painted walls. It was a depressing landscape in which only the towering palm trees stood unharmed, like silent witnesses to a senseless devastation.

My mind swirling with mixed emotions, I waved my company badge at Ahmed, the security guard at the checkpoint, to access my office building area.

'*Marhaba*! Welcome back!' he said brightly.

'*Shukran*!' I said, struggling to raise a smile, too disturbed by the mindless destruction I'd just seen.

Surprisingly, there was no sign of the slightest damage anywhere inside this large area. I unlocked the entrance door to the building and stepped in. After a long year of hoping and praying to return to Libya, the joy at stepping into the reception hall was indescribable. My Libyan colleagues greeted me warmly, and I was delighted at being back amongst them, immensely relieved that none had come to any harm although each had a poignant story to tell. They recounted how they'd fled the compound towards their hometowns at the start of the conflict, and how some had lost family members. All were hopeful that a new Libya would emerge from the chaos with peace and prosperity for its people, and that it would find a dignified place amongst the rest of the world. Some of their stories were heartbreaking and tough to listen to. What could I possibly say to a Libyan grieving the loss of a close family member in a war supported by my own government? I only knew that war was never the answer to settling anything, and that it was always counter-productive.

I learnt with astonishment that some expatriates didn't leave the compound during the whole period of the conflict, and had to be regularly evacuated towards other cities nearby when the fighting grew too intense inside the compound. I learnt that my manager, Mr Fahmi, wouldn't be returning to SOC, which was sad as his perpetually cheerful disposition and ready laughter made the office a convivial environment to work in. Since no replacement had been found for him and work was rather scarce in these unique post-war circumstances, working hours were, unofficially, substantially reduced. This was most helpful to the many employees like me who were left to sort out the cleaning up of their houses themselves. Although it seemed that the administrative buildings in Area 1 had suffered no damage, there was a long road ahead to fix up the residents' houses. But, in the midst of all this destruction, a cheery and buoyant ambience reigned across the compound at the war being over, and at the premise of a brighter chapter on the horizon for the country and its people. Libya had been hit to its core, but it was ready to rise again. I felt honoured to be part of the reconstruction process, albeit in my own humble and minuscule way.

I'd already been warned that my house was in a 'bad way', but had no idea of just how bad it was. I decided to go and assess the damage for myself at the end of my first day back at the office, but not before making a short diversion to the beach first. My heart began beating suddenly faster, as if about to reunite with a lost friend as I felt the warm rays of the sun on my face and the tickle of a soft breeze on the back of my neck. The beach was as it had always been—pristine and untouched by the folly of man. Unlike the devastation around me, no bomb could possibly defile the finesse of its white sand or the depth of its shimmering blue waters. I sat on a bench and watched the waves softly rolling onto the sand, and soon my whole being floated in a sea of tranquillity. I thanked God that the war was over, and prayed for a stronger Libya to rise up from the chaos.

Uplifted by the immaculate, timeless vista before me, I became convinced that it was only a matter of time before the houses were rebuilt, and the compound regained its unique atmosphere of before the war. I could only foresee good ahead. After a moment of silent contemplation, I made my way towards Secretary Street.

That morning, I learnt from work colleagues that because of its size, my house had been used as a base for some of the fighters, just like Mary's next door. Both houses were left in a deplorable condition, stripped of all furniture and personal belongings. I approached the street with a mix of dread and excitement, then let out a huge sigh of relief—there was no sign of external damage to any of the garden walls on the small cul-de-sac. A few houses were in need of maintenance, but that predated the war.

From the outside, my house looked as I'd left it all those months ago, except that its iron gate was now wide open. *The palm trees need trimming,* I thought as I noticed their droopy branches hanging dolefully like more casualties of the recent turmoil. I stepped into the yard and immediately recognised a handful of personal items of clothing scattered around, half-buried beneath dried mud and dead leaves—my favourite black and green sweatshirt, a pink summer dress, a cream shirt, a handy fifteen-minute recipe book, some family photos…

I picked up the muddy photos then noticed that behind the screen door, the door to the house was also wide open. A wave of dread suddenly washed all over me. I decided there and then that I wouldn't let whatever awaited inside affect me in any way, then pushed the screen door into the living room. My jaw dropped at the horrid, depressing squalor before me. The empty room appeared twice as large, and it had been stripped of all furniture, furnishings and floor coverings. All that remained was a wretched pile of burnt trash in the middle of the bare floor. I stood, numb, in utter disbelief, too afraid to venture into the other rooms. Despite Nasser's warning about the condition of my house, I hadn't expected such a shocking, filthy sight.

Totally disheartened, I started towards the kitchen. The bulky American-type refrigerator, the electric cooker, the washer–dryer had all gone. Nothing was left apart from the bare wall cupboards. I made my way towards the two bedrooms and they too had been emptied out. All my clothes and personal belongings had disappeared. The only items of clothing left were those half-buried under the mud and dead leaves in the yard.

While there was nothing remotely uplifting about the state of my house, I told myself that I'd often thought of decluttering anyway—although this wasn't quite the extreme method I'd had in mind. Parts of the floors and walls were smeared with a thick, pinkish slime that turned my stomach. The kitchen and bathroom were in a foul, disgusting condition. The kitchen sink was covered with that same thick, pink slimy mess, and the bath tub had been used as a toilet. I felt physically sick as I surveyed the filth that now replaced the exotic haven this house had once been. I wondered why SOC had recalled its expatriate workers before it had fixed up their accommodation. And how could the company consider it acceptable to offer me a temporary house that couldn't be locked up? Where was I supposed to go until my own house was fit for habitation again?

In spite of the fact that I'd prepared myself for the worst, I realised I had a proverbial mountain to climb before I could realistically move back into my house and feel settled again. Our services department, in charge of the maintenance of the houses, was swamped with the rebuilding work required around the compound, and all its efforts were concentrated on other priorities that didn't include the maintenance of the houses on Secretary Street. I couldn't figure out why my calls to the department for help with cleaning and basic furniture led nowhere until I was told unequivocally that its principal mission was to assist Libyan employees and their families first. I was taken aback by the response, but had to accept the department's policy after the war that the Libyans had just lived through. This was an extremely sensitive time during which any fuss from expatriates over the loss of furniture or personal belongings was likely to be considered indecent. But, crucially, it meant that if I expected to move into my house in any reasonable time, then I'd have to rely solely on myself for its cleaning, maintenance and furnishing.

I learnt a short time later that my house had been broken into the day I left the compound with Hiba on our way towards Egypt the previous year. I bitterly regretted the absence of my first manager, Mr Bayda, and how his forceful, yielding manner and sense of fairness would have ensured that expatriates received equal assistance with the restoration of their houses. He was that missing, all-important *wasta* I so badly needed, now more than ever. In my helplessness, I kept reminding myself that these were exceptional circumstances, that I had to consider my situation within the context of a war in which people had died. These sobering reminders invariably calmed my pent-up frustrations and put into their true perspective the loss of my belongings, the condition of my house or the lack of help from the services department. Left with no other choice for the maintenance of my house, I resolved to take advantage of the reduced office hours to start fixing it up myself.

I'd spent my first night back inside the compound at the medical clinic, but by the end of my second day, it looked like there would be no immediate alternatives to my accommodation problems. I reminded myself that beggars couldn't be choosers, and resigned myself to making the most of my hospital bed at the clinic until my housing issues were sorted out, hopefully soon. But, despite my best intentions, this wasn't to be. The manager of the clinic, Mr Salah Ibrahim, had been unaware that I'd occupied a bed at his clinic until I bumped into him as I prepared for my second night there. It was the end of the day, I'd just taken a shower and, bundled in an oversized bathrobe, wet hair wrapped in a towel, was making my way towards the consultation room that had become my home.

Just as I was about to open the door, Mr Ibrahim suddenly appeared out of nowhere, like some hair-raising vision. Eyes like daggers, he shot a dark, angry look at my direction, but said nothing. Instead, he huffed and puffed his way straight into Mary's office, a few doors away. I walked into the consultation room and waited for the storm. I heard him ranting and raving, and I knew that what was coming my way wasn't going to be to my advantage.

'What is *she* doing at the clinic?' he yelled. 'Who gave *her* permission to stay here? I want her out *now!*'

His over-the-top reaction didn't surprise me one bit—I even expected it. A few years before the war, this same Mr Ibrahim telephoned my office to speak to Mr Fahmi, my manager at the time, who'd just given strict instructions to hold his calls for a while.

'Do you know who I am?' Mr Ibrahim insisted irately as I promised that Mr Fahmi would return his call as soon as possible.

Incensed at what he perceived to be *my* refusal to connect him, he rudely slammed the phone down on me. He grudgingly held on to that exchange and bore a petty animosity towards me ever since. Each time he came to meet with my manager, he made a point of ignoring my presence. It was unbecoming and immature behaviour on the part of a senior member of SOC management, but it didn't bother me one bit. Luckily, I was healthy enough not to have to visit *his* clinic, so our paths rarely crossed. But even with the dramatic changes that the compound was going through as a result of the recent war, which required support and goodwill from its residents, Mr Ibrahim's hostility towards me was reignited as soon as he set eyes on me. He felt it unashamedly justified to order me out of the premises despite Mary's pleas that I had nowhere to go. And I *really* had nowhere to go. There was no other temporary house I could occupy, and all my neighbours on Secretary Street were either housed at the clinic, or sharing houses with others. I was technically homeless in a foreign country barely emerging from a war. In truth, being kicked out of the clinic didn't inconvenience me too much. Besides expecting it at any time due to its manager's spiteful attitude towards me, I wasn't keen at all on spending my nights on a hospital bed, surrounded by anxiety-inducing equipment. While I had no roof over my head for the night, I still had no intention of going back to the temporary house with its missing front door lock and broken windows.

I was indignant at having been callously ordered out of the clinic, but was grateful for the only option I had for the night—the office couch. I quickly got dressed, threw the few items of clothing I had at the clinic into a bag, hurried back to the temporary house to grab the colourful blanket and pillow, and set off towards my office. I waved my company badge at the security guard at the checkpoint, who looked decidedly puzzled at my untimely presence. I was relieved that he asked no questions as I was in no mood to offer any explanations. He merely stood there, half smiling but utterly confused, whilst I struggled to hold on to the blanket with one arm and my overnight bag and pillow with the other... And he had good reason to be confused—it was nearly six o'clock in the evening, all the offices were closed, but, most importantly, workers, especially female, didn't normally show up for the night clutching their bedding.

I unlocked the entrance door to the building and stepped into the pitch dark hallway. It was deathly quiet. All of a sudden, I felt a vague malaise at the thought of spending the night in an empty building surrounded by other empty buildings. The presence of the security guard at the nearby checkpoint was reassuring, but he wasn't visible from my office window. The one-level modern structure comprised a dozen offices, a couple of washrooms and kitchens. Each office was locked, which was comforting, but it wasn't enough to fully ease my mind. The sun was setting fast, and darkness would soon engulf the compound. I struggled to shake off the sense of foreboding that was slowly rising inside me. I couldn't decide whether I was more worried about some spooky, ghostly happenings, or someone breaking into the building in the middle of the night—I wasn't sure which would be worse.

I hurried around the whole floor to ensure all doors were locked, then made my way to my office. Exhausted, deeply exasperated at this turn of events, I plonked the blanket and pillow on the reception couch right outside before locking myself in and making a cup of tea. There was no supper that night. I was in for a sleepless night ahead, but didn't mind too much as long as it was uneventful. I switched on my computer and worked into the night to delay the dreaded moment I'd have to lie on the reception couch outside my office door. I gave in just before two o'clock in the morning, and under the warmth of the colourful blanket, tried hard to block any scary thoughts from my mind. Throughout the night, my sleep-deprived brain remained on alert for the slightest noise, imagining all kinds of fanciful threats.

At long last, the first call to prayer broke into the heavy silence of the night to put a welcome end to it. The faint light of dawn trickled through the window blinds and, with it, the firm realisation that I wouldn't spend another night in these conditions. There was no breakfast that morning. I wearily hauled myself to my feet to ready myself for work before my colleagues started arriving. When they did, they were shocked to learn that I'd spent the night on the reception couch, and took it upon themselves to find me an appropriate housing option. The consensus was for me to stay with a Libyan family until my house was fixed up, a suggestion I wasn't too keen on. It wasn't the ideal solution, but these weren't ideal times.

Without hesitation, Younes, one of the senior workers in the department, offered me a roof with his family. I was touched by his generosity, but decidedly frustrated that I was forced to rely on a work colleague I hardly knew for accommodation. Younes' house was only a short walking distance from my own, and I had no choice but to gratefully accept his offer. I lived with Younes' family for a month, sharing a bedroom with his young daughter, Nuria, who, in typical teenage fashion, spent most of her nights texting friends on her tablet. His wife, Amal, a bubbly Egyptian woman with a permanent smile on her face, was a soap opera enthusiast, who spent hours reviewing the latest developments in the daily romantic Turkish series she watched avidly with her daughter. Despite her time-consuming hobby, Amal was a fabulous cook who enjoyed preparing delicious meals.

From the first day I stepped inside her home, she welcomed me with open arms and fussed over me like I was her most valued guest. I was extremely thankful for the family's hospitality, but couldn't help feeling that I intruded on the life of an ordinary family with their own problems to solve after the war they'd just been through. I'd decided earlier on to spend as little time as possible there, and to redouble my efforts to clean up my house. Every morning on my way to work, I'd stop at my house to pour gallons of bleach and mountains of scouring powder everywhere to be washed off after work. As there was still little going on at work, I'd spend the morning at the office until about midday then head back to my house for cleaning chores until early evening.

After several weeks of this tedious routine, the house finally looked ready to move back into, but for one major problem—there was no electricity, no telephone, no bed, no refrigerator, no cooker, nothing, not even a chair to sit on. Each day, I called at our services department for the reconnection of the electrical supply, and any second-hand furniture that would enable me to move in. These were admittedly difficult times, but it was unfair that SOC repaired its employees' houses in such an inequitable manner. Nothing happened for expatriate workers unless they had *wasta* to intercede on their behalf, and I was certainly discovering its importance at this time of great need. My first and second manager had filled that role for me, but now that they'd both retired, I was firmly relegated to the 'no *wasta*' category. As a lone woman, the thought of being without this vital support in these tough times in Libya was deeply unsettling, especially when at the best of times one was nobody without it.

After several attempts to pressure the services department to reconnect the electricity supply at my house, they finally did, eliminating the main hurdle keeping me from moving back in. Despite no decent second-hand furniture being available, I was desperate to regain possession of my house without any more delay. I'd already painted all the interior walls a clean, pure white, deciding to tackle the furniture problem my own way. I purchased half a dozen cot mattresses from a furnishings store in Area 3, enough cloth in a dark burnt orange colour, and designed my own Arabic style sitting area, which would also double-up as a sleeping area. I picked up floor coverings and curtain fabrics from the Area

3 Saturday market, and entrusted a seamstress with the task of putting it all together.

Within days, I had a set of comfortable sofas-cum-beds, and brand-new curtains for all the windows in the house. A couple of coats of varnish gave a new lease of life to a second-hand coffee table and a dresser I'd salvaged from the services department, and my house began to take shape. After a few more days of relentlessly chasing the department for decent kitchen appliances, I finally moved in. I purchased a new television set, and, slowly, began to feel at home again.

Soon thereafter, a rumour started circulating that, at the end of the war, people—including some from outside of the compound—had taken advantage of the many unlocked houses to help themselves to the furniture and belongings inside. These expeditions had been called 'going shopping in Brega'. Whereas many Libyan employees had retrieved items for safekeeping until their owners returned to their houses, I hadn't been that lucky, and had lost absolutely everything. It was inconceivable that SOC hadn't locked up the houses that had been broken into, leaving them to be ransacked while their owners were still out of the country. It was reckless negligence on the part of the company, but, again, a petty argument when viewed in its wider context.

After months of my work department plodding along without a manager, a Mr Mehdi El-Abadi was finally nominated as its head. I was slowly settling into my house and looking forward to also enjoying a more stable work environment. Mr El-Abadi, a quietly spoken, self-effacing man, was the complete opposite of my two previous gregarious managers. Unlike them, he was also a chain smoker who was never without a cigarette hanging precariously from his lips, which didn't bode well for the staunch anti-smoker that I was. Even though all the office buildings inside the compound had no smoking policies, several managers openly flouted the order. Mr El-Abadi was one of them, and unashamedly so. Communication with my two previous managers had been effortless, but was sadly non-existent with Mr El-Abadi. Although my office adjoined his, apart from the brief *Salem* greeting in the morning, he wouldn't utter a word to me all day if he could avoid it. Trying to initiate a conversation only resulted in a polite, monosyllabic response that reflected his reticence to engage in any exchange. In all my working years, I'd never known such a reserved and uncommunicative manager. The resulting radical shift in the office dynamics took some time to get used to, but I viewed it as just another change to adjust to in the post-war life inside the compound. Indeed, the consequences of war were unforeseeable, impacting adversely on so many critical levels that my new manager's taciturn disposition in the office had to be the most insignificant of them all.

Life inside the compound resumed somewhat sluggishly, with SOC painstakingly clearing up the bombed-out sites and fixing up its employees' houses. Despite the difficulties I faced with the maintenance of my house, my excitedness at being back in Libya never waned, and I looked forward to spending many more years in the new post-war Libya. A painful chapter of the country's history book had been turned, and I was hopeful that the future would bring long-term stability and prosperity for the country.

The western leaders involved in the Libyan war had spoken of the freedom that Libyans would enjoy as a result of the devastation inflicted upon them, which had brought about the demise of their leader. So far, nothing in the country had changed for the better, and some of my Libyan colleagues seemed at a loss to grasp the meaning of this new-found freedom they were now supposedly living under. On the contrary, they now lived under a palpable sense of insecurity and uncertainty about the future that hadn't existed before.

As time went on, it became clearer that things weren't as they'd been before the war, and that the concept of this newly earned freedom was not only confusing, but badly misunderstood. For some, it signified a licence to do anything they wanted, when they wanted. On a few occasions in the office, I witnessed one or two employees arriving in the morning, openly stating that they would do no work on that particular day for the simple reason that they were now 'free' to do so. They accepted that in order to be paid, they had to physically show up, but they surmised that it was part of their new rights as liberated citizens to refuse to work on any given day. It was mind-boggling, but I hoped that my new manager would soon clear up the misunderstanding. I suspected that Libyans would realise, in time, that even in the world's most democratic nations, the freedom of every citizen was controlled and manipulated to varying degrees by the powers that be. They might even come to realise that they'd been no more *enslaved* than many other nations around the world who simply *think* they are free.

In the early days of the war, firearms had been widely distributed to the population by the government and, consequently, most Libyans inside the compound kept some at home for protection. Some discreetly carried guns on them during office hours, creating an uneasiness that trouble could erupt at any moment. But locals felt justified in carrying guns during this transitional period before the advent of the stability and security promised to them as a reward for the war. But in the meantime, the sense of safety which had prevailed in the compound during the Gaddafi era had disappeared to make way for a precarious insecurity that was only going to get worse. While only a Libyan citizen knew what it was really like living under Gaddafi's rule, I'd lived in Libya in the utmost safety for over ten years, and had become well acquainted with the country's customs. Whatever was said of Gaddafi's eccentricities or alleged crimes, I only saw people living in a basic degree of comfort often denied to the average citizen in some western nations. Not once did I encounter beggars living rough on the streets of the Libyan cities I visited. Despite their undoubtedly controlled lives under the leader's autocratic rule, there was a prevailing air of tranquillity and social order, which was emphasised by the innately relaxed and peaceful nature of the Libyan people. No doubt that below the surface, many resented the authoritarian regime they lived under, and felt that they were being short-changed. The lifting of the sanctions and the slow opening of the country to the outside world from 2003 no doubt revealed to the Libyan people the extent of their repressed conditions under their leader's regime. They observed the meteoric rise of the Gulf states into world-class economies whilst they seemed like the impoverished inhabitants of a mega-rich country bursting with natural resources. But despite the label of vicious dictator invariably attached to his name and the notoriety surrounding his rule, Gaddafi implemented valuable social reforms to benefit his countrymen, and had ambitions to unite the whole of Africa under the banner of the 'United States of Africa'.

Under his rule, education and medical care were provided for free, with the country boasting one of the best healthcare systems in the Middle East and Africa. Before he took power in 1969, only twenty-five percent of Libyans were literate; under his rule, eighty-seven percent were, with students given the opportunity to further their studies abroad at government expense. Gaddafi funded and carried out the world's largest irrigation project—the 'Great Man-Made River'—to make water readily available to all Libyans across the entire country. Libya had no external debt, had its own bank, and provided interest-free loans to its citizens. Couples received a substantial cash payment on marriage. Electricity was free for all. Cars were made affordable to all thanks to large government subsidies, while the price of petrol was as low as a few pennies per litre.

Regardless of Gaddafi's alleged shortcomings, these social measures were geared towards the betterment of his people—hardly the mark of a vicious dictator. Libya might have needed social and political reforms, but it hadn't needed a disastrous war to stunt its progress for the foreseeable future. The disastrous post-conflict social and political unrest in the country couldn't possibly be worth the war imposed upon it. Social reforms had already been in the pipeline before the war, and who knows what might have happened had the 'liberating' western coalition not interfered in the country's affairs. Any social or political problems Libya might have had were strictly for the Libyans to sort out between themselves, whilst the 'war of liberation' imposed upon them was but a smokescreen for a much bigger scheme engineered from outside of the country's borders. Libya was subjected to a deliberate destruction by a coalition bent on safeguarding its own interests. That truth was the first casualty of war was evidenced time after time by the recent armed conflicts started under false pretexts by powerful nations against weaker ones, with their deceptive lies ultimately being exposed, but not until the premeditated military onslaught had taken place.

In Libya's case, diplomatic mediation had been suggested to prevent a war, a seemingly wise and rational move vetoed by the European block and the US. Before Gaddafi's untimely demise, there had been rumours of talks between Egypt and Libya to form an alliance. A plan seen unfavourably by those powers whose interests lie in that region remaining economically stagnant and politically in the hands of western-backed dictators. Gaddafi's widely rumoured plan to quit selling his country's oil in the euro or US dollar, instead demanding payment in a new currency linked to gold, was his downfall. In his typically grandiose manner, he'd declared himself the 'King of African Kings', making no secret of his ambition to form a united African continent, with its whole population trading solely in the new African gold dinar. He'd actively pressed other African and Middle Eastern countries to join him in the plan. According to the International Monetary Fund, Libya's central bank had, at the time, an asset base in excess of a hundred and forty tons of gold in its vaults. Gaddafi's plan held hugely profitable economic implications for the African continent, but catastrophic ones for western countries. His plan was deemed as having the strong potential of throwing the world economy into chaos, leading one prominent European leader to brand Gaddafi as 'a threat to the financial security of mankind'. By only trading in the gold dinar, African nations would have been empowered to stand up to external exploitation and take themselves out of debts and poverty by controlling the pricing of their precious resources themselves. The spectre of the gold dinar on the economic world stage was suggested by many specialist observers as the primary reason behind the urgent foreign intervention in Libya.

Gaddafi was making strong waves in the powerful western nations' political waters, becoming a significant threat that had to be removed. Did he sign his own death warrant with his ambitious gold dinar project? By rearing its head in early 2011, the Arab Spring provided the perfect excuse to 'liberate' the Libyan people. It was a sovereign nation's legitimate right to rise up within its borders to demand a change of government, but for another nation to arrogantly pretend to be assuming the role of saviour by demanding new leadership under the threat of military intervention had to be unacceptable and strongly condemned under any law. It was highly revealing that once the western countries achieved their objective of overthrowing Gaddafi and, better still, facilitating his assassination, they threw in the towel and left without a glimpse at the havoc they were leaving in their wake. It was mission accomplished for them, but the start of chaos and instability for the Libyan population that might not be overcome in the near future, if Iraq and Afghanistan were recent examples to go by.

These self-appointed saviours weren't the solution, but the problem itself. In 2009, Britain, France and other European states sold Libya nearly $500 million worth of weapons. For what purpose? The interests of regional peace? What had wars achieved other than wrecking untold havoc, creating more deadly conflicts, and bringing in social and political mayhem for decades to come? What had they achieved other than inflicting pain and suffering on those parts of the world? Wars hadn't improved the lives of the populations in those regions, and had only resulted in Iraqi children not going to school, or an Afghanistan awash with drugs. There seemed to be a covert policy in some powerful nations to keep certain parts of the world in a state of deliberate stunted political and economic development. It was ironic that these aggressive wars emanated from so-called free, democratic countries bent on imposing their will on weaker nations. The consequences of wars being impossible to reverse, no doubt their true legacy will become clearer with the passing of time. Meanwhile, and in the name of so-called freedom and humanitarian concerns, it had been Libya's turn to be annihilated.

As the compound slowly resumed its operations in the midst of the country's shaky post-conflict recovery, a disturbing development took place on 11 September 2012, when gunmen attacked the US liaison office in Benghazi, killing the US ambassador, one official and two CIA agents. The attack was swiftly condemned by the Libyan interim leader, Mr Mohammed Magarief, who pledged to bring the attackers to justice. Inside the compound, the news caused much concern to its residents, and I shuddered to think what other deadly fallout from the recent conflict might blight the country over the coming days, weeks or months.

Inevitably, unrest gradually spread across the whole country, with former rebel fighters regrouping to form militias bent on asserting their role as 'guardians of the revolution'. Frequent clashes erupted between rival groups, leading to yet more chaos. Although the insular compound was sheltered from the troubles going on outside of it, the war did bring disorder to it in the form of the local tribes.

Aware of the strong, traditional force that tribal leaders represented in his country, Gaddafi, upon seizing control in 1969, astutely formed a union of tribal leaders—the People's Social Leadership Committee, charged with keeping in line tribal members. When the Brega compound was built in the 1960s, the tribes living on the land were paid off to relocate elsewhere. Peaceful throughout the Gaddafi era, as soon as the 2011 war ended, the tribes began revendicating ownership of parts of the compound and making demands for jobs and housing for their members. While SOC had already recruited hundreds of employees from these local tribes since the end of the conflict, it soon became a regular occurrence for tribe members to forcefully take over houses inside the compound, regardless of whether these were already occupied or not. Bent on inflicting maximum disturbance until SOC met their demands, they routinely stormed the office buildings too. As these disruptions grew more frequent, I feared for the once peaceful, ordered environment inside the compound that slowly disintegrated by the day. But in spite of these tribal disturbances, life continued ticking by cautiously, each passing day gently pushing the memory of the war a little farther away and strengthening the hope that any lingering security complications would be resolved in the not too distant future.

By May 2012, neighbours on Secretary Street started complaining of incidents they were encountering. Lynda's and Jackie's houses had been broken into and personal valuables stolen. Then local youths began harassing the nurses as they made their way to and from their shifts at the medical clinic. These were unsettling activities that had been unheard of before the war. Although these incidents had been duly reported to SOC each time they happened, they'd been routinely ignored by the company. No doubt that it had bigger fish to fry so soon after the war, but its lack of response bothered my neighbours and I greatly. It was hugely disheartening that there now appeared to be a 'before the war' and an 'after the war' scale to gauge life inside the compound. More break-ins at nurses' houses on the street followed in June, September and October 2012. Then I decided to contact the company chairman after an incident at my own house.

It was just before eleven o'clock in the evening on Friday, 1 November 2012. I'd been fast asleep until I was brutally woken up by Mary's loud screams from her house next door.

'Two men in your garden! I've called security!'

I opened my eyes, still too dazed from sleep, not sure I'd heard correctly, but I felt no panic. I doubted whether anyone could break into my house easily, not with its bolts, padlocks, door grille and steel-shuttered windows, but it wasn't time for complacency either. I jumped out of bed, rushed into the living room to dial the security department's number. I then pulled the curtain back slightly and peeked into the well-lit garden. All was quiet, with no sign of any intruders.

Within seconds, a security guard arrived and I stepped out to meet him. Mary was already recounting to him how she'd seen two men breaking into her car, which was parked right outside her house. Mary was no pushover. She'd yelled at them in no uncertain terms and they fled by jumping over the wall into my own garden. The security guard walked around the yard and, at the foot of one of the palm trees, found an axe, two screwdrivers and one leather sandal, which one of the men had lost as he escaped from the scene. An axe? I was extremely unnerved that these thugs had carried such

113

a deadly tool, and shuddered at how close Mary and I might have come to real harm.

'I'll report the incident to management first thing in the morning,' said the guard, 'and we'll make more rounds around your street throughout the night.'

Yet another incident report to be filed, which would lead nowhere, like all the previous ones. I asked him about management's response to the earlier reports.

'Umm… You know, it's difficult… We report everything to management, but we never had these problems before the war,' he said, clearly ill at ease.

'OK, but why is nothing being done?' I pressed on.

He sighed, shrugging dejectedly. 'Everyone has guns… Management's afraid to do anything…' he said quickly, a helpless look all over his face.

That was quite a disturbing revelation. If the company was 'afraid' to put a stop to the increasingly thuggish conditions inside its walls because 'everyone has guns', then there was no hope for a return to the safe, before-the-war life the residents had once enjoyed.

My first task on arrival at the office on Sunday morning was to write to the SOC chairman on behalf of all my Secretary Street neighbours. I set out the list of all the incidents that had occurred over the past six months on our street and requested appropriate security measures. I had no idea at the time that I was giving the company a prescient warning of a far more serious crime that would be committed seven months later, one that would have a huge impact on *my* life.

Like the previous incident reports, my memo to the chairman didn't receive a response either. I made several attempts to speak with the security manager, Mr Khaled

Hatami, who initially ignored my calls until a month later when he called me in the office.

'Incidents? What incidents?' he asked. 'I've never heard of any incidents on your street!' His curt, dismissive manner set the tone for the rest of the conversation.

'No, you *do* know,' I said calmly. 'At least five reports were filed by myself with the chairman and your own office over the past six months, but you never responded…'

'I know nothing about these reports,' he insisted, refusing to acknowledge any incidents on Secretary Street. 'What incidents are you talking about? You're so exaggerating…'

'I'm not. I suggest you meet up with the women on Secretary Street and hear it directly from them. How's that?'

'All I know is that we haven't heard of any foreign woman dying on that street yet!' he joked.

I couldn't believe my ears. How could the company's security manager be so flippant and dismissive of the security concerns employees reported to him? I was shocked and hugely offended by his comment.

'So, you're waiting for someone to *die* before you do anything?' I said. 'OK, Mr Hatami, let me make something very clear to you. You and SOC have been warned repeatedly, and you will be held directly responsible for any harm to any one of us on Secretary Street!'

Click. I'd barely finished my sentence that he abruptly ended our discussion by hanging up on me.

Mr Hatami's offensive remark disturbed me so much that I discussed the issue immediately with my manager, Mr El-Abadi. He revealed that SOC management had initially considered putting a permanent security guard on Secretary Street, but that the idea was ultimately vetoed as too impractical. And since SOC had figured out no other alternatives, it looked like, as far as the company was concerned, the matter was closed. Again, I thought of my first manager, Mr Bayda, and how he'd mobilised a guard outside my house for two days just to deter some stone-throwing kids. I desperately missed his no-nonsense, radical solutions to any issues.

Faced with our management's apathy, my neighbours and I resolved to be extra vigilant with our safety, being only too aware that these incidents had instilled a disquiet into our life on the street that hadn't existed before. I feared that our carefree days inside the safety of the compound were coming to an end as lawlessness slowly forced its way in; I felt an increased sense of foreboding that it was only a matter of time before serious harm befell one of my neighbours on the street. It was foreseeable, but preventable if only SOC paid attention. But in spite of my fears, I never imagined for a second that I'd be the victim of the next serious crime, and that the scene was being set for the traumatic moment that would change my life forever.

THE FATEFUL DAY

Friday, 7 June 2013 was the first day of the weekend and it began like any other Friday in the compound. The morning was sunny and warm, with the heat of another glorious summer's day preparing to bear down on the compound. It was the kind of morning that usually got me out of bed at dawn for yoga practice on the beach with either Sandy or Mary, but not on that particular day as I had to be in the office instead. I periodically worked on Fridays to finalise with our London agency the last-minute arrangements of Libyan employees travelling for assignments abroad. I enjoyed working on Fridays. The office was usually empty, and I'd work leisurely with music playing in the background, before a lunch of a spicy burger and fries from the nearby beach restaurant was delivered to my desk.

That day, I arrived at the office at around ten o'clock, and worked until about three in the afternoon when I made my way home. Outside, the air from the stifling heat was so thick it could be cut with a knife. There was a stillness all around as the scorching sun beat down on the compound and kept the residents inside the coolness of their homes. The road was completely deserted as I walked the short distance to my house. I hurried indoors to escape the sticky heat, had a quick shower, changed into light tracksuit bottoms and T-shirt before stepping out into the yard for some light pottering around until supper time. The air was still heavy and hot and, except for the effervescent chirping of the birds, there was silence all around. I breathed in the pungent aromas of the basil and rosemary plants, and rejoiced at being back at the compound after the recent war. I felt an overwhelming sense of contentment wash over me as I counted my blessings. Basking in the tranquillity of my surroundings, my heart overflowing with optimism, I reflected that despite the incidents of the last few months, it was only a matter of time before the peace and security that had prevailed before the war would return to the compound.

Shears in hand, I walked towards the cascade of pink blooms spilling from the oleander tree in Mary's garden onto mine. Mary left on her vacation early that morning. She often sat in her garden with friends, sipping cold drinks into the warm evening for hours on end, their loud bursts of laughter ringing through the stillness of the air—a casual, reassuring picture about to be shattered forever. Had Mary left on her vacation just a day later, she'd have been entertaining her friends in her garden that afternoon, and the tragic moment that was about to unfold wouldn't have taken place.

Lost in no more taxing thoughts than what to have for supper, I started pruning the unruly branches of the oleander tree before turning my attention to watering the parched potted plants. That's when I heard a car drive by my house and park right outside it. The garden wall was too high for me to see who'd driven in, but my curiosity was piqued. I'd noticed Hiba's car parked outside her house on my return from the office and, with Mary on leave, I could think of no other car that would usually be parked on our street. I peeped through the small gap in the garden gate, but could only make out that it was a dark grey car. I assumed it was a visitor to one of the other houses then returned to watering my plants.

Within seconds, someone pounded loudly on my garden gate, before a man's voice asked, in Arabic, for water to wash his car. Alarm bells immediately rang as local men weren't expected to be on Secretary Street as a general rule, let alone to wash their cars. I hurried towards the gate and locked its padlock before shouting that I had no water to give, despite it flowing under the gate onto the pavement. He repeated his request, throwing a five-gallon plastic bottle over the top of the garden wall. His insistence irritated me, but I wasn't concerned one bit for my safety at that point—it was full daylight, the gate was padlocked and there was a six-foot-high wall between us. I still felt completely safe despite his annoying presence behind the wall. It didn't cross my mind that things would get worse quickly, and they did in a flash.

As I picked up the plastic bottle to throw back over the wall, a man's head suddenly appeared at the top of the wall. I was transfixed for a split second then frantically aimed the water hose I held in my hand at him whilst screaming for help at the top of my lungs. My mind, blissfully calm just a moment earlier, was now in total disarray. In a heartbeat, the scene had changed from one carefree moment pondering what to have for supper to one of life-threatening danger. My confused brain froze then retreated into slow motion whilst, at the same time, chaotic thoughts raced through it. I couldn't believe what was unfolding before my eyes, but I had no doubt that I was in serious danger. I was in a terrifying nightmare I couldn't possibly wake up from because it was only too real. I gasped for breath and began shaking uncontrollably as I remembered that no one was likely to hear my screams at that time of day on a Friday, the quietest day in the compound as many locals left for the weekend. I thought of Mary who'd have been sitting in her garden with her friends, and how they'd have jumped to my rescue. I was alone, helpless and doomed.

Neither my screams nor the splashing water deterred the man as he leapt over the wall with frightening agility, and landed heavily on top of me. My prescription glasses flew to the ground in the scuffle, causing my vision to blur instantly. I was still screaming so he violently slammed his hand over my mouth before positioning himself behind me and locking his arm in a tight stranglehold around my neck.

'Shut up! I have a knife and I'll slit your throat if you scream again!' he said.

From the corner of my eye, I saw the movement of his arm as he reached into his back pocket for the knife, which he then pressed against my back. It all happened so fast, but in that split second it took him to jump over the wall. I'd noticed that he was young, probably in his mid-twenties, and had dark, longish hair under a brown and beige army style cap similar to those worn by rebel fighters during the war. He was of average height, thin build, and wore a dark blue chequered shirt and dark trousers. He was of a nondescript appearance, with nothing distinctive about his physique that I'd remember later.

Dazed, I felt like a rag doll, my whole body suddenly weak and shivery. I never knew such knee-buckling desperation as I shuddered at what this thug was about to do to me. Would I live through this nightmare to see my loved ones again? Was this man going to rape and run, or rape and kill? I was petrified, nauseous and faint all at the same time. I was powerless, my body paralysed with fear, but my confused brain still raced with zillions of jumbled up thoughts. In those brief seconds, I understood how fleeting life could be, how there was nothing like the threat of imminent death to make one so desperate to live. It was often said that a person's life was supposed to flash before their eyes when death was near. Mine didn't and I quickly took it as a sign that I wasn't destined to die just yet. That was vaguely encouraging, but my life was still firmly in the hands of a total stranger with clearly evil intentions, who had invaded my most private space and was now in control of whether I lived or died. I wondered how much physical pain my attacker would inflict on me, how being stabbed would feel, how dying would feel... My knees buckled as he pushed me, like a lamb to the slaughter, towards the doorway to the house.

'I won't hurt you if you do as I say, but believe me, I'll slit your throat if you scream again!' he said.

I was in a state of near collapse at the prospect of being alone with this criminal inside the house, where no one could possibly hear my cries. The mind-numbing thought that I was going to be raped, with no idea of whether I'd be alive or dead by the evening, was simply too much for my disorientated brain. While the overwhelming certainty that I was unable to physically fight back an aggressor dawned on me at the worst possible moment, I felt to my core that I didn't want to die either. All my instincts screamed for me to submit in order to stay alive. I decided not to antagonise him and, just like I would've clung onto a life-saving raft, I clung to his words that he wouldn't hurt me if I stopped screaming. I wasn't even sure I had the strength to scream anymore. I thought I'd appeal to his better nature instead. In a quivering voice, I pleaded with him that I was old enough to be his mother, even his grandmother, and that God was watching him. My words only infuriated him and he pushed me roughly towards the doorway.

'Shut up! Just shut up!'

He sounded so enraged that I felt time had come for a prayer, that last resort of the fearful or doomed. That irritated him even more and prompted him to violently kick the screen door before shoving me into the living room and dragging me into the small hallway towards the bedroom. The room was in darkness. The window shutters were down to seal away the sunlight and keep the room cool in the summer heat. This compounded my blurred vision, but I felt strangely glad that the scene about to take place was going to be so hazy that, just maybe, it'd become that much easier to forget later—if I survived what was coming. I'd noticed his bloodshot eyes earlier and, although he hadn't smelt of alcohol, I worried he could be on drugs. He also reeked of the strong stench of gasoline, and the sickening smell lingered in every pore of my being for weeks after the attack, despite the scores of showers to deterge myself completely of it, and of the whole experience. What if he had some drug-related disease? But did this really matter if I was about to die?

With the assault over, the rapist proceeded to initiate a casual conversation, like what had just happened was no more than a tryst between two consenting people. His voice was calm and relaxed as he asked which office I worked at and, bizarrely, if I was from the Philippines. I had no intention of entering into chit-chat with my rapist, but knew that I had to tread carefully and not provoke him into an adverse reaction. As I frantically racked my battered brain for a way to make him leave the house, the sudden, loud shriek of the telephone on the bedside table interrupted his monologue. I had no idea who might be calling, but help was surely at the other end of the line. I was desperate to answer it, but he quickly picked up the receiver and slammed it back down again.

'It's my neighbour!' I said. 'I'm expecting her. She must be on her way to my house right now.'

I hoped that the thought of a neighbour on her way to my house would prompt him to leave as fast as he could. It worked. He sprang out of bed, arranged his clothing, sped out of the room, but not before calmly saying that he'd come back later. For a second or two, I wished he would as I'd have ensured that the whole security department would be waiting for him. The immense relief that my life had been spared, that the nightmare was over, was indescribable, giving me the proverbial wings to run behind him to lock the screen door. I watched him jump over the garden wall like a scared cat. All of a sudden, uncontainable rage exploded inside me before I telephoned the security department.

I was near collapse by that point, but I opened the living room window to scream for help at the top of my lungs. Strangely, in the midst of all my agony, a feeling of euphoria crept up to remind me I was still alive, a ray of light and positivity to focus on in spite of the pain. My disorientated brain was locked in an out-of-control mode, switching from waves of utter misery and rage to elation, even gratitude. Gratitude? Had my spirit been so beaten down that I felt pitifully thankful to my rapist for sparing my life? It was a surreal moment where immense, but fleeting, relief was quickly usurped by wild, unbridled fury. Zillions of fast, dizzying emotions battled furiously inside me. My head was spinning in disbelief at what had just happened. I'd been out in the yard less than an hour earlier, happy and optimistic about the future, but before the afternoon was over, I'd been plunged into an ordeal that would turn my whole life on its head for years to come. My fears that serious harm would befall someone on Secretary Street had become a reality, but I hadn't envisaged—not for a split second—that I'd be the victim.

At various times over the past months, I'd made SOC aware of the security concerns on my street. After what had just happened to me, I felt raging indignation towards the company for its sustained recklessness, which had facilitated my rape. SOC's downright negligence made it answerable for my rape, just as I'd warned its security manager that the company would be held accountable for any harm to anyone on Secretary Street. His only reaction to my words had been to slam the phone down on me.

THE AFTERMATH OF THE RAPE

The scourge of rape, present in all societies from time immemorial, is a tragic indictment of our so-called civilised times as it continues to plague women's lives. The definition of rape has varied over the years to be understood as largely the act of forced sexual intercourse on a woman, or a man, through physical violence, or the threat of injury or death. The elements of lack of consent and coercive nature are crucial to this definition. Most rapes are perpetrated by men on women, with statistics demonstrating that the vast majority are committed by people known to their victims. It is a crime common throughout our modern world despite the advent of progressive societies in which women's rights have advanced significantly. I'd often pondered my likely reaction in the event I found myself in the hands of a would-be rapist—I believe most women have. Over the decades, self-defence classes run by experts advocating basic techniques to stave off an attacker or, at least, ensure that rape didn't lead to serious injury or death, sprung up everywhere like mushrooms. A sad testament of the inability of even the most modern societies to protect women once and for all from the violent physical abuse meted out to them. Since I didn't possess one aggressive bone in my body and abhorred any form of violence, I strongly suspected that I'd freeze up from sheer terror and choose the path of least resistance—submission to save my life. I hadn't been wrong, and found out in a real-life nightmare what I'd always feared—that I'd be unable to stand up to an attacker, especially one armed with a knife. However, to lessen the odds of ever finding myself in such a situation,

I followed to the letter all the usual safety rules inside and outside of my home, dare I say to the point of paranoia, and was careful never to place myself in circumstances where my physical well-being could be compromised. I just wasn't a risk taker with my life.

Unbeknownst to me at the time, Hiba, whose house stood opposite mine, had seen the rapist scaling my garden wall, but, unfortunately, the thought that she was watching a criminal live in action didn't cross her mind. After all, such things didn't happen in our compound, not even after the recent incidents. Luckily, the scene had raised enough concern in her mind to phone me moments later when, receiving no response, she'd walked across to my house just in time to see the rapist return to his car. Her intervention had been too late to save me from the rape, but it might have saved me from a worse fate as it was her call that had prompted the rapist to flee, and I was incredibly grateful for that. She arrived at my gate as I stood at the window, still screaming hysterically. I ran out onto the garden and unlocked the garden gate to let her in. Only then did I notice that the entire left side of my face was terribly sore and bruised, the result of the rapist slamming his hand over my face after jumping over the wall.

'Oh my God! Yes, I saw someone climb the wall, but I didn't think of it as danger. I thought that you'd locked yourself out and that he was helping you. I'm so sorry,' she said, the sorrowful expression on her face and broken voice betraying her pain at having misread the situation so dramatically, and not calling for help in time.

She recounted how she'd crossed the pavement towards my house to come face to face with a young, dishevelled man rushing towards a car parked right outside my house. His suspicious demeanour prompted her to ask him what he was doing on the street, and he mumbled a few words she couldn't make out then sped off. But not before she'd taken a good look at him, his car and number plate. Hiba telephoned the security department again before driving me to the nearby medical clinic, where scores of security officers awaited our arrival. It wasn't six o'clock in the evening yet. As the eye witness to the rapist scaling the garden wall, but also a friend, Hiba insisted on being by my side throughout the police interviews I had to go through at the clinic. I was relieved that her fluent Arabic would spare me from using my own rather sketchy version, especially in these traumatic circumstances.

The news that a 'foreign woman' had been raped in Area 1 spread like wildfire around the compound. I couldn't believe I was *that* woman. My office manager, Mr El-Abadi, and Mr Fathi Belkacem, the services manager, rushed to the clinic as soon as they heard.

'How many times did I warn you that something bad would happen? And what did you do? Nothing!' I yelled. 'You're all responsible for this!'

Both men stood there helplessly, looking sombre, at a complete loss for words other than repeating how sorry they were. I had no doubt that they were, but it was way too late. I was examined by a Serbian doctor, Dr Martina Dorjevic, who sent trace evidence of the rape to the clinic's laboratory for processing. The time I spent at the medical clinic after the rape remains hazy in my mind, but I never forgot the moment Dr Dorjevic asked me to sign a document. I was so distraught and shook so uncontrollably that I couldn't even hold the pen in my hand. As she tried to calm me down, my cell phone rang. It was a high-ranking British official calling from

London. I thought of how quickly the news of the rape had travelled all the way to the UK. He expressed his sympathy, promising the embassy's full support, but I was too distressed to be able to hold a coherent conversation, or even remember his name later on. But his phone call so soon after the rape left me in no doubt that the British Embassy would step up to take matters into its own hands and bring me redress.

In the middle of an interview with an officer from the Brega police station, an urgent call came on his radio that a 'nervous man' had been stopped at the Area 3 checkpoint in a car fitting the description Hiba had given the security guards. At that stage, I knew absolutely nothing about the rapist, or that he was a newly recruited SOC employee and, bearing in mind his nondescript physical appearance, I had no idea whether I'd even seen him before. The man had been taken to an office building around the corner from the medical clinic, and Hiba and I were immediately escorted there to identify him. It was getting dark outside as, flanked by three security guards, we walked out of the clinic and into the parking area of the small office building next door. Hiba pointed to the dark grey car parked there.

'That's the car I saw the man drive away in…' she said without hesitation.

Even though I felt sick at the thought of facing the rapist again, I was hugely relieved that he'd been caught so quickly. What followed next proved to be another ordeal to go through so soon after the rape. Hiba and I were ushered into a small office where two young men sat behind desks, and two others stood awkwardly by a window. All four looked tense and edgy. The three security guards positioned themselves by the door entrance to observe the proceedings—a far cry from the identification line-ups depicted in television crime series. It was nerve-racking standing so close to these four jittery men whilst Hiba and I scrutinised them.

Straight away, I eliminated three of them for being either too chubby, too short or dark-skinned. The fourth man strongly resembled the rapist in age, height, build and in that same nondescript physical appearance, but he was dressed completely differently, no longer wearing that brown and beige camouflage cap or the dark chequered shirt and jeans he had on at the time of the crime; instead, he wore a zipped-up dark brown leather jacket, and, even more importantly, his longish hair of a few hours earlier was now styled in a freshly shaven crew cut. While I was pretty sure it was him, I hesitated making a definite identification for the simple fact that DNA was available to prove his guilt. Hiba had no such hesitation.

'Him…' she said, pointing at the fidgety young man standing clumsily in front of us.

She was adamant it was the man she'd spoken to as he dashed to his car after the rape. He looked at her, saying nothing then quickly looked away. I continued staring at him, without a word, and he repeatedly averted his eyes from mine. He just stood there, hands clenched at his side, head hung down like a naughty schoolboy summoned into the headmaster's office. He turned away each time our eyes met, at one point walking to the nearest desk and crouching behind it, in a bizarre attempt to escape our accusatory eyes. I asked him to remove his jacket and he obliged, revealing a clean light grey vest that looked like it'd been put on very recently. It appeared that in order to prevent his identification, he'd rushed home after the rape, had a haircut and changed his clothes before being stopped at the Area 3 security checkpoint.

Hiba repeated to the guards that she was sure it was the man she'd seen and spoken to on our street. I could only say that I was very confident it was him, but that his radical change of appearance and clothing made me reluctant to be more categorical. The loss of my prescription glasses as he'd jumped over me was enough to make my recollection of him blurry at the best of times, but this was compounded tenfold by his complete change of appearance. And I wasn't concerned one bit by my hesitation since DNA evidence would confirm his guilt in due course.

The fact that both Hiba and I pointed at this particular man caused one of the three others—the chubby one—to become agitated. He stood up to take the suspect's defence, yelling that the man hadn't left the office all afternoon and, therefore, couldn't have committed the rape. His aggressive outburst, despite the presence of the security guards standing at the doorway, scared me stiff. I was already badly shaken, and didn't need any more stress. Concerned that things might take a nasty turn, I told the guards to end this confrontation. As we were led out of the building, one of the three security guards revealed that the dark grey car in the yard that Hiba had recognised belonged to the man we'd both singled out. We then returned to the clinic to continue our interviews with the waiting security and Brega police officers.

Once all the necessary formalities were completed, Hiba and I were driven to the Brega hospital outside of the compound, where I was examined by a midwife as a doctor wasn't available. It was after midnight when we finally returned to Hiba's house. I was physically and mentally exhausted, drained of all energy, stunned and thoroughly bewildered at how quickly tragedy had struck. I hadn't been in some rough part of town of some dangerous foreign country, alone, late at night, but in my garden, in the middle of the day, in the safety of a fortified compound when evil came for me. How could a peaceful moment in the privacy of my own home end so dramatically? I had no answers.

Hiba and I sat on her sofa, barely speaking. Suddenly, just before one o'clock in the morning, her phone rang. A security guard was on his way to pick me up for yet another examination at the same Brega hospital, but by a doctor this time. Despite the late hour, Hiba insisted on coming with me. After this third examination, the female Libyan doctor, Dr Nawal Sayed, verbally confirmed to the police officer accompanying us that the 'physical evidence was consistent with rape'. It was nearly two o'clock in the morning by the time Hiba and I were back at her house. My sleep that night was troubled and agitated, and it would remain so for a long time to come.

Arrangements were made by the local police for an interview the following day with an investigating judge, Mr Salah Nasri, at the Brega police station. Hiba, as the eye witness, was also summoned to attend. Although Mr Nasri, a tall, serious-looking man, didn't speak any English, no translator was made available. Since my command of the Arabic language didn't extend to describing a rape situation, Hiba was relied upon to translate the exchange between Mr Nasri and I, just as she'd done during the interviews at the medical clinic the previous evening. The eye witness to a crime translating the exchange between the victim and an investigating judge would be inadmissible anywhere else, but not in Brega, and so the interview was allowed to proceed without a second thought.

Mr Nasri took note of my deposition and ordered a forensic examination at a hospital in Ajdabiya for the next day. I bulked at the prospect of yet another examination. Mr Nasri expressed his surprise that no security guard had visited my house after the rape to collect evidence or retrieve the plastic bottle the rapist had thrown over the garden wall. He immediately ordered a security guard to return to the house to collect the plastic bottle for fingerprint analysis. Faced with such basic disregard of the most elementary evidence-gathering procedures by both the compound security and the local police officers, I reflected that I was dealing with inexperienced officers, and felt thankful that the British Embassy would soon be involved. At that early stage, I had every confidence that justice would prevail in no time at all. My case couldn't be easier to wrap up—the rapist had been identified, an eye witness was available and, most importantly, DNA evidence was being processed to prove his guilt. What could possibly go wrong?

Early on the morning of Sunday, 9 June 2013, an SOC chauffeur picked up Hiba and I for the one-hour drive to the Ajdabiya hospital for my fourth physical examination in forty-eight hours. To this day, the mere recollection of this examination makes my blood boil. I woke up that morning, shaking and in floods of tears; just lots of silent, unstoppable tears. To compose myself in time for my hospital appointment, I took one of the two Valium tablets I'd been given at the clinic the day before. Despite my reluctance at taking any type of antidepressants, I made an exception that morning due to the distraught state I was in. The last time I took half a sleeping pill was during the armed fighting inside the compound in March 2011, and it had rendered me quasi-comatose for the night. This time, the pill had no effect on me whatsoever, and my whole body was still shaking and my tears still flowing as the chauffeur pulled up outside the hospital. I was led into a consulting room to be greeted by a stern-looking Sudanese male doctor. I asked him if Hiba could be allowed in for support, but he refused point blank. I sensed not a shred of empathy from him as he fired questions at me about the rape, and scribbled down my replies in a notebook. Then he looked up.

'Now be quiet. Take your clothes off and lie down,' he said sharply, pointing to the examination table.

For a brief second, I struggled with all my might to contain my gut instinct to tell him to get lost, and walk out of his office. But even in my disconsolate condition, I was only too aware that if I wanted my day in court, then I had no choice but to submit to all the questioning and physical examinations thrown at me. When the Brega investigating judge ordered this examination the previous day, I'd simply assumed that it would be similar to the three I'd had in Brega. But this one was different—it was cringeworthy and thoroughly humiliating. It lasted no longer than a few seconds but felt like an eternity. The most degrading seconds of my entire life. I was mortified. The Libyan nurse assisting the doctor never moved from the chair on which she sat silently in a corner, her gaze firmly fixed onto the floor, clearly too uneasy to look anywhere else.

Once the examination was over, the doctor handed me a prescription for a wash medication and some Xanax pills, then sent me on my way. I left the hospital utterly deflated, like an unbearably heavier weight had just been loaded upon my already overburdened shoulders—a weight that I feared

I'd have to carry around with me for the rest of my days. I returned to the compound with my heart broken into a million pieces, and the feeling that I'd been violated all over again. All my requests for copies of my statements to SOC security and the Brega police, and of the medical examination reports, consistently fell on deaf ears.

As soon as I was back behind my desk later that day, I received a call from a Mrs Jane Hanson at the British Embassy in Tripoli. Mrs Hanson was going to be my contact at the embassy. I was massively relieved by her call, confident that the embassy would somehow keep a close eye on the proceedings until the case was settled. Mrs Hanson requested a timeline of the events leading to the rape and any other relevant information. Unfailingly sensitive and sympathetic, Mrs Hanson called at least once a week for updates, proving the ideal listener as I uninhibitedly poured out my thoughts and fears since the rape. I was incredibly grateful for her support and thanked my lucky stars that I had the might and authority of the embassy by my side at such a terrible time.

Later that day, Dr Martina Dorjevic called. She'd examined me at the clinic right after the rape and wanted to share the conversation she'd had with a technician at the laboratory to which she'd sent the DNA sample for analysis. The technician informed her that the sample showed no trace of DNA evidence whatsoever.

'Well, I suggest you look again! It's there, so do your job and find it!' she told him. 'And call me when you do!'

I was extremely uneasy at the sample being handled by the laboratory of the company not only employing the rapist, but to be sued by his victim. Dr Dorjevic had worked for SOC for over two decades and didn't hesitate revealing that she was only too familiar with the company's unscrupulous methods at times. She also warned me that the manager of the clinic, Mr Ibrahim, was pushing for SOC to 'close the case for lack of evidence'. I felt my heart tighten in my chest.

'Don't let this happen,' she said. 'You'll need your embassy to intervene, that's for sure.'

I thanked her for her concern, and assured her that I had every intention of making SOC face its responsibilities in my rape. I then contacted the British Embassy in Tripoli to report Dr Dorjevic's comments and ask for assistance to ensure that the vital DNA sample wouldn't go missing.

The next day, Dr Dorjevic called again with official confirmation, by the laboratory, of DNA evidence, and that the sample would be sent to a laboratory in Benghazi for further analysis. I was hugely relieved that a seemingly independent laboratory would be handling the sample, but couldn't help feeling nervous as long as it remained in SOC's hands. In the meantime, I was glad to have been examined by a foreign doctor unwilling to be intimidated by the clinic manager, and keen on ensuring that SOC respected their due diligence.

The clinic manager's efforts for the case to be closed were reprehensible, but not surprising. He was the same Mr Ibrahim who had ordered me out of the clinic the previous year after finding out I'd spent one night there after the war. Dr Dorjevic told him it wouldn't be advisable for SOC to obstruct the proceedings when DNA evidence was available to confirm the rapist's guilt, and while the British Embassy kept a close eye on a crime against one of its nationals.

'I want to make sure your case isn't covered up. And I'll testify in court if necessary!' she said.

I was incredibly grateful for Dr Dorjevic's support and, again, reassured her that I had no intention of letting SOC silence my rape. I had no idea at the time of the many obstacles that would be erected along the road ahead, and the multitude of struggles that awaited.

Late in the afternoon of Monday, 10 June 2013, two solemn-looking men walked quietly into my office just as I prepared to leave for the day. I'd never seen either of them before.

'*Salem!*' they said in unison.

'Mr Said Barak, SOC chairman…' said the shorter of the two men before pointing to the man beside him, 'This is Mr Ryad.'

Finally! I thought. The SOC's elusive chairman who hadn't bothered replying to my memo of the previous year warning him of escalating incidents on Secretary Street. It took the rape of one of his employees inside his area of control for him to react. He was flanked by Mr Ryad, a member of SOC's management committee. They stood awkwardly by my desk, looking sheepish, the strained smiles on their faces failing miserably to mask their obvious discomfort.

'Umm… We've come to tell you… umm… how sorry we are at what happened,' said Mr Ryad slowly, as though he was gauging the likelihood of an angry outburst from me.

The chairman nodded in agreement. 'If you… umm… need,' he said in heavily accented English before looking at Mr Ryad to take over the speech.

'Yes. If you need anything, just let us know…' continued Mr Ryad.

I was surprised at how nervous they both looked, but I didn't say anything. I had nothing to say. The onus was on them to explain the company's negligence that had led to my rape.

'There's just one thing,' said Mr Ryad hesitantly before mustering enough courage to spell out in one quick breath the real reason behind the presence of these senior executives in my office. 'We ask you... umm... not to post what happened on Facebook.'

My jaw dropped to the floor. The SOC masks had fallen. The chairman and his sidekick were on a damage limitation exercise to prevent the fallout that a post about my rape, on a global social media platform, might have on the reputation of one of the biggest international oil companies in Libya. Suddenly, I had no doubt whatsoever about the veracity of every single warning about SOC's intention of brushing my rape under the carpet. My heart sank at the unsettling realisation that SOC wasn't remotely interested in justice, but only in safeguarding its interests and reputation by silencing a case in which its negligence could be exposed on a media platform.

'I don't use Facebook,' I said, in total shock at their brazen request.

I was part of a generation for whom the display of one's private life on social media platforms for the whole world to see was anathema. At the time, the thought of posting my rape online never crossed my mind, not for a millisecond.

'*Shukran*! Thank you!' said the chairman, his demeanour suddenly upbeat.

'If we'd known you'd be so approachable, we'd have come to see you much earlier in the day,' cooed Mr Ryad, clearly no longer fearing any outburst from me.

They then turned on their heels and left. I sat at my desk, trying to take stock of the situation I was in, and felt nauseated by it all. The chairman's visit to my office revealed SOC's attitude towards my rape, but it also highlighted the company's awareness that it had a responsibility in it through its failure to heed the security concerns I'd brought to its attention. But regardless of SOC's intentions, nothing could extinguish my determination to seek redress from the company, or pursue it all the way to the courts if necessary. In fact, the company's efforts to silence me only fired up my resolution to expose and prosecute this crime by all possible means. The only saving grace I could see in my sorry predicament was the British Embassy by my side, and its indispensable support to achieve my goal. Coincidentally, access to Facebook was blocked for a few days following the chairman's visit to my office.

Days later, a retired senior SOC executive, Mr Fahim Bari, called me in the office one morning. Mr Bari had retired from the company several years earlier after a lifetime of service, but his stellar reputation as a man of integrity and high morals lived on in the compound. He expressed his shock at the rape before warning me that a 'very good source' within SOC had informed him that the company was setting wheels in motion to cover the case, and that I should be prepared for 'anything and everything'.

'Keep in touch with your embassy at all times,' he said. 'They're your only chance of getting justice in Libya... Trust no one! Absolutely no one!'

Mr Bari's words were intensely disturbing, and they reinforced the importance of the involvement of the British Embassy. They also opened my eyes to the troubling fact that my case was being undermined by adversaries from within the company, who were bent on silencing it. The rape of a foreign worker reflected too negatively not only on SOC and its international reputation, but on Libya as a whole, as I'd soon learn. I was incredibly grateful to Mr Bari and to all those who hadn't hesitated to step forwards to warn that I was dealing with opponents for whom truth and honesty were easily set aside in favour of lies and self-interest.

On my return to Libya following the 2011 war, I'd started keeping notes of all incidents happening on Secretary Street, but now that I'd been raped and seemed caught up in a web of deceit, it was crucial that I kept the most meticulous records of all the events surrounding the rape and its aftermath.

I spent part of my time in the office trying to locate a Libyan lawyer to represent me, and educating myself on the criminal legal system in general. I discovered with disbelief that foreign police forces were under no obligation to investigate a crime on their home soil against a non-national. This astonishing piece of information made the involvement of the British Embassy in Tripoli even more critical if the rapist was to be prosecuted, and SOC made accountable for its responsibility.

Despite SOC's alleged attempts to suppress it, the rape had sent shockwaves around the compound. The company issued a statement on Sunday, 9 June 2013 condemning 'this ignominious crime', but, more importantly, confirming that the company had 'taken all measures necessary… to guarantee the application of the laws and regulations… to punish the offender….'. This was encouraging news so soon after the rape, or was it just a smokescreen? I'd lived and worked for the company for over a decade, and the nature of my work duties brought me in contact with many employees. They all had a hard time coming to terms with the fact that such a heinous crime could take place in their midst, even after the recent war and the sense of insecurity it had brought to the compound. And they found it just as difficult to accept that one of their own had committed such a crime against a 'foreign guest' they'd known for so long. There was a daily steady stream of people coming to my office to offer support, some expressing their downright 'shame' that a Libyan was responsible, a few even breaking down before me as they spoke of their sadness at the rape. I received messages of support from people in the compound I'd never even met. One local foreign company offered financial support towards the legal proceedings. I was immensely thankful for this generous offer, but turned it down, so convinced that my case would be a piece of cake for any lawyer to settle. A statement from the '17 February 2011 Coalition' was sent to the chairman denouncing the rape and demanding the 'quick processing of the criminal by the justice system... to be punished as an example to others'.

I was deeply touched by the way everyone rallied around me, and believed that in the face of all this support inside the compound, SOC would have no other choice but do the right thing vis-à-vis the rape, and make the compound safer for all its residents.

Early one morning, one of my trusted work colleagues, Malik, entered my office, looking less perky than usual, and announced that a number of people inside the compound were discussing taking justice into their own hands by punishing the rapist themselves. I was mortified at the prospect of being directly responsible for any harm inflicted on anyone, including my rapist. The punishment of a crime by another crime was an abhorrent proposition, and I made it clear to Malik to let it be known that I was against any illegal action to be taken in my name. Instead, I relied wholeheartedly on the Libyan justice system and the British Embassy to obtain redress through the appropriate legal channels.

Despite my weakened physical condition since the rape, I insisted on being in the office every day. Taking time off to spend inside the compound was no option, and I was determined not to leave on my London break until all the formalities required by the Libyan authorities were completed. In the meantime, I decided to organise a protest gathering outside the chairman's office. It required prior authorisation from management, but I was sure it wouldn't refuse me this little favour. Coincidentally, early on the day that the chairman had come to ask me not to post the rape on Facebook, I'd submitted the proposed date of Thursday, 13 June 2011 for the gathering, a date which was, as expected, promptly authorised by management. With the help of a small team of supportive colleagues, I called other employees in other areas of the compound, asking for their participation to achieve maximum impact. All promised to attend, and it looked like numbers on the day would be high as everyone wanted the rapist apprehended, as well as a security upgrade.

Two days before the scheduled date, I received a call early one morning from a member of the personnel department advising that the gathering could no longer be held on the proposed date of Thursday 13, but had to take place at ten o'clock on that very morning. This last-minute change left me with barely an hour to contact all the participants. It was clearly an underhanded attempt to derail the protest, stifle my voice and that of all those who'd planned on attending. As a consequence, less than two hundred people showed up, a far lesser number than that expected on the initially agreed date of two days later.

At the gathering, I was deeply touched by the many people holding placards screaming their support for me. It was another surreal moment when I had to come to terms, all over again, with the fact that I was the subject of this meeting. The chairman made an appearance to express his sadness at the rape, adding that 'no such crime had happened in the compound before'. That wasn't an encouraging start because most residents were aware of at least two rapes which had occurred decades before my arrival in Libya. Both had allegedly involved expatriate women assaulted by local male residents of the compound, and both crimes had been swiftly dealt with by the company by terminating the women's employment and putting them on a one-way flight back to their home countries. The chairman couldn't possibly be ignorant of this indelible stain on the company's track record.

Two nurses from Secretary Street stepped in to challenge his statement. Natalia had been the victim of an attempted sexual assault at her house six years previously. Her manager advised her at the time against pressing charges as they'd automatically lead to her dismissal from the company. The second nurse, Elena, spoke of the relentless harassment she experienced at the hands of local youths targeting her house for stone throwing and doorbell ringing at any time of day or night.

The chairman nodded as each woman took turns to speak, and he looked genuinely embarrassed at hearing what had been going on in Secretary Street, but said nothing.

I asked him why he hadn't responded to my memo of seven months earlier detailing the latest incidents. Again, he had no comment to make, merely nodding his head as a clue to his growing uneasiness at being unable to come up with acceptable answers. After listening to both Libyan and expatriate employees' tales of discontent, he promised that security around the compound would be immediately upgraded. I reflected that sometimes it was necessary for a terrible event to happen before a bad situation was finally improved; maybe this was such a case.

At the end of the meeting, a group of female Libyan co-workers surrounded me, pleading with me not to let SOC intimidate me into giving up my fight for justice. Like everyone else in the compound, and possibly even more so, they felt strongly that the rapist had to be prosecuted and the company held accountable. I couldn't agree more.

'You're lucky to have a foreign passport to guarantee you justice,' said Amina. 'So, please don't let SOC stand in your way. The rapist must go to jail... and the company's also responsible!'

'Here in Libya, there's no justice for victims of rape,' continued Amel. 'They have no voice here... so please, use your passport to get justice for yourself!'

At that very moment, I felt, indeed, extremely 'lucky' too. How immoral and unjust that an innocuous document was someone's key to a justice denied to others purely because they were born elsewhere. But these women's heart-rending pleas highlighted the critical need for a change in the way rape was dealt with in their own country. As a foreigner in their homeland, I was deeply touched that they'd opened up to me on this taboo subject, and I promised them not to give up my fight, not suspecting for one instance the long, hard struggle ahead of me despite my 'luck' at holding the 'right' passport. Suddenly, my rape was no longer just about me alone; these women had transformed it into a moral obligation towards them, one that filled me with overflowing determination that justice would be served in their name too. On the numerous occasions that I felt overwhelmed by the legal difficulties facing me, my promise to my female Libyan co-workers never failed to spur me on to continue pushing ahead.

Rape is a major taboo in Libya, a crime that dare not speak its name, but just because it isn't openly acknowledged or discussed doesn't mean it doesn't happen. Rape knows no social, cultural or geographical boundaries, and happens anywhere and everywhere. In Libya, it is perceived as the most humiliating stain on the lives of the victims, and is invariably concealed under a shroud of secrecy to prevent bringing 'dishonour' to their families. The 'shame' that is automatically heaped onto the victims only serves to keep the crime conveniently silent, while these misplaced sensitivities result in the violation of the human rights of half of the population. The fear that rape victims, suddenly viewed as 'damaged goods', could be either rejected by their families or destined to a life of lonely spinsterhood is a powerful motivator to keeping the scourge of rape buried deeply under a wall of silence. Under such crippling societal pressures and the crushing weight of their families' honour placed on their shoulders, it isn't surprising that victims are unwilling to report crimes of sexual violence to authorities. But these attitudes only lead to judicial impunity for the rapist, a hushed 'deal' behind the scenes between families, consisting of financial compensation or, in some specific cases, marriage between the rapist and his victim.

How could any decent, level-headed person ever place 'shame' on a rape victim's shoulders instead of on the rapist's? A radical societal change in thinking is clearly long overdue before the rights of the victims of sexual violence in countries like Libya are recognised, respected and addressed by granting them the dignified care and redress they're entitled to. Societal change is a painstakingly slow, tremendously ambitious project, but surely one worth fighting for when it involves half a country's population being abused and cheated of their rights. I soon learnt through my rape ordeal that what I felt personally—my mental anguish, despair and frustrations—was only important to *me* while, conversely, it was only by using my experience that I could impact *others*, and hopefully make a difference in their lives. Keeping the issue of sexual violence silent doesn't make it go away—it simply makes the disease fester and grow out of sight. If my experience could lead to the tiniest positive change to benefit just one victim, then what happened to me would have been worthwhile, and I could live with that.

Upon my return to the compound following the 2011 war, I'd transformed my house into a comfortable home, but the thought of living in it after the rape wasn't an option I was willing to entertain. As supportive as ever, Hiba invited me to share her house until I was allocated a replacement by SOC. In my darkest hours of need, Hiba proved to be someone I could rely on, and I'll be forever grateful for her friendship.

The day following the protest outside the chairman's office, Hiba and I were in her kitchen preparing supper when the doorbell rang. Mr Hatami, the SOC security chief, stood, all smiles, outside the gate. This was the man who, during a telephone conversation seven months previously, had accused me of 'exaggerating' the incidents I'd reported, joking that no foreign woman had died on the street. He'd come with his deputy security chief, Mr Hadi Amani, looking for ideas to improve security on the street. It was ironic, even comical, but I wasn't amused one bit. His offensive comment was still fresh in my mind, and I couldn't think of anything I wished to discuss with him. I suggested he read my memo again as it had contained all the tips he was now seeking. Then I reasoned that if my rape could bring about a security overhaul inside the compound, then it was surely worth putting my anger aside. I took a deep breath before listing the basic steps which would immediately enhance the security on Secretary Street—from the restoration of lighting to the redundant lamp posts, to higher garden walls and the locking-up of the derelict empty houses standing wide open as an invitation to criminal activity. Both men agreed the measures would be easy to put in place, promising to start the work without delay.

Other suggestions such as surveillance cameras were deemed too expensive, while a permanent security guard was considered impractical as 'everyone in the compound would want a security guard on their street too'. Instead, Mr Hatami promised to arrange for a security car to patrol our street more often than it currently did. I pointed out the futility of such a measure as it took no more than half a minute for a patrol car to slowly drive along the small cul-de-sac that was Secretary Street. Unless SOC showed serious commitment to providing adequate security, then the compound would remain set for more crime to happen in these shaky post-war times.

Again, I couldn't help recalling the good old days when my first manager posted a security guard outside my house for two days to deter some stone-throwing young kids. Those were the good old days in Brega, but, sadly, they seemed like a whole lifetime away.

Promptly the next day, Mr Amani, the deputy security chief, walked into my office with a broad grin all over his face. He was an outgoing, happy at all times character, ready to burst into fits of laughter at the slightest opportunity.

'I've an offer for you that you can't refuse!' he said with a twinkle in his eyes. 'How about a family house with brand-new furniture?'

I wondered what SOC had up its sleeves. Was the company trying to keep me sweet? Mr Amani launched into describing the offer in more detail—a spacious four-bedroomed house with a large garden, located on a tiny cul-de-sac of half a dozen properties, all occupied by Libyan families. He admitted that the property was in bad shape inside, but that it'd be completely refurbished to my taste within weeks if I accepted the offer.

'I'll think about it,' I said.

A four-bedroomed family house sounded way too big for one person, but I was prepared to discuss the offer with Hiba, with the idea of possibly sharing it together. We went to view it after work that same day. It was a typical Libyan family house, with massive rooms, and a huge wrap-around garden. It'd clearly been designed for a large family, and could easily have accommodated the majority of my Secretary Street neighbours in it. Not only was it way too big, but I feared that its considerable size would make me feel even more vulnerable than I'd been since the rape. Besides, despite the house being just a stone's throw away from my own, I'd miss my neighbours on Secretary Street and the way we kept a close eye on one another. Now more than ever, I needed to be surrounded by people I fully trusted and Secretary Street provided just that. However tempting the offer had been for a brief second or two, I felt no qualms declining it.

In mid-June, Mrs Hanson called with the uplifting news that the embassy had contacted the Libyan Foreign Ministry for a meeting to discuss my case. Suddenly, my spirits soared, and I had no doubt that such a meeting could only lead to a resolution of my slam-dunk case and to the rapist being locked behind bars in the blink of an eye. I informed her, however, that I'd received several reports from reliable sources within SOC of the company's intentions to stifle the case, and I reiterated my fears that the DNA sample would go missing if left under the company's supervision. Mrs Hanson advised me to contact a Libyan lawyer, and promised to send me a list of lawyers to choose from.

That same day, the French consul in Tripoli, Mr Jacques Martin, called me at the office. Although of dual French and British nationality, I was in Libya as a British citizen, and was, therefore, somewhat surprised that the French consul had tracked me down all the way to Brega. Mr Martin said that the French Embassy was aware of the rape and that it would be following the case closely. My spirits skyrocketed at his words. I had the embassies of two major European powers behind me—how lucky was that! I was ecstatic, and a million miles from thinking that anything could go wrong. Despite SOC's rumoured intentions, my belief that the wheels of justice couldn't possibly be obstructed was reinforced by Mr Martin's authoritative tone. With my case under the spotlight of two powerful embassies, I felt supremely confident that I was on my way towards the light at the end of the proverbial tunnel. For all it was worth, for the first time since the rape, I slept surprisingly well that night.

But within days of Mr Martin's call, Mrs Hanson informed me that the British Embassy had advised its French counterpart that it would handle the case itself, which put a swift end to any involvement by the French authorities. It was a step taken by the British Embassy without prior consultation with the primary interested party—myself— but it didn't bother me at the time since I believed I was in the best of hands with the British authorities by my side. But I'd have ample opportunities in the years ahead to regret the setting aside of the French Consulate by the British Embassy.

Within days of the rape, I consulted with a lawyer in Ajdabiya, the nearest town to Brega. Mr Ali Jalil had been recommended to me by an expatriate colleague as 'speaking good English, a bit grumpy, quite expensive, but well worth it', and one who had 'won all his cases against SOC'. Unfortunately, despite my colleague's glowing endorsement, by the end of my brief meeting with Mr Jalil, I felt decidedly reluctant to be represented by him. Mr Jalil was an elderly, stylishly dressed, serious-looking man who'd practised law for decades, as evidenced by the number of framed certificates hanging on the walls of his plush office. Although he came highly endorsed and I had no cause whatsoever to doubt his expertise, his abrupt manner made me uncomfortable, and gave me cause for concern.

'Did you identify the rapist?' he asked bluntly whilst peering at me through gold-rimmed round glasses.

'The eye witness did, but I—'

'No. *You, you!* Did *you* identify the rapist?' he growled, wagging an impatient finger in my direction.

I felt like a hardened career criminal being grilled by the most aggressive prosecutor in town.

'I'm pretty sure it's him and there's DNA evidence to prove it,' I said in an attempt at explaining my slight hesitation at categorically identifying the rapist—the loss of my prescription glasses as he jumped over me, his standing behind me as he held me in a stranglehold until he pushed me into the darkened bedroom, his complete change of appearance at the identification process…

Mr Jalil listened carefully for a brief moment, his eyes boring into me. The impassive look on his face told me he wasn't convinced one bit by my explanation.

'You need to know something about Libya,' he started. 'There isn't *one* court in the whole country that would accept a woman not being able to identify her rapist… *Not one*! It's just not credible!'

He'd dismissed all my arguments off hand and, without further ado, had delivered his final verdict. The case was closed before it had even begun.

'It's just not credible!' he'd dared say.

His insulting words rang in my ears, and offended me greatly. Seething and on the verge of tears, I stood up to respond to his slur on my integrity.

'Well, you're wrong! It *is* possible because it *has* happened to me! Maybe it's your court system that needs reviewing!'

Desperate for legal representation that was proving so difficult to secure, I launched into a do or die tirade to plead my case before him. I repeated that my eye witness had identified the rapist, but that because of his drastic change of appearance, I relied on the DNA evidence to prove his guilt. Mixed with the loud pounding of my heart was a tiny voice in my head whispering that I needed a lawyer to believe me and fight my case with conviction, and that Mr Jalil didn't fit the bill.

'OK,' he said, nodding his head slowly. 'I'll represent you, but not before October. I'm going on holiday this week until then. Call me again in the first week of October.'

His curt, abrasive manner hadn't warmed him to me one bit, but, even more importantly, I wasn't prepared to wait four long months for legal representation, and decided to look elsewhere. But my visit to Mr Jalil hadn't been a stressful moment in its entirety as I'd learnt that Libyan protocol required the British Embassy in Tripoli to directly request the Libyan Foreign Ministry to instruct the public prosecutor to initiate the necessary criminal proceedings, information which I relayed to Mrs Hanson the very next day.

As promised by Mrs Hanson, I received the list of lawyers, as well as a leaflet on Support for British Nationals Abroad. Surprisingly, the list of lawyers proved to be an out-of-date list of law firms located in either Tripoli or Benghazi. The majority were unreachable, and the handful that answered were either business lawyers or outside of the Brega jurisdiction. Little did I know then that I'd spend a significant amount of time over the coming years searching for legal representation, and that committed, ethical lawyers were like gold dust.

I'd been briefed by Mr El-Abadi, my office manager, that he'd be my point of contact between all the Libyan parties dealing with my case, and that I was to approach him with any issues regarding it. Bearing in mind his difficulties to communicate at the best of times, I suspected this exercise wasn't going to be a smooth ride. Regardless, I set aside his reluctance to engage and probed relentlessly for answers, feeling at times like a downright irritant. To his credit, he was never anything other than kind and patient. Mrs Hanson suggested I inform SOC of my struggles at securing legal representation and, whilst I didn't expect the company to recommend a lawyer to sue them, I wasn't going to keep to myself the difficulties I faced in a crime that SOC had facilitated.

Early one morning, I walked into Mr El-Abadi's office and approached his desk through the faint clouds of smoke already engulfing it. Dressed in SOC's dark blue overalls, he sat hunched over a pile of papers, a cigarette hanging loosely from his lips. I sat opposite him, preparing to pour out my latest frustrations.

'You know that the chairman came to my office the other day to ask me not to post the rape on Facebook...' I said.

Mr El-Abadi nodded then stubbed his cigarette inside the half-full ashtray.

'But since that day, his office has ignored my calls...' I continued. 'It looks like business as usual for SOC even after the rape of one of its employees! I'm trying to find a lawyer, but Brega is outside the jurisdiction of all those I've contacted. I just don't know what else to do...'

Given the glaring conflict of interest between SOC and myself, I suddenly felt incredibly foolish to be unburdening myself to someone on the wrong side of the fence. Mr El-Abadi listened with genuine concern then dialled the number of SOC's legal manager, Mr Ali Tahar. I had no illusions that Mr Tahar would assist me in locating a lawyer to sue the company he represented, but I had nothing to lose by hearing the expert opinion of the company's own legal manager. The conversation between both managers took place in Arabic, on loud speaker, and I understood the grim gist of it.

'Look, it's easy… There must be strictly *zero* involvement from the company. *Zero*! No discussions with her or anyone else on the subject!' snapped Mr Tahar. 'It's a personal matter between her and the man. Nothing to do with SOC!'

I hadn't expected his assistance, but neither had I anticipated such hostility and downright dishonesty from someone supposed to uphold the law. Fury began coursing through my veins. It was shocking that in its attempt to muzzle the rape, SOC had no qualms in declaring it a *personal matter* between the rapist and I. I was disgusted at the cunning and duplicity of it all. My manager looked equally astounded by Mr Tahar's comments.

'Hold on now,' he said. 'This *personal matter* is the rape of an SOC employee by another SOC employee, inside her SOC house, inside the SOC compound. How is SOC not involved? It *is* involved whether it wants to admit it or not. SOC *was* responsible for her security at the time she was attacked! The company can't deny responsibility! There's nothing *personal* about any of this and you know it! I suggest you discuss this further with the chairman and get back to me!'

He then put an end to the call by slamming the phone down.

I was completely taken aback by this vehement display of defiance from my usually mild-mannered manager. His forceful tone was so out of character that, for a brief moment, he no longer was the retiring, uncommunicative individual I'd had such a hard time engaging with.

'This is so wrong! And from our own company lawyer! It isn't acceptable! But don't worry, I'll speak to the chairman myself,' he added as he furiously puffed on his cigarette.

I hugely appreciated my manager's acknowledgement of SOC's responsibility in the rape, and that he hadn't hesitated to say so in such an emphatic manner to Mr Tahar. I felt caught up in a conspiracy of deceit, trapped between the legal manager's stance of 'strictly zero involvement' and that of the clinic manager of 'closing the file for lack of evidence'. The prospect of my case being settled any time soon seemed fraught with obstacles deliberately erected behind the scenes by some SOC players, but I was encouraged by my manager's stance, hopeful that there would be other good people out there for whom truth and morality mattered, who would support my quest for justice.

I thanked Mr El-Abadi for his support then prepared to leave his office, when he gestured for me to remain seated. Slowly, I sat back down, dreading what was coming next.

'The DNA sample is on its way to Benghazi for processing,' he started. 'The results are expected in a week or so. We've kept another sample at the clinic, just in case... Also, an official warrant for the arrest of the rapist has been issued.'

I hadn't expected such encouraging news and was delighted that SOC, despite its intentions, appeared to be allowing due diligence to be carried out unhindered.

'But... umm... there's something else...' he said hesitantly, looking suddenly uncomfortable. 'We're a hundred percent sure... that the man who was arrested at the Area 3 checkpoint is... the rapist.'

That was interesting, but no real news to me. I already *knew* he was the rapist, and there was even DNA evidence to prove it. But if SOC was now 'a hundred percent sure' that he was, then the company would have to go through the legal process to expunge its responsibility in the crime.

'How can you be sure when the DNA results aren't available yet?' I asked, my heart racing wildly at the thought that closure might be even closer than I'd wished for in my wildest dreams.

He seemed to shrink into his seat before looking away to avoid my inquiring eyes. 'Umm… I can't tell you right now, but I promise I will one day… *Insha'Allah.*'

What was that supposed to mean? I had no time to waste waiting for that 'one day' to come when I already feared my days in Libya were counted. It was the kind of frustrating and pacifying statements that irritated me at the best of times, but, with the seriousness of my predicament, it made my blood boil.

Of course, that 'one day' never came. Sadly, that discussion was to be the longest exchange I'd have with my manager about my case, or anything else for that matter. There was to be no more feedback from him despite my relentless attempts for answers about outstanding issues such as the perpetually untraceable DNA results. He invariably commented that he had 'no information', but that he'd 'find out and get back to me'. These words became a mantra he reeled off each time I asked a question. Gradually, I realised that his initial defiance of the company's position towards my case had dissipated, and that he finally sided with SOC. As advised by its legal manager, the company was merely deploying its strategy of 'strictly zero involvement' and, sadly, there seemed to be no one within SOC management with a modicum of integrity and decency willing to challenge it.

A few days following that last discussion with my manager, Malik, my trusted Libyan colleague, informed me that the rapist was affiliated with the main tribe in Brega.

'He and most of the management,' he'd added before dropping the bombshell that the rapist had confessed his crime to his tribe.

Suddenly, the penny dropped. That was how my manager had been 'a hundred percent sure' of his guilt. And if my manager was also part of this tribe, then he'd been clearly too embarrassed to reveal to my face that he and the rapist were members of the same club. I was already aware that tribe members were brothers-in-arms, that their loyalty to one another could, if necessary, transcend the moral prescriptions of fairness and impartiality, and I feared that my case would fall within the boundaries of that necessity to allow loyalty to a criminal tribe member to supersede his victim's right to justice.

The picture taking shape before my eyes was a murky one in which deception and scheming combined to inhibit the due process of the law. Was I being given the run-around by SOC management because it closed ranks around the rapist, a tribe member? With this invaluable *wasta* on the criminal's side, how could I possibly compete single-handedly against such a system? I was appalled by it all. More than ever before, I regretted Mr Bayda's departure, and how he'd have ensured that proceedings were handled fairly. But, despite this latest challenge, I had every reason to be confident—the rapist had his tribe to protect him, but I had the British Embassy and the incorruptible force of the law by my side.

While I waited for any news of progress from either the British Embassy or the Libyan authorities, I decided to start a petition for improved security around the compound. It was my way of reminding SOC that I was still intent on making it face up to its responsibility. The petition gathered nearly three hundred signatures, far fewer than expected due to the reticence of many who feared reprisals from the company if they were seen to be overtly supporting my battle. I could understand their fears—the compound's residents

156

were also SOC employees with families, and their priority was to protect their jobs and livelihood. But I felt that I'd accomplished quite a coup when no less than the chairman's wife agreed to sign my petition. I'd stepped onto the company coach to Benghazi one afternoon to circulate the document amongst the passengers for their signatures. I'd never met the chairman's wife before, but was delighted to realise later that she'd added her name to the petition. Although I suspected the whole exercise would prove futile in the end and that the petition would, in all likelihood, find its way through the chairman's office shredder, the security concerns of the residents had to be brought to the company's attention, with a demand that an overhaul of its security measures be implemented. The chairman himself had promised as much at the 10 of June gathering, and who knew whether it wouldn't prevent another rape.

I was at the medical clinic one morning, a week or so after the rape, when I was approached by Dr Hawa Khalifa, a young Libyan doctor who led me discreetly into the nearest consultation room. *What now?* I wondered as my heart started beating a little faster since I no longer expected good news from anyone.

'There's a rumour circulating that you need to be aware of...' she whispered.

I sighed, waiting for her to continue.

'Some people are saying that there's no way a Libyan man would have committed such a crime. They say that you must have known him, and invited him into your home...'

I breathed a sigh of relief as I'd anticipated much worse. I wasn't the least bit surprised at Dr Hawa's words. Just as some within SOC management closed ranks around a tribe member, some locals were showing the same blind loyalty towards a fellow countryman. Undermining the credibility of the victim by tweaking the facts of a crime in an effort to dismiss it, or at the very least minimise its impact, was a time-honoured practice played out in courtrooms around the world by the most celebrated—albeit unscrupulous—lawyers to get their guilty clients off the hook, to the detriment of truth and justice. In fact, it wasn't always about justice, but rather about winning at any cost.

Even though I wasn't overly perturbed by the rumour, it still left a bitter taste in my mouth at what was being said behind my back by people who clearly didn't know me. Besides, not only was there an eye witness who'd seen him scale the wall, but the rapist had confessed his crime to his tribe and, by extension, to SOC itself. Basic common sense also dictated that, had I been acquainted with him and invited him to my home, then I surely would have spared him the effort of jumping over the garden wall while I frenetically sprayed him with the water hose and screamed blue murder!

I had to rise above such ignorance and dismiss the rumour for what it was—malicious, gratuitous gossip. I had to keep my eyes firmly fixed on the end goal, and not be distracted by petty rumours. In fact, it only strengthened my resolve to drag the rapist in front of the courts and show the rumour mongers that one of their own had, indeed, committed 'such a crime'. Months later, my British attorney would warn me that SOC might well attempt to sully my reputation as part of a defence strategy, and to be extremely cautious as the company might even go as far as hacking into my personal emails!

I'd been in regular contact with Mrs Hanson at the British Embassy for a few weeks since the rape, and although

I appreciated her support, I couldn't help noticing that she never had any progress to report, but told myself that it was still early days.

Months later, with the benefit of hindsight, I'd come to realise that my discussions with Mrs Hanson had filled me with such a false sense of security that I never doubted that the embassy would be actively working behind the scenes to bring closure to my case. Without hesitation, I'd shared with her the most minute details surrounding the rape and its aftermath. I held nothing back. To keep SOC on its toes, I took every opportunity to remind management of my regular liaison with the embassy, and of its involvement in the case. I believed it to be so myself. Initially, SOC had expected the embassy to be closely monitoring the proceedings—a logical assumption given the seriousness of the crime against one of its nationals. While SOC had felt pressured to carry out the necessary due diligence, it had also expected an imminent visit from an embassy representative in the days following the rape, a protocol in serious cases. When such a visit failed to materialise over the next couple of weeks, then months, SOC's attitude began to slacken—could it be that the mighty British Embassy was powerless to act after all?

Unfortunately, the explicit message behind the embassy's lack of decisive intervention immediately following the rape was that it wasn't too concerned about the crime committed against one of its nationals. And the message was swiftly heeded by both SOC and the Libyan authorities who relaxed their investigations even further. In the midst of such *laissez aller* around me, my main worry was that the DNA evidence would be conveniently lost by SOC. I repeatedly pleaded with the embassy for assistance in securing this vital element of the case and its unfailing response was that the embassy couldn't make such a demand from the company, and to contact a Libyan lawyer instead. This response would have been totally legitimate had SOC—a subsidiary of a Libyan government entity—not obstructed the normal course of due diligence. While a couple of telephone calls were made by the embassy to SOC in July and August 2013, and a letter sent in April 2014—nearly a year after the rape—requesting an update in respect of security measures, it was all way too little too late.

The crux of the matter was that the embassy had failed to intervene at the appropriate time to address the matter effectively with both SOC and the Libyan Foreign Ministry. By failing to provide firm support to a wronged citizen, the embassy also failed to send the unequivocal message to SOC, to the Libyan authorities and to the British expatriate community in Brega, that the British authorities paid unreserved attention to the crimes committed against their nationals abroad. These failures would have far-reaching consequences on the way my case would be handled subsequently by both SOC and the Libyans authorities.

The lack of solid involvement by the British Embassy also proved a missed opportunity to arrive at a resolution of the case during a more stable political period. As the post-war situation in Libya steadily descended into more chaos, there were clearly far more urgent issues to deal with in the country than the rape of a foreign woman. Weeks after the rape, I asked Mrs Hanson the reason why a visit to the compound by an embassy representative hadn't materialised, especially after I'd learnt that the embassy could arrange for a representative to be present during police interviews, medical appointments, etc. Although I appreciated the embassy's constraints and limitations after the recent war, its response in December 2013 that embassy staff had to 'abide by travel restrictions put in place in Libya for security reasons' felt rather lame. At the time of the rape, a whole year before the Libyan political situation began to dangerously deteriorate, SOC operated two daily return flights from Tripoli to Brega on which hundreds of employees travelled in all safety. And yet, the British Embassy had deemed it too risky for one employee to carry out their diplomatic duties outside of the comfort of their office. Was I expecting too much from my own country's embassy? Who could it help if it was powerless to assist a rape victim? The lack of a visit by an embassy representative coupled with its non-committal stance were the determining factors that set the tone for the way SOC, and the Libyan authorities, would subsequently handle my case. It was massively frustrating because my rape couldn't have been more of an open-and-shut case to settle. Even before the rapist had confessed to his tribe—the ultimate in direct evidence—he'd been identified as an SOC employee and resident of its compound, an eye witness was available as well as DNA evidence, and yet, the Libyan authorities refused to prosecute him without pressure 'from above'—namely the British Embassy— which, for some reason, the embassy was unwilling to exert.

Each passing day brought its load of setbacks to slowly open my eyes to the mounting obstacles ahead of me. I couldn't fight this battle alone against the corruption and dishonesty of my opponents, and desperately hoped that I'd soon find a lawyer willing to travel with me on this tortuous road to justice.

Part of my office routine was hunting for any news from trusted work colleagues about the rapist, which I could then pass on to the embassy, or to my Libyan lawyer, once I managed to locate one. Within days of the rape, I was given the rapist's name and even his company payroll number. I learnt that he lived in Area 3 of the compound with his parents and siblings, that he was known, at least by sight, to most of my Libyan colleagues. The close-knit environment of the compound made my fact-finding missions about the rapist rather easy, and my supportive colleagues quickly turned into willing informants, ready to provide me with the latest information about him. I learnt that he'd been released from custody by the police for 'insufficient evidence' after two days, before being suspended from work by SOC.

Each bit of information was eagerly passed on to the British Embassy. Upon his release from custody, he immediately absconded from the compound for a few weeks before resurfacing with another change in appearance—he'd completely shaved his hair off. I didn't believe I'd ever seen him before the rape, and only had the faintest recollection of him after it. As soon as I heard that he was now free inside the compound, I feared running into him. I was certain I wouldn't recognise him, and became suspicious of any young man remotely fitting his nondescript physique. During my lowest moments, my imagination plotted frightening scenarios in which he'd stalk me, or even murder me, to put a stop to the legal proceedings I planned against him. So far, he'd been allowed to get away with rape, so why not with murder? I was unaware at the time that there'd be no need for him to resort to such extreme measures since he benefited from the most invaluable *wasta* from not only his tribe and SOC, but the Libyan system itself. He seemed untouchable anywhere in

Libya, but regardless of how bleak my case appeared, I had to find a way to bring him to justice.

Only too aware of SOC's intentions to suppress the rape, I grew fearful that the company would seize the first opportunity to terminate my employment contract. By firing me and permanently keeping me out of Libya, SOC would kill two birds with one stone—it would put a stop to the civil case I planned against it, and keep silent the indelible injury that the rape of a foreign employee would inflict on its international reputation. Faced with the grim prospect of losing my job at any moment, a race against time began to locate a Libyan lawyer to start the legal process.

Once the rapist confessed his crime to his tribe, it was only a matter of time before he freely admitted it to all and sundry, but despite his confession, he remained free to come and go inside the compound. SOC had suspended him from work to appear to be doing the right thing as it believed the British Embassy was monitoring the situation. I was told later by Ayman, another work colleague keen on opening my eyes to the futility of fighting my case in his country, that 'a Libyan will never be prosecuted in Libya for a crime against a foreigner because that's just the way things are here'. Ayman didn't comment on the unfairness or otherwise of this Libyan state of affairs, and simply wished to convey the hopeless reality of my case in Libya. But I really wasn't interested in getting into a battle against a whole system; I merely wanted plain and simple justice. If it were true that such a covert policy existed in Libya to protect homegrown rapists, then I'd be willing to challenge it with any Libyan lawyer prepared to redress this outrageous wrong. Was it such an outlandish notion in Libya to expect a rapist to be prosecuted for his crime? Was it really asking too much? With each passing day, I sensed dark, malevolent forces lurking within the once enticing environment I'd felt privileged to call home for so many years.

It was devastating that the rapist had been released from police custody after forty-eight hours for 'insufficient evidence', despite having been quasi-identified and DNA evidence being processed. However dispiriting my predicament appeared to be, I still felt confident that he'd be returned to jail as soon as I found a Libyan lawyer to send him back there once the DNA results provided indisputable evidence of his guilt. The case was being undermined by the Libyan authorities themselves, and it was tremendously frustrating that it was all happening under the nose of a nonchalant British Embassy. The rapist's release from police custody had emboldened him enough to admit to the rape to his tribe first—which included many within SOC management—and so convinced him of his immunity from prosecution that he now freely discussed his crime with anyone who'd listen. I was aware that he was still suspended from his job with SOC, and was frequently seen around Area 3 of the compound where he lived, but I certainly didn't expect the bombshell that hit me one morning.

One of my colleagues-cum-informants, Saleem, walked into my office, full of effervescence, and declaring that he had 'big news'. I held my breath in nervous anticipation of the next piece of information coming my way.

'He says he's willing to pay you compensation,' he said, pausing for a second or two before looking away uneasily. 'And even marry you...'

My jaw dropped all the way to the floor. I was speechless. I stared at Saleem, eyes wide with disbelief at the enormity of what I'd just heard. I felt humiliated to the core while my blood boiled with rage. The protection granted to the rapist by both SOC and the Libyan system had so bolstered him that he now mocked me publicly.

'He also said that members of his tribe will approach you soon to discuss reparations.'

Suddenly, my anxiety levels rose sky high at the prospect of round-table discussions with members of the rapist's tribe. I was immensely relieved that no contact was ever made after a few weeks, but questioned my personal safety in an environment where the judicial process was so openly flouted, where a rapist was allowed to roam freely under the protection of a tribe fully aware of the harm I represented not only to its protegee, but to its own reputation.

The regular reports from my work colleagues about the rapist had always been difficult to hear, but, to add more insult to injury, it was crushing that he now insulted me in public. I soon noticed that people I didn't know visited my work department purely to take a peek at the 'raped woman'. I felt gossiped about and pointed at by strangers, but held my head high despite the torment going on inside me. From that point on, I kept my office door shut to shield myself from prying eyes. It was massively unjust that the rapist was so galvanised by his apparent immunity that he openly spoke of his crime while his victim was turned into a figure of curiosity by some.

As events unfolded with time, it became increasingly clear that the rape of a foreign woman was of no consequence to the Libyan authorities, but being aware of the local ways and customs, I couldn't help feeling it would've been a totally different matter had a Libyan woman been raped. Archaic traditions and pressures might have prevented her voice from being heard inside a courtroom, but, behind the scenes, the full weight of her tribe would've fallen hard on the rapist to obtain swift reparations. As a foreign victim of rape, my tragic reality was that my case was of no importance to the Libyan authorities, but, most crucially, it was of no importance to the very institution that had all the power to make a real difference and on which I'd naively relied upon for support: the British Embassy.

Nearly three weeks after the rape and with still no luck in finding a Libyan lawyer to represent me, my morale hit rock bottom, and I felt the desperate need to escape from the compound and the country altogether. All the lawyers I'd contacted had cited the jurisdiction issue as the reason for not taking on the case. Only that grumpy lawyer in Ajdabiya, Mr Jalil, had agreed to represent me, but not until October, a timeframe I considered too impractical. I feared having to retain him purely out of a lack of alternatives, and having to contend with his sharp manner and preconceived ideas about rape.

I was preparing to leave the compound within days when a work colleague casually handed me a piece of paper on which was scribbled the telephone number of a Mrs Selma Hussein. He told me she was a well-known Benghazi lawyer, and a highly respected one at that. I was so desperate for legal representation that I didn't even worry whether Brega was within her jurisdiction or not, only hoping that she could speak enough English. I vaguely remembered her name on the embassy's lawyers' list, but that she couldn't be reached on the listed number. I called her immediately, and was hugely relieved that she could speak English well. I introduced myself before briefly outlining my case to her. She sounded warm, friendly and confident that she could handle the case. My heart leapt with joy. Coincidentally, Mrs Hussein was about to leave for London herself, and suggested meeting there during the first week in July 2013. I was elated. Suddenly, I no longer felt alone, and all my recent frustrations began lifting to make way for hope surging through me like a much-needed soothing balm. I wanted to trust in the infallibility of the justice system everywhere, and refused to give any credence to the outlandish policy of not prosecuting the Libyan rapists of foreign victims. Up to now, the wheels of justice had been painfully slow to start turning, but I had to keep faith that justice was bound to prevail in the end. Didn't it always?

Before leaving the compound for London, I requested to be allocated another house on Secretary Street as I couldn't continue living on the site of my rape. There were several smaller, empty houses on the street, and one could easily be fixed up to accommodate me. My manager promised that one would be ready by the time I returned from leave. I was glad to have had enough patience to submit to all the police interviews and medical examinations required before my departure, in spite of my weakened physical condition and urgent need to flee the country. I had ensured that nothing was left amiss, and was leaving the compound confident that progress would be made in my absence.

I flew out of Libya at the end of June 2013, three weeks after the rape. I desperately needed to put aside everything that had happened, and concentrate instead on regaining enough strength to face whatever awaited upon my return. Top of my list was a visit to my London doctor as I'd been increasingly worried about my health since the rape; I felt permanently nauseous, on edge, and could hardly sleep. My family doctor, a sympathetic, caring man, reassured me that all my physical symptoms would subside within weeks, but that the psychological trauma of the rape would likely stay with me for the rest of my life. As a self-diagnosed hypochondriac, I was far more concerned about my physical health, believing that I could handle my mental health myself or, if necessary, with help from a psychotherapist. I'd already planned a programme of self-help and meditation to begin as soon as my physical condition improved. My doctor diagnosed post-traumatic stress disorder, but didn't recommend the use of any anti-depressant medication, advising psychotherapy instead, which suited me perfectly as I favoured a more holistic approach to health.

Since I wasn't going to be in London long enough to see a therapist on a regular basis, I'd have to find one in Libya as soon as I returned—only hoping that a Libyan psychotherapist would be far easier to find than a Libyan lawyer... I understood only too well that my overall physical and mental fitness would be key to my recovery, promising myself to attend the gym at the compound even more assiduously on my return. I was prepared to commit to the most strenuous fitness programme to help me face the legal battle that I knew awaited me in Brega.

It was during this time that a fleeting thought about forgiveness first crossed my mind. I was infuriated with myself that I could think of forgiving a criminal for turning my life upside down, and pushed the irritating thought away each time it popped up in my mind. But as much as I resisted the idea, it persisted until I finally recognised that forgiveness had to be the foundation to my recovery and the tool to reach ultimate freedom. I had to find it in me to forgive my rapist. There was no escaping it if I wanted to regain the sense of peace that the rapist had robbed me of. I had to forgive for my own sake, and love myself much more than I loathed the rapist. And one other thing was crystal clear in my troubled mind—if my doctor was right that the psychological trauma of the rape would live with me forever, then I had to find a way to unburden myself of its toxic effects. It made sense that I couldn't embark on a recovery programme and expect a positive outcome whilst I bubbled over with simmering rage. The reasons behind my decision to forgive were quite easy to rationalise, unlike the practical process of it all. How on earth would I begin to forgive the perpetrator of the most heinous crime against me? Was I even capable of such compassion towards someone I despised so much? I still struggled to even come to terms with the fact I'd been raped and was drowning in a psychological tsunami, but I was rational enough to recognise that I had two paths ahead of me: one towards never-ending heartache, and another towards healing and peace. The choice was simple and mine alone to make.

The ordeal of the rape had turned a light off inside me, draining me of all positive energy; I suspected I couldn't possibly emerge totally unscathed from it, but I was determined to reduce its effects to the barest minimum. The rage inside me was a soul-destroying dead weight that I refused to drag through the rest of my days. For my own sanity, I had to free myself of it, and find a way to block the likely descent towards dark depression. My whole being vacillated between emotions I never knew possible before.

For a few days following the rape, I felt that although I didn't want to die, I didn't want to live either; it was the closest to being dead without having died. My whole being had been gobbled up inside a bottomless pit of misery and despair from which I saw no way out. I accepted that the trauma of the rape would be forever seared in my mind, but while I would never be able to erase its memory, I still had the power to lessen its poisonous impact. I was in control of either allowing this traumatic, life-defining event to haunt me for the rest of my life, or disable its destructive force and free myself of the pain and bitterness it had unleashed in me. I had to make the conscious effort to end the constant replaying in my head of that harrowing moment to stop it from latching onto my soul until it became a permanent memorial to one tragic afternoon on a glorious summer's day.

The die-hard optimist in me had always managed to bounce back from life's challenges relatively unscathed, and I didn't want to become so embittered by the rape that I'd lose the ability to keep on looking towards the light, even when plunged into the darkest situations. I refused to let the anger inside me blind me to the good that was still out there. Nothing positive could possibly come from holding on to gloomy, depressive thoughts that would only keep me from embracing the good in my life. I decided to free myself of my inner pain by simply slamming the door shut on it. It didn't mean I'd give up my legal fight against the rapist or SOC. Not at all. Forgiving didn't mean forgetting or throwing in the towel. It didn't mean pretending that the trauma never happened. It didn't mean that the slate would be wiped clean as if by magic just because I'd vowed to forgive the actions of a criminal. No, forgiveness was for my own sake first and foremost, and meant that I'd open the door wide for mind, body and soul healing to release the corrosive power of a traumatic event. I had to retake the reins of my life, and not remember that day with never-ending anguish. I refused to be soured by it, resolving instead to label it as the lowest point in my life, a nasty, vile event of the past that held no power over my present or my future. Like everyone else, I wasn't immune from life's tragedies and, like everyone else, I carried painful personal stories. Experience taught me that life held much pain within it, that it could be both tragic and amazing all at once. I'd known the tragic, but now looked forward to the amazing part. I remembered reading once that each time a person forgave a grievance, they would heal a wound of their own; a premise I found so inspiring that I promised to keep it in mind during my undoubtedly challenging journey towards forgiveness.

As a self-declared hypochondriac, I was also very concerned by the health stresses that could be triggered by traumatic events, and dreaded a potential impact on my physical being as a result of the rape. Forgiving was about lifting this hefty, all-round destructive burden off my shoulders, and I was ready to start the process. Although the memory of that day could never be erased from my mind, I wanted to be able to recall it without feeling its debilitating, soul-crushing impact. For a brief but endless moment when time had stood still, the rapist had held my life in his hands with such absolute power that I had no idea whether I'd live or die. But I'd been lucky to survive, and now had to focus only on that positive fact, and not grant the rapist a second more of my time. For my own sake, I was ready to open the doors of forgiveness and let the healing begin, feeling sure that only good things would derive from it. The preservation of both my physical and mental health was the main catalyst for my decision to let go of my rage and forgive the rapist, but my deep faith in God had also steered me towards that path. I had to accept the imperfect world which had created my rapist, but most importantly, how could I ask for forgiveness of my own sins when I couldn't find enough humility and compassion inside me to forgive the sins another human being committed against me? Yes, forgiving was the only way to regain my peace of mind and, as soon as I stopped resisting the idea and fully accepted it, I felt a huge weight lifting off my shoulders.

But I was soon to find out that being willing to forgive and going through the process of forgiveness were two separate things—the first was an abstract concept arrived at with the best intentions at heart, while the second was the torturous, emotional process that held untold inescapable pain within it. At times, I fiercely rebelled against the whole idea of forgiving, and struggled to find enough strength to hold fast to my forgiveness plans. I was embarking on a process that would be excruciatingly slow and painful, but I looked forward to emerging from it as a spiritually cleansed new me, strengthened by an ordeal that was supposed to weaken me forever. I began researching the most basic coping mechanisms that could lighten the emotional burden I was under. There were times at the height of my forgiveness crusade when I imagined meeting the rapist, and the words I'd speak to him. It was easier to think of him as a young, lost soul in need of guidance than the remorseless, arrogant criminal he was. Even during the darkest times following the rape, a part of me hoped that he would regret the terrible choice he made that day to brutally assault a defenceless woman in her own home, and that he would change the direction of his life. But I also hoped that, for the sake of society at large, he'd be prosecuted for his crime by his country's authorities, for if they continued to look the other way, then he, and others like him, would use this immunity from prosecution as an open licence to rape. In the meantime, and whatever happened to him, I needed, for my own sake, to be kind to myself by letting go of that traumatic event once and for all, by calling on the healing power of forgiveness, and placing my struggles, if not in the hands of the inadequate British Embassy, then firmly in God's. My experience taught me that one could move emotional mountains with the power of faith and forgiveness. Another lesson I'll forever be grateful for.

In the early afternoon of Thursday, 4 July 2013, as arranged by Mrs Hussein in Brega, she and I met outside the Starbucks on Borough High Street. I'd been standing outside the venue for barely a few minutes when an attractive woman in her early forties, smartly dressed in an elegant cream-coloured trouser suit, approached me.

'Bahia?' she asked.

I nodded, smiling.

'Selma Hussein. Call me Selma,' she said brightly as she extended a perfectly manicured hand towards me.

We entered the venue and sat at a table by a large front window. After exchanging a few banalities, we ordered coffee then turned to my rape saga. I handed Selma a copy of the case documents as she sipped on her cappuccino, then launched into an abridged version of the events of that fateful day, barely a month ago. Every bit of information my Libyan colleagues-cum-informants had given me about the rapist was relayed to her. She listened intently, nodding her head at times, whilst taking copious notes.

Despite the reports of SOC's plan to quash the rape, and the rapist being loose inside the compound, the circumstances of the case made it an especially easy one to wrap up—the rapist had been identified, he'd admitted to his crime, there was DNA evidence, an eye witness... I failed to see what could possibly go wrong. All that was needed was a lawyer to start the judicial process. Little did I know that things would get worse very quickly.

'My advice is to pursue SOC for damages. You've got a strong case, and your memo to the chairman months before the rape is material evidence of the company's negligence,' she said, holding up the document in her hand.

She took another sip of her cappuccino before adjusting the designer sunglasses perched on her stylishly coiffed head.

'No, SOC will not want a case like this to land in court. That's for sure... It will settle before,' she added with confidence.

'OK, that's good to hear. What about the rapist?' I asked, a little puzzled that she hadn't mentioned the principal villain in this sorry tale at all.

'The rapist? Oh, forget him! There's no point filing anything against him,' she said with a dismissive hand wave.

'Huh? What do you mean "no point"?' I asked, eyes wide with disbelief. My heart suddenly began beating erratically at the inconceivable notion of my rapist being let off scot-free.

She looked at me intensely for a few seconds then sighed heavily. 'Why? Because this is Libya. And in Libya, he won't spend one day in jail for rape, that's why.'

My mouth fell open in shock. I was utterly flabbergasted. Each time I thought things couldn't get any worse, something always happened to show otherwise. I felt like I'd just been run over by a speeding monster truck. I'd never heard of a rapist being handed carte blanche by any authorities anywhere in the world. Was it that, in Libya, it wasn't a case of 'innocent until proven guilty', or even 'guilty until proven innocent'? No, in Libya, in my case, it was 'innocent even if guilty'!

Incredulous at what I'd heard, I closed my eyes for a brief moment to let the enormity and implications of her words fully sink in. How could such injustice be possible in the twenty-first century? Was it Selma's confirmation of that covert Libyan policy that absolved Libyan rapists of crimes against foreigners that Ayman had spoken of? I'd chosen not to believe Ayman, but to hear it being quasi-confirmed by a lawyer was a crushing blow. What else would go wrong? How could an identified rapist be let off the hook by the authorities whose duty it was to prosecute? How could such a deeply religious society tolerate such a blatantly outrageous state of affairs? I was prepared to forgive the rapist for my own sanity, but I could never accept the justice system absolving him of his crime and denying my entitlement to justice. Regardless of my intentions to forgive the rapist, I needed him to be prosecuted and punished under the law. Was it too much to ask? Even with forgiveness thrown into the mix, there simply could be no peace without justice.

Selma assured me that she knew the system in Libya inside out, and that suing SOC for 'negligence and failure to provide duty of care' was the best way forward—the only way. 'Forget the rapist!' she'd announced matter-of-factly. *Easy for you to say,* I thought.

In spite of my shock and while I was relieved that a civil lawsuit could be filed against SOC, I knew with every fibre of my being that the rapist being granted immunity was something I could never accept. Selma's comment about the rapist escaping punishment troubled me greatly. I was outraged at the scandalous injustice of allowing a rapist to walk free from his crime. If Libya was truly a place where the law didn't prosecute rapists, then I wondered why Selma, as the prominent big city lawyer that she was—and a woman to boot—wasn't fighting this outrageous, crippling injury to her gender. If one battle was worth fighting for, surely this was it.

The hopelessness of my case flashed before my eyes, making me wonder how competent Selma would be at handling the rape of a foreign woman when she appeared to be so accepting of such an injustice to her womenfolk. But, since Libyan lawyers weren't exactly knocking on my door to represent me, I had no other choice but to trust in her experience and knowledge of the laws of her country—at least for the time being. She agreed to represent me, and I hoped for the best. I'd always had an unwavering faith in the justice system, but I could feel it slowly crumbling with each obstacle I encountered. This policy of not prosecuting rapists in Libya was extremely perplexing since sexual violence crimes were criminalised under the country's own domestic laws. Libya might not share the same judicial culture with Britain, but it was party to most of the principal universal human rights treaties, including the Convention on the Elimination of All Forms of Discrimination Against Women (CEDAW). It had a legal obligation under international law to 'prevent and prosecute rape and other forms of sexual violence', and Article 407 of the Libyan Penal Code criminalised 'sexual intercourse with another by force, threat or deceit'. There it was in black and white.

I decided to trust solely in the unequivocal rule of law, and rejected Selma's comment about the rapist being legally untouchable in Libya. If the law protected the rights of rape victims, then I had to believe it was firmly on *my* side, and not on the side of my rapist. I had no idea how, but I was determined that the Libyan rape laws wouldn't be flouted in my case, confident that with the support of the British Embassy, I'd achieve my goal.

In spite of my case having all the elements to make it an easy one to settle, it was hampered by the Libyan system itself. While each passing day brought its load of setbacks to show me how bumpy the road ahead was going to be, I was sure that my struggle could only end in victory. The question that hadn't crossed my mind was: victory for whom?

The meeting with Selma over, I made up my mind that for the rest of my time in London, I'd put to one side anything connected to the rape, and focus instead on regaining my physical strength. I gorged on all kinds of vitamins and supplements to boost my energy, and get rid of my persistent bouts of nausea. My research into ways to take my mind off the rape and deal with the resulting stresses highlighted the therapeutic benefits of... house cleaning! I could have thought of more indulgent choices such as island-hopping in the Caribbean or retail therapy in Milan, but if the uninspiring, tedious cleaning of my house could heal my torment, then I was game.

Each morning, without fail, I prepared to lose myself in hours of washing and scrubbing in anticipation of the soothing effects of deep, silent concentration as it worked its magic on my traumatised mind. Of course, I was aware that I was cleaning far more than the odd dusty surface, and was more than willing to immerse myself into the most monotonous domestic chores imaginable if they could switch off my memory of the rape, and cut me off from its pain. My sense of vulnerability had gone through the roof since the rape, so much so that I imagined danger at every turn. I considered installing metal grilles to all external doors and windows at my London house, totally unconcerned by the conspicuous look such additions would lend to the house. My safety concerns were being magnified in my head until they took on a whole new dimension—one that allowed for a touch of paranoia to creep up at times.

After six long weeks in London, time came for my return to Brega. My break had been well spent—my house was gleaming from top to bottom, and I'd managed to overcome my nausea thanks to the tons of vitamins I'd gobbled down. At no point during this vacation did I count the days until I was back at the compound. In fact, I dreaded the thought of reimmersing myself into the overwhelming situation that the rape had thrown me into, but my return to Libya was essential if I wanted my day in court. I reflected that matters could only improve now I'd found a Libyan lawyer to work alongside the British Embassy. So far, nothing had seemed to proceed smoothly, but I still strongly believed that the British Embassy would step in to ensure justice was served. Or so I naively thought.

On my first morning back at work, I rushed into Mr El-Abadi's office full of anticipation of news of any progress. I hoped against hope that some magic wand had cleared away all my problems during my absence.

'Any news about the DNA?'

He looked at me, eyes wide with feigned surprise. 'Oh... You're still thinking about this?'

He'd sidestepped a direct answer with a highly offensive question of his own, and for a second or two, I stood speechless, frozen to the spot. I could hardly believe his condescending, inconsiderate words.

'What?' I spluttered. 'You think I'm being over-sensitive about my own rape? Yes! I'm "still thinking about this"! And I won't stop until it's resolved! You can tell that to management from me!'

'I really don't know anything,' he said pathetically, 'But I'll find out if you want me to.'

I stormed out of his office and sat at my desk, steaming with fury, wondering how much longer SOC would allow me to remain in Libya if I persistently pushed for my case to be addressed. I had a strong feeling that the countdown to my days started ticking shortly after the rape. Mr El-Abadi had said that the DNA results would take a week or so, but, nearly two months later, he seemed totally unconcerned about their whereabouts. Instead, I was met with his amused stare, and brushed off like I was fussing over spilt milk. His dismissive response offended me no end. Would he display the same flippant attitude if his wife or daughter were assaulted? Had he really expected me to have put the rape out of my mind? Of course not; it had been his way of letting me know that, as far as the company was concerned, the rape was yesterday's news, that the subject was closed. To SOC and the Libyan authorities, my rape had been inconsequential, a petty inconvenience to set aside without a second thought. Mr El-Abadi was my contact about all issues relating to my case, but apart from his conversation with the SOC's legal manager during which he'd voiced his disapproval of the company's stance, he now acted like a willing participant in SOC's strategy to repress the rape.

Surprisingly, Mr Hatami, the security manager, who'd accused me of exaggerating the incidents on Secretary Street months earlier, walked into my office later that morning to discuss, yet again, additional security measures to put in place on Secretary Street. His distasteful comment that 'no foreign woman had died on the street yet' was still at the forefront of my mind, and I was reluctant to discuss anything with him. I reminded him, with some impatience, that the basic measures we discussed two months earlier still hadn't been implemented. I wasn't fooled one bit—his visit was nothing but a mollifying ploy by SOC to give the impression it was actively looking to improve security on my street. But, again, I remembered that if security could be improved, then it was maybe worth playing the game. I set my reluctance aside, and suggested emergency panic buttons inside the houses, directly linked to his department. There'd been one incident the previous year when a local man attempted to break into the house of a nurse, Sylvana, as she lay in bed early one morning. He hadn't succeeded, but an emergency button would've made a huge difference to her, or, indeed, to me at the time of my rape.

'An emergency panic button? Well, that's just like a cell phone, isn't it?' he said, smirking.

I ignored the sarcasm in his voice, and calmly explained the difference to him. He promised to research this further then get back to me. I didn't expect to hear from him again, and I wasn't mistaken. I was growing accustomed to SOC's deceitful attempts at pretending to be doing the right thing when it had no intention of delivering. Not even after a brutal rape had taken place within its walls.

That same day, I realised my return to the compound hadn't been expected by everyone, and I was stunned to hear that the majority of my work colleagues had been certain I wouldn't return to Libya.

'We were shocked to see you back,' said Saleem, my trusted work colleague.

Rather perplexed, I asked him why.

'A Libyan woman wouldn't have come back to work because... umm, you know... the shame of it...' he replied matter-of-factly.

That infuriating, misplaced 'shame' again. His words really touched a nerve inside me, leaving me appalled by such archaic, senseless attitudes. I'd worked with Saleem for many years; he was a soft-voiced, straight-talking man, and I knew he hadn't meant any slight by his comment—he was merely exposing the cultural divide between us.

'Well, firstly, I'm not Libyan and, secondly, I don't feel *shame*,' I said as calmly as possible. 'The *shame* you so conveniently dump on the victim should be on the rapist and all those protecting him... You guys had better get used to it because I'm not leaving until I've had my day in court!'

The idea of feeling 'shame' for being raped was not only alien to my thinking, but massively insulting. Why should I feel 'shame' for what a criminal did to me at knifepoint? Such an outrageous judgment thrown at the victim only reflected the attitude of Libyan society when confronted with the issue of sexual violence. But, even in seemingly more progressive parts of the world, rape still was the only crime for which the blame and responsibility were, at times, placed squarely onto the victim's shoulders. Instinctive judgment of the victim often occurred, with the serious risk of impacting on the investigation and subsequent trial of the rapist. Such biased judgment, steeped in archaic and irrational thinking, had no place in a just society, but no doubt it would remain far easier to legislate new laws than to change people's deeply entrenched mentalities.

The idea of not returning to Libya hadn't crossed my mind for a second as my presence in the country was a prerequisite to any court action against the rapist or SOC. Failure to return would merely bring a swift end to my legal plans; I had no option but to be in Libya to initiate the judicial process, regardless of the bumps along the road that I now fully expected to come across.

Within days of my return, Malik, one of my trusted Libyan colleagues-cum-informants, confided in me that he was related to an officer at the Brega police station, and suggested paying him a visit to enquire about my case. Another example of Libyan *wasta* at play, slyly opening doors to confidential information being given to outsiders. I insisted on accompanying him and hearing any news first-hand. We drove to the police station in his car immediately after work, and met with the officer in question who had nothing to disclose other than the highly significant statement that the Libyan authorities 'would do nothing unless instructed from above'. The next morning, I relayed this information to Mrs Hanson, confident that the British Embassy would be the nudge 'from above' the Libyan authorities required.

Contrary to my manager's promise that a house would be ready on my return to the compound, this wasn't so—just as Saleem had revealed, it seemed no one had expected my return to the compound! Hiba, ever the supportive friend, offered that I continue sharing her house which, again, I was grateful for. But within a few short weeks, SOC had refurbished Elena's old house for me to move into. Elena was a gentle Serbian nurse who'd occupied house number 1557 for several years before being driven out by the unsettling changes to our once peaceful street. The situation took a toll on her when local youths began targeting her house for relentless stone throwing and doorbell ringing. Her morale, already at a low point, was broken to the point of no return when a local man attempted to break into her next-door neighbour's house. Still in bed early one morning, Sylvana was awoken by the sound of someone trying to force her front door open. Petrified, she telephoned the security guards at the nearby medical clinic then opened a window and screamed for help. Undeterred, the man continued trying to force her door open for a moment longer before finally fleeing. This incident right next door to her house was the final straw for Elena who resigned shortly thereafter. The incident, duly reported to SOC management, was met with its usual apathy.

I looked forward to moving out from Hiba's house into my own, and bring a semblance of normality into my unsettled life since the rape. House number 1557 was located at the back of Secretary Street, at the end of a row of about eight small properties, all tucked behind high boundary walls, and occupied by foreign medical personnel. The house to the left of mine was derelict and empty, and to the right was a plot of vacant land. My priority was to transform this house into a mini fortress, making it impenetrable to any potential intruder as I reinforced the metal grilles fitted to both the front and back doors with a variety of security locks, padlocks and door alarms I'd brought in from London. All this paraphernalia made me feel perfectly safe during the day, but once darkness fell, it wasn't enough to prevent me from turning into a jumpy, over-anxious person that I didn't recognise or even like being.

Realistically, no one could break into the house, but although reason and logic told me so, nothing could appease my over-active imagination once night fell around me like a looming menace. Each evening, the tedious ritual of barricading myself inside would begin, and nothing but the first light of dawn could dissipate my nervousness, and settle my restless mind. I felt certain that my rapist would find out where I'd moved to and return. 'I'll be back later!' he'd said before running out of the house after the rape, and his words were engraved in my mind. At times, I feared he'd be lying in wait as I left the house for work in the morning, or as I returned in the afternoon, ready to inflict more harm.

On several occasions, well-meaning colleagues warned me that my life could be in danger if my persistence at seeing the rapist prosecuted became too obvious. I'd made no secrets to them that I no longer felt safe in the compound, that I was constantly on the lookout for potential danger, and that I hardly slept at night. They were genuinely concerned about my safety, and, with most of them keeping weapons at home, it didn't take long before they suggested I too had a gun for protection. It all seemed surreal. I had enough problems as it was, and certainly no aspiration of suddenly turning into Calamity Jane! Just as I'd suspected that I would freeze up if faced with a rapist, I knew that I could never own a gun or, worse still, fire it at anyone. I'd never even touched a real gun before. No, keeping a firearm under the mattress wasn't an option I was prepared to contemplate, not even under my circumstances.

I thought I'd made my point quite clear until one tenacious colleague, Eissa, took it upon himself to convince me otherwise. Unannounced, he arrived at my house one Friday afternoon. His visit surprised me as we interacted only at the office.

'*Salem*! Before you say anything, please just look at this,' he said, handing me the light blue plastic bag he carried.

I took a peek inside the innocuous-looking bag, and immediately thrust it back into his hands.

'Nooo! I've told you I don't want a gun!' I barked.

'You need it! We're all worried about you… Please, just listen for one minute,' he pleaded as he removed the black, ugly weapon out of the bag.

It was gruesome—nothing like the dainty, pocket-sized handguns with mother-of-pearl handles that the heroines of Hollywood movies carried discreetly in their elegant purses.

'Are you mad?' I cried out. 'I don't want it anywhere near me! Take it and leave!'

'We've all got guns at home. Even my wife knows how to use them,' he continued, undeterred. 'Just let me show you. It's very easy!'

The potentially disastrous consequences of this crazy moment dawned on me fast. It'd only take an SOC patrol car to drive by and find Eissa fiddling with a firearm in my garden for me to lose my job on the spot, before getting me into serious trouble with the local police. Eissa's presence was massively detrimental to my interests and there was no way I'd risk losing my job and, with it, my day in court. I was determined not to give SOC any reason whatsoever to put me on a one-way flight to London before then. But Eissa wasn't giving up easily, repeating that all locals had guns at home, and how their wives and sisters knew how to use them. That may be so, but I was certain that no expatriates had guns at their homes, and I had no desire to start a trend. Ignoring my protests, he proceeded to demonstrate the easy steps to handling a gun by first loading and unloading the bullets inside.

'Please, just hold it,' he said, sounding like a salesman desperate to off-load the latest gadget on a reluctant housewife.

'Nooo! I... don't... want... it! Take it and leave, or I'll call security!' I shouted, knowing full well I wouldn't call security and initiate my exit from Libya myself.

Finally, Eissa calmly placed the loaded gun back inside the blue plastic bag, put the bag carefully on the garden table and, quick as lightning, darted out of the gate into his car and sped away. I stood there, dumbfounded, staring at the bag with its lethal weapon on my garden table. I wracked my brain for a way to safely dispose of its deadly content, seething at being thrust into a potentially critical situation I'd never asked for. Until I figured out a way to get rid of the bag, I thought it wiser to move it inside the house. It was surprisingly heavy, and it made my skin crawl just touching it, knowing that it was loaded. I pushed it under the coffee table before my imagination went into overdrive, suspecting Eissa of being involved in the latest SOC ploy to justify my sacking. Nothing made sense anymore, and I feared that anything could happen simply to cut short my time in Libya. The bag remained under the coffee table the whole weekend, and I even refused to leave the house, just in case SOC plotted a timely search whilst I was out.

Strangely enough, I never felt so apprehensive and fearful as during that weekend when I had a lethal weapon for protection. I could think of no safe way to dispose of the gun, so I planned to return it to Eissa on Sunday morning. As I prepared to leave my house for work, I picked up the bag with its ugly contents, buried it at the bottom of a large shoulder bag, and set off on the short road to my office. Mouth dry with fear, legs shaking, I waved my badge at the armed security guard at the checkpoint, half-expecting the shrill of metal detector alarms to ring wildly as I hurried by. But nothing happened and I breathed a huge sigh of relief, before rushing into my office, calling Eissa and plonking the bag firmly into his hands.

'I only tried to help,' he said sheepishly.

'Just take it and go...'

The gun episode put me under such mental strain that I just wanted an immediate end to it. I sat at my desk, slowly feeling the pent-up tension I'd been under the whole weekend finally subside. Needless to say, I was never approached again with any gun offers by anyone.

There was one great benefit to my move to house 1557—its location right opposite the new women's gym. A gym on my doorstep was a bonus, and I promised myself to use it daily to maintain a relatively sound body and mind despite the circumstances. I knew that the only effective solution out of my ordeal would be for the rapist to be prosecuted and for SOC to be held accountable, but until such time, I counted on the gym to help me overcome any hurdles that awaited along the way.

In the summer of 2013, the SOC chairman, Mr Said Barak, left the company and was replaced by Mr Ali Rahman.

I hoped wholeheartedly that the new chairman would prove more willing than his predecessor to engage with Selma, my Libyan lawyer, to settle the situation that had arisen between SOC and I as a result of the rape.

So far, SOC had completely sidelined Selma, and her attempts at communicating with the company continued to be ignored. SOC, one of the largest oil companies in Libya, employed thousands of foreign workers, and a rape of a worker inside its residential compound was bound to be detrimental to its international standing and reputation. All along, Selma's only objective had been to meet with the chairman to discuss an out-of-court settlement. She didn't consider any other options other than negotiations, which had suited me initially. She'd had no doubt that SOC would soon join her at the negotiating table, but the company had other plans that entailed simply shutting her out until she gave up. A letter to SOC had received no response, whilst her access to the compound was repeatedly denied by the company. Her subsequent attempts to contact the chairman led nowhere, and since she couldn't enter the compound without SOC's authorisation, she remained on the sideline, unable to progress matters. While she hadn't expected such a contemptuous reaction from a company of SOC's standing, she was still convinced that the company would choose to avoid a trial by coming to the negotiating table in due course. The waiting game had begun.

By keeping her at arm's length and refusing to engage with her, SOC were merely putting into practice its strategy of 'strictly zero engagement' with anyone about the case, and showing no intention whatsoever of entering into any negotiations at any point. The company seemed to view any discussion about the case as an acceptance of its responsibility in the rape while, conversely, its refusal of any dialogue would absolve it of any legal liability.

Incredulous that she'd been treated so shabbily by the company, Selma asked me to compile a package of documents and photographic evidence, anything that would show security flaws on Secretary Street. Already in a state of semi-permanent anxiety since the rape, the idea of playing lead detective in my own case didn't fill me with enthusiasm. But I was only too aware of my hapless circumstances, which left me no choice but to agree to take on that role and gather all the evidence Selma needed to move the case forward. It was a nerve-racking mission which, I knew only too well, could land me into hot water with SOC. Every evening, I waited for the right moment just before darkness fell to sneak out of my house on snooping expeditions around my neighbourhood, a small camera concealed under the conveniently long sleeves of my *abaya* to secretly snap photographs and record videos. It took several attempts over a couple of evenings before I was fully satisfied with the quality of my snapshots and videos. All that was left to do was to compile all this testimony into one package to be delivered to Selma in Benghazi.

On several occasions, Selma expressed her frustrations at the company's disdainful attitude towards her, and her certainty that only the intervention of the British Embassy would force SOC into some form of engagement. Unfortunately, the British Embassy wasn't showing much interest in my plight and, for some unknown reason, was withholding the much-needed support that I and Selma had expected all along. Although I was in regular communication with Mrs Hanson, she still had no progress to report. I was routinely informed that the embassy was in contact with the Libyan Foreign Ministry, which was great news, but there never seemed to be any feedback forthcoming. Gradually, a pattern emerged from my regular liaison with Mrs Hanson, consisting of weekly or twice-weekly telephone calls during which expressions of sympathy and placating statements were made, but always falling short of the one thing my case so badly needed, and which the embassy could've so easily provided: unambiguous and effective intervention.

The longer I interacted with the British Embassy, the more I suspected it had no protocol in place to deal with rape crimes against nationals abroad. SOC was a subsidiary of the National Oil Corporation of Libya (NOC) which controlled the country's entire oil industry, itself owned by the Libyan government, and yet, I was expected to believe that the British government had no diplomatic leverage to apply in order to support one of its nationals, a victim of a serious crime in a country to which it handed millions in yearly financial aid. I wrote to a long list of British government ministers and political figures, appealing for their assistance, from William Hague, to Philip Hammond, to David Cameron, to Boris Johnson, to Theresa May, to Jeremy Hunt and Sajid Javid amongst others. Those who deigned respond all used that typical, conciliatory political language in their replies that offered nothing of any substance to progress my case. The empty rhetoric was invariably the same, and no longer meant anything to me. In fact, I saw it for what it really was: a patronising attempt at pacifying me whilst they continued to do nothing other than figuratively patting me over the head until I gave up the fight and disappeared.

The then prime minister, Theresa May's response went the extra mile when she added a touch of contempt with her suggestion to contact the Legal Ombudsman if dissatisfied with the level of assistance I'd received. Such a flippant response from a powerful woman was a slap in the face, which only added yet more insult to injury.

As events slowly unfolded, I began to view the British authorities' failure to get involved in my case within the context of the recent armed conflict in Libya in which they had participated. I became convinced that their failure to lend assistance to a national in need was the direct result of the British government's unwillingness to disrupt its diplomatic post-war relations with Libya. The rape happened at a sensitive time, less than two years after the end of the war in Libya and, for its own political reasons, the British government elected to be indifferent to the violation of one of its citizen's rights by a country it recently helped 'liberate' and into which it poured millions in financial aid with no questions asked. I'd always believed that justice was an inherent right, not a privilege, and that human rights were fundamental, universal rights to which every person was entitled to in virtue of his or her basic status as a human being. It was a no-brainer that there existed a legal and moral obligation on every governmental institution to respect and protect the rights of its citizens, and that these rights were independent from any diplomatic or trade considerations. And yet, it looked like both the Libyan and British authorities had allowed their diplomatic considerations to interfere with their obligations towards a citizen with an inherent right to justice. My case was taking on unsettling political undertones, and I was deeply troubled by the hypocrisy of a system willing to deny its citizens justice when other self-serving interests prevailed over their human rights.

The cold, unpalatable truth was that I'd been abandoned at the hands of the Libyan authorities and their corrupt system, with the tacit acquiescence of the British authorities. How else could I explain the rapist being free at large, and likely to remain so, whilst SOC made no secret of its intentions to suppress my case. Despite being the victim of an easy crime to solve, I was caught up in the behind-the-scenes scheming of all those who were duty-bound to assist. By reneging on their duties towards my case, both the Libyan and the British authorities became complicit in my rape fiasco. If the deliberate withholding, by an individual or institution, of any action to resolve a crime resulted in the undermining or suppression of the due process of the law, wasn't that akin to aiding and abetting a crime, albeit after the fact? Were the authorities troubled at any time that their denial of a rape victim's right to justice would only provide a rapist with both immunity and a pass to potentially rape again? Were they satisfied that a subsidiary of a government entity had shirked its responsibility in a serious crime against a national? No government worth its salt would display such blatant dereliction of duty. I was appalled by the systematic apathy I encountered from both the British and Libyan authorities, and became convinced that my case was ignored in the name of their diplomatic relations.

The passing of time and unfolding of events only reinforced the belief that I'd been forsaken at the mercy of the corrupt Libyan system by a British government sitting tightly on the fence while I pleaded for help. It was a crushing, demoralising conclusion to arrive at, one which could only exacerbate both my mental disposition and my future legal struggles.

As the prospect of a positive end to my case appeared bleaker with each passing day, my determination to continue pressing ahead never wavered and, despite it all, I still remained generally confident that, ultimately, justice would prevail. I was in this optimistic frame of mind when I was invited to a meeting with the National Council for Human Rights (NCHR) at its Benghazi office. I learnt later that this meeting had been arranged by a work colleague who was acquainted with a worker at the council—*wasta* at play again. Every day, I prayed for even the tiniest step forward in my case, aware that help might come from the most unlikely quarters, and was always ready to seize every opportunity just in case it led to a breakthrough.

The meeting took place on a Sunday morning in September 2013. The NCHR building was a state-of-the-art fortress guarded by an array of security surveillance cameras in every corner. I was led through a maze of corridors and security points to the office of the head of the council, Mr Ibrahim Khatemi, a distinguished, middle-aged man sitting comfortably behind a large desk inside an impressive den of high-tech equipment and latest mod cons.

Smiling, he offered me a seat before expressing his sadness that a 'guest' to his country had not only been wronged by one of his compatriots, but been treated 'so appallingly afterwards'. It was encouraging that Mr Khatemi could be objective about my case and appalled by the treatment I'd received so far. Bizarrely, it reaffirmed to me that I wasn't expecting too much by demanding justice after a rape. I handed Mr Khatemi a copy of my case documents—which I never seemed to leave home without these days—and filled him in on the rape saga. He listened intently, took a few notes then promised to liaise directly with the Libyan government on my behalf. His words were like music to my ears.

He then introduced me to Ines, a senior member of his team, who opened up about the deteriorating social and political climate in Libya resulting from the recent armed conflict. Ines elaborated on the NCHR's staunch commitment towards security and justice for the Libyan population despite the increasing post-war difficulties. She reiterated her boss' statement that the NCHR would contact the Libyan government on my behalf before declaring that she was at a loss to understand why the British authorities weren't actively involved in the case.

'I'll tell you one thing for sure... This is Libya and as a foreigner in this country, unless your embassy steps up, you'll get nowhere. I'd even say that in your case, only pressure from *outside* of Libya will bring results...' Her voice trailed off to emphasise the hopelessness of my predicament without the British Embassy's active engagement.

By that stage—three months after the rape—I had a pretty good idea where I stood with the British Embassy, and didn't hold much hope of concrete assistance from it. The embassy's non-committal posture was beyond my comprehension, but it was only too real. I asked Ines about mediatising my case.

'If you do this and remain in Libya, then, without a doubt, your life will be in serious danger,' she replied without hesitation.

Upon my return to London a few weeks after the rape, my intention had been to contact the media with news of the rape, but I was advised against it first by Selma then by all subsequent lawyers. I'd been hugely ambivalent about keeping my rape under wraps as it was a fact that media exposure was a tried and tested mechanism to trigger a reaction from unresponsive public figures or authorities. In most cases, only the fear of public scrutiny, outrage or embarrassment through mediatisation could shake things up and bring about results.

Despite my doubts, I chose to trust in my lawyers' expertise and heeded their advice, a decision I bitterly regretted as the passing of time dramatically reduced any impact my case might've had at the opportune time. I recognised far too late that a post on a social media platform might've set the wheels of justice in motion, and, again, lamented my failure to realise this significant, missed opportunity at the right moment. Instead, I'd naively put my trust in the Libyan judicial system and relied on the British Embassy's full support, which never materialised.

A few days following the meeting at the NCHR, my manager informed me that I was to be interviewed by another investigating judge, a Mr Salah Toufik, at his office in Benghazi. Again, I was more than willing to submit to all the requests from the Libyan authorities if it meant that my case could be progressed.

Early on the morning of Thursday, 12 September 2013, I set off for Benghazi with Mabrouk, the SOC driver. Hiba's presence, as the eye witness, hadn't been requested this time. Besides being the eye witness, Hiba had doubled up as a translator during all the interviews with the SOC security officers and the Brega police. Mr Toufik, a giant of a man in his mid-forties, spoke very little English and, again, no translator was available. While he and I struggled to communicate with one another in a mixture of pidgin English and Arabic, the scene that ensued took on a decidedly surreal dimension. As it happened, Mabrouk and the investigating judge knew each other personally, which was enough for him to be invited to sit through the interview. Once he noticed the language struggles between Mr Toufik and I, Mabrouk took it upon himself to step in as a translator despite his own non-existent English. The three of us muddled along until our laborious exchange thankfully drew to an end, and Mr Toufik announced I had to be fingerprinted and provide three mouth swabs to be sent to a laboratory in Italy for DNA comparison.

Suddenly, I found this request highly suspicious. Why was my own DNA needed at this stage? What happened to the sample taken immediately following the rape months earlier? And why were my fingerprints needed in the first place? If one person needed fingerprinting, it was surely the rapist, not me! What next, a mugshot of the victim? I expressed my objection to these tests to Mr Toufik before calling Selma, my Libyan lawyer.

'Oh no, don't worry! It's normal procedure in Libya,' she said.

Nothing made sense to me, and while I was strongly tempted to refuse to submit to these tests, I was also unwilling to disobey an investigating judge in case it rang the death knell for my case, and so I reluctantly agreed to being fingerprinted and mouth swabbed. Mr Toufik said he expected the results by the following week—a highly dubious timing since there still was no news of the results of the sample taken at the Brega clinic three months earlier.

The sudden need for my fingerprints was something I couldn't rationalise, and the thought of my DNA profile and fingerprints being on file *somewhere* in Libya still concerns me greatly today. I never heard from Mr Toufik again, or received any report on this second DNA sample. Mr El-Abadi, my office manager, knew nothing; my lawyer Selma knew even less as she was still kept at arm's length by SOC; and the British Embassy in Tripoli didn't want to know, clearly at ease with the status quo. I was in a legal impasse, completely at the mercy of a system that was revealing itself to be more underhanded and corrupt by the day. There just seemed to be no one in authority I could turn to. I became steadily more discouraged, spending all my free time at the gym to keep my growing frustrations and despair at bay. The dismal reality of my case appeared clearer with each passing day—I was alone in a battle against a Libyan system bent on standing in the way of justice while the indifferent, inactive British Embassy stood in the background.

Unsurprisingly, the lack of headway in a case that should have been so easy to settle began to take a toll on me. I barely slept at night, my mind incessantly rehashing the latest events or frantically searching for ways to advance the case. My fears that the rapist would return were intensified by my house being sandwiched between a derelict property and a vacant plot of land, making me feel dangerously cut off from my closest neighbours.

Just after one o'clock in the morning, on a quiet night at the end of September 2013, the loud shriek from the back door alarm jolted me brutally out of a light slumber. At that time, I spent my nights on the living room sofa, fully clothed, just in case anything happened. I immediately jumped from the sofa and dashed towards the back door. While there was a padlocked grille fitted on the outside of the door, the alarm on the inside would be triggered by the slightest touch to the outside door. I let it shriek whilst I dialled the security department's number. An officer arrived within seconds and, torch in hand, proceeded to check the pitch dark area behind the house, which could only be accessed by climbing an impossibly high fence. He found nothing amiss, and promptly concluded that it was probably 'just kids playing'—a highly improbable statement considering the time of night and the height of the fence.

I spent the rest of the night speculating on what might have set the alarm off, and went to work the next day with another sleepless night under my belt. My lack of sleep was becoming a norm, and made me wonder how long I'd last under these physically and mentally draining conditions. I seemed to be permanently worn-out by a situation that held no hope in sight, living in such a state of anxiety that I saw danger everywhere. On a few occasions, I even worried that I might be heading towards paranoia, but it was difficult to appease my mind and feel safe when alarms at home went off at night for no apparent reason. My efforts to locate a psychotherapist to alleviate my anxieties led nowhere as none were available in Brega. I'd have to travel to either Benghazi or Tripoli—a three-hour drive and a one-hour flight away respectively—to consult with one. The distances involved made therapy too impractical to consider and so, more than ever, I relied exclusively on my meditation sessions and fitness routine at the gym to ward off any adverse effects on my body and mind that the rape and its aftermath could inflict on me. I obsessively spent all my free time at the gym and, like an addict, depended on my daily fix of endorphins to keep me going.

As events unfolded with more disappointments and let-downs, the gym and my spirituality became my alternatives to psychotherapy. I was slowly losing faith in my fellow man and, instead, placed my trust in God alone. It was in Him that I renewed my strength to continue with my struggle and deal with the hurdles erected by those who chose to turn their backs on me instead of ending my turmoil.

In November 2013, a well-known Libyan newspaper, the Libyan Herald, ran an article about a three-day conference which had taken place in Tripoli the previous month on the subject of sexual violence in Libya. It had been organised by an Italian NGO—No Peace Without Justice (NPWJ)—with support from the Italian and British Embassies. It was attended by representatives of the United Nations Support Mission in Libya (UNSMIL), countless civil society organisations, members of the judiciary, international NGOs, foreign embassies… Taking place just four months after the rape, this conference was a huge missed opportunity to bring my case under the spotlight as it were, and I felt immense frustration at finding out about it after the fact.

I read with astonishment the reported statement from the head of the East Tripoli Prosecution Office, Mr Nuri Bakai, that 'not a single case of rape had been reported to the Attorney General in Libya since the revolution of 2011 which would have triggered an investigation by the prosecutor's office'. My heart sank deep inside my chest. I wasn't even a statistic in the Libyan books! I was non-existent. Invisible. No wonder my case was going nowhere. Mr Bakai added that this was 'probably because sensitivities around rape meant that victims were reluctant to report attacks'. But I'd had no such 'sensitivities' or 'reluctance', and had reported my rape to every possible authority, local and foreign alike, and I was still excluded from the statistics! I seethed with rage at this bare-faced lie from a senior Libyan official.

I was extremely disheartened that all efforts to counteract the constant setbacks since the rape had amounted to nothing but a waste of time and energy, and had led absolutely nowhere. All because powerful, unscrupulous players behind the scenes insisted on stifling my case. I promptly forwarded a link to the newspaper article to Mrs Hanson at the British Embassy in Tripoli and waited for her reaction.

Her response that the embassy was 'disappointed' and would 'make representation to the general prosecutor's office' was too feeble to be of any consolation to me whatsoever, especially as I recognised that familiar, placating tone between the lines that implied that nothing concrete would be forthcoming.

Of course, I received no feedback as to this latest representation to the general prosecutor's office. Bearing in mind the British Embassy's support of the conference organisers, I suspected it had occupied a front row seat at the conference, and heard that deceitful statement first-hand. But, in line with the embassy's unwillingness to intervene in my case, that lie from a senior Libyan official was bound to have no effect on the embassy.

The article went on to state that one of the conference participants was a Libyan organisation that provided counselling and financial support to rape victims. One of its aims was to also facilitate marriage between rape victims and revolutionary fighters, especially those who were amputees. The core principle behind such a project was undeniably commendable, but I couldn't help feeling greatly troubled by it as it revealed not only Libyan society's attitude towards rape, but the depth of the so-called 'shame' that was placed automatically upon the victims. Rape victims were seen as 'damaged goods' that could be married off only to physically challenged men, clearly also viewed as 'damaged goods'. I found it offensive to both groups of people, who were simply victims of tragic circumstances. The article made for uneasy reading as its implication—however unintentional—was that no Libyan rape victim or physically disabled man, as 'damaged goods', could realistically be worthy of an 'un-damaged' person. The crippling stigma surrounding the issue of rape stood like a gigantic barrier in the way of the just and humane treatment that victims needed. Only a radical change in society's perception of the issue of sexual violence could bring about the justice and care that victims were rightfully entitled to, but the road towards such a colossal change inside a highly patriarchal society would, no doubt, be fraught with humongous obstacles.

It was now five months since the rape, and there was still no trace of the DNA results sent to SOC's laboratory for processing all those months ago. The rapist was free around the compound whilst Selma, hands firmly tied by the company's refusal to even allow her into the compound, appeared at a loss to figure out her next move. My manager, Mr El-Abadi, was as evasive as ever, merely repeating that he'd get back to me, while the British Embassy in Tripoli rehashed its mantra for me to speak to my Libyan lawyer. I informed Mrs Hanson from the outset that Selma had been sidelined by SOC, making her unable to proceed with the case. In the middle of this deadlock, I resembled a hamster frantically going around in its cage, desperately searching for a way out of this vicious circle. Every door I'd knocked on had slammed shut in my face, and I no longer knew who to turn to.

Surprisingly, before the end of November 2013, and totally out of the blue, Selma received a letter from SOC stating that, 'what happened was not their problem, that security in the compound was adequate, and that no such incident happened before'. The wording of the letter was identical to the words spoken by the SOC's legal manager during his telephone conversation with my manager a few weeks after the rape. At least, there was no ambiguity about the company's position vis-à-vis my rape. While SOC had made no secret that it intended to refute any responsibility, it was still deeply disheartening to see it printed in black and white on official paper. The letter was straight to the point, and implied not the slightest hope for an amicable arrangement. As far as SOC was concerned, there was no case to discuss. But in spite of the bleak outlook facing me, I still desperately clung to the idea that, even with a helpless Selma and a lethargic British Embassy, I had the full force of international law by my side, and, therefore, the certainty that a way would be found to challenge SOC and prosecute the rapist in the courts.

Massively frustrated by the lack of any progress being made, I contacted the British Home Secretary at the time, Mr William Hague, for his assistance. With all the difficulties I'd encountered so far from every quarter, I simply couldn't fathom how a powerful institution like the British government could remain so passive in the violent crime against a national, when it held all the powers to make a significant difference. I trusted that there had to be at least one person amongst all these high-powered people at the top, who would care enough to intercede in my case. With renewed but cautious optimism, I eagerly awaited Mr Hague's response.

Finally, in the midst of all the doom and gloom, there came a piece of news from Selma that I believed to be quite a breakthrough at the time. Days before she received

SOC's letter of November 2013, she'd reached out to the then chairman of the National Oil Corporation, (NOC), Mr Nouri Belreen, to discuss my case. The mighty NOC, a Libyan state-owned entity, controlled the whole of the country's oil industry, and was, to put it simply, SOC's boss and owner. Selma apprised Mr Belreen of the case, deploring the company's unwillingness to engage with her, or to allow her access to the compound. Suddenly, it all clicked into place in my head. By sending that letter to Selma, SOC had merely obeyed its boss' orders to make contact with her. But while it merely rehashed the company's well-known stance of rejecting all responsibility, the NOC chairman assured Selma that SOC would indeed pay damages if negligence in its duty of care was proven. Mr Belreen promised to write to her, and to SOC, to confirm NOC's position. I'd become wary over the past months of setting my hopes too high, but could this be the lucky break 'from above' that the Brega police officer had referred to? I certainly hoped so. I was elated by NOC's reaction and by its chairman's apparent willingness to play fair. NOC's decision would supersede any prior statements made by SOC in its shameful efforts to distance itself from the case. On several occasions, I requested from Selma copies of this all-important correspondence from both SOC and NOC, but while she promised she would, she consistently failed to do so.

As part of my quest for assistance, I contacted a number of human rights organisations and legal firms in the UK. After my fruitless experience with the Libyan system, I'd finally accepted that real progress would only come from outside of Libya, just as Ines at the NCHR in Benghazi had told me. I was still ignorant of the fact that the jurisdiction issue would be the major stumbling block in my case, and that it would be near impossible to locate an English law firm willing to enter into litigation with a subsidiary of a state-owned corporation in a country like Libya, especially after the recent war. I learnt with shock that there was no legal obligation for a Libyan company on its home soil to respond to a UK court summons in respect of a crime committed in Libya, and that there was no law in existence to obligate it to do so. The company could flout the court order and default on any trial outside of its borders, safe in the knowledge that it was immune from any legal consequences. I was appalled that such nonsensical flaws existed to make it possible for foreign companies to evade their legal liabilities under the nose of the international legal community. Basic moral decency, ethics and justice clearly had no place in the equation. Just as I'd deplored the impunity granted to the rapist by the Libyan system so far, I now had to accept that the absence of appropriate legislation on cross-border crimes would ultimately also grant impunity to SOC. Just as society's attitudes towards the issue of rape had to change in order that justice for the victims became a systematic process, urgent reforms to legislation on cross-border crimes also appeared to be long overdue to end the scandalous immunity given to foreign criminals that enabled them to evade their responsibilities towards their foreign victims.

One day in early 2014, Mr Fathi Belkacem, the SOC's general services manager, took me aside in his office and broached the subject of the letter SOC had sent to Selma in November 2013, in which it rejected all responsibility in the rape. Mr Belkacem was one of the managers who'd rushed to the medical clinic immediately after the rape.

'I want you to know that I, and many others, don't agree with the contents of the letter sent to your lawyer,' he said. 'SOC *is* responsible! We're all behind you.'

I didn't doubt the sincerity behind his words for a second, but, at this juncture, they sounded rather hollow to me. I'd heard it all before—empty words and false promises that led absolutely nowhere. What I needed was tangible legal action to put the rapist in jail and make SOC face its responsibilities. I was no longer interested in, or comforted by, inconsequential words and gestures, however well-meaning. I thanked Mr Belkacem for his comment and left his office.

One of the institutions I contacted after the rape was Amnesty International, the prominent human rights organisation. Imagine my delight when a Mrs Lynda Johnson called me one day in December 2013, requesting copies of all the case documents to present to the organisation's lawyers! That such a prestigious institution would be prepared to look into my case boosted my spirits that all wasn't lost. It transpired, months later, that Amnesty International had spoken with Hiba as the eye witness and written to the SOC's chairman who, true to form, hadn't bothered responding, confirming the company's unflinching stance of engaging with absolutely no one about the case. Clearly, SOC was taking full advantage of its privileged status as a subsidiary of a state-owned corporation—the ultimate *wasta*—and of the inadequacies in cross-border crime legislation, to shamefully evade its responsibilities, but it was incomprehensible that the law enabled it to do so, and show nothing but contempt to anyone prepared to investigate my rape.

Despite its best intentions and efforts, Amnesty International could do no more for my case. With all the more urgent injustices and suffering going on around the world, I readily accepted that the organisation had far more critical issues to deal with, and was grateful that it had attempted to assist me at all. My case was massively hindered by the jurisdiction issue that made cross-border crimes in a country like Libya quasi-unprosecutable, and granted impunity to criminals while foreign governmental authorities looked the other way. It appeared that unless some form of political pressure 'from above' was brought to bear on the Libyan authorities, then all my efforts to bring closure to my case would be vain, and, for some reason, this pressure was resoundingly absent.

Early in January 2014—seven months after the rape—I contacted the Foreign Office in London just in case it'd be more inclined to assist than its lethargic counterpart in Tripoli. It responded within days that it would instruct the embassy in Tripoli to send a 'chaser note verbale to the Libyan authorities asking how the case was proceeding and to raise the question about the location of the DNA samples'. I was baffled that the British Embassy in Tripoli needed to be nudged from London to do its job, but, most importantly, the Foreign Office promised to get back to me about a potential meeting between myself and the Libyan Ministry of Foreign Affairs. I'd chased the embassy in Tripoli for such a meeting on several occasions, but, despite promises, a meeting never materialised. Hoping that the Foreign Office in London might be more apt to deliver, I waited patiently for a date to meet with the ministry.

The package of documents and photos that Selma had requested was now ready to be delivered to her. It took a little while, but I gathered every scrap of evidence that she would need into a folder—from doctors' certificates to every bit of correspondence with SOC, to an array of photographs and videos showing neglect on Secretary Street. In mid-January 2014, I travelled to Benghazi to hand over that all-important package to her. Sitting in a quiet corner inside the large, empty reception area of SOC's Benghazi office, Selma flicked through the documents and photographs, nodding her head from time to time. I observed her silently, waiting for her verdict.

'You have strong evidence,' she said. 'Your memo to the chairman months before the rape… well, it just says it all…'

My heart started beating faster as I imagined the end of my nightmare inching closer. Then came the first unexpected blow.

'But a Libyan court is likely to award you only a token amount in damages…'

I looked at her with surprise, dreading what other pieces of depressing news she had in store for me.

'Let me explain why,' she continued. 'It would be, umm, unfair to award you anything else just because you're a foreigner while Libyan women get absolutely nothing.'

I was astounded by her comment. She'd delivered it in such a matter-of-fact, almost logical way that I wondered whose side she was on, whether that was also her own considered judgment. She had no idea how shocking or insulting her words had sounded. I was overwhelmed by the hopelessness of my situation—the Libyan authorities refusing to prosecute the rapist unless instructed 'from above', the passive British Embassy, SOC stubbornly keeping Selma at a distance, and, to make matters even worse, it now looked like she didn't have my best interests at heart after all. She missed the point that I was the victim of a violent crime committed in her country, by one of her fellow compatriots whom the system of her land protected and didn't consider worth prosecuting 'because this is Libya'. From the start, Selma had accepted as gospel that the rapist wouldn't be arrested, let alone tried and convicted, purely 'because this is Libya'. She consequently never mentioned him, keeping him totally out of the loop, the only objective she aimed for being the settlement of damages from SOC. Was I supposed to accept this amoral, outrageous Libyan state of affairs, and just move on?

In spite of her status as a prominent lawyer committed to the pursuit of justice and enforcement of the law, she'd declared it 'unfair' that I should be compensated purely because I was a foreigner—and she was certainly right on that point. I had to be compensated not because I was a foreigner, but because I'd been wronged and that justice demanded it, just as it demanded it for all the Libyan rape victims in her country. Justice shouldn't be a privilege for the lucky few by virtue of their nationality, but a basic fundamental right for all. A victim's nationality should have no part in the equation. I was sickened by the prolonged denial of my human rights by the very system designed to protect them, which, instead of redressing a wrong, only exacerbated my ordeal further.

'Also, SOC might argue that you chose to return to Libya after the war... that the rape was part of a *force majeure* situation,' she continued.

'Well, yes, I did return to Libya when SOC called me back at the end of the war the previous year,' I said. 'But I wasn't raped on the battlefield, I was raped inside my home in my employer's secured residential compound! So, *no*, my rape wasn't an act of God, but the act of a rapist employed by SOC! Besides, by SOC recalling its foreign staff to work, it also clearly accepted responsibility for their safety, just as it had done before the war.'

It was frightening to measure the absurdity of the arguments that SOC could use to evade legal liability. As our meeting neared its end and I thought things couldn't possibly get any worse, Selma revealed that she'd been instructed by SOC that any case documents be forwarded to their lawyer in Benghazi, a Mr Yunes Suleyman.

'Frankly, I'm not hopeful that things will move forward any quicker with him. He's already told me he doesn't want to handle the case. And he doesn't speak any English at all.'

Some of the documents were indeed in English, but surely their translation was no major problem. I was more concerned that my case was in the hands of a hostile lawyer who'd already voiced his reluctance at dealing with it. Selma expected to hear from him within a month so I'd just have to sit tight until then, hoping against hope that his advice would be for SOC to come to the negotiating table. I asked Selma again for copies of the letters from SOC rejecting responsibility, and from NOC confirming damages would be paid if negligence was proven. These letters were of paramount importance as evidence to be included in my package of case documents. Again, she promised to forward them, but didn't.

As my frustrations grew at the lack of any progress so many months after the rape, I emailed the Foreign Office in London with my intention of mediatising the case. I reiterated my strong objection to my taxes being handed to Libya in financial aid—an admittedly futile argument— but I was so desperate that I was ready to use anything if it could yield a positive response. The Foreign Office replied with the suggestion of a meeting in Tripoli between myself and the British Embassy. A meeting with the party that had been dragging its feet since the rape left me rather cold at first, but while I was totally bewildered by the embassy's passivity, I still desperately hoped for a breakthrough that only the embassy—as the pressure 'from above' required by the Libyan authorities—could, realistically, bring about. More aware than ever of the hopelessness of my predicament, I agreed to the meeting, just in case.

As I was scheduled to leave Libya on a London break at the end of January 2014, the meeting was arranged for the day before my departure. On my way to the British Embassy, I stopped at the NOC's offices to deliver a copy of all the documents, photographs and videos I'd compiled for Selma. As SOC's boss and owner, and especially as the NOC's chairman seemed willing to play fair, it was important that he had all the case documents at hand. The chairman being unavailable, I left the package with his secretary. At no time did NOC either acknowledge the package or comment on it. It was hugely disappointing, and only served to strengthen my suspicions that there was a consensus amongst the Libyan authorities to simply ignore my case until the time came when I was permanently removed from the country, a plan made all the more likely by the British Embassy's apathy.

Following countless telephone exchanges with Mrs Hanson since the rape, I finally met with her and the vice consul, Mr Paul Marston, at the embassy's offices in Tripoli. Both were warm, courteous and extremely pleasant as they offered a sympathetic listening ear to the grievances I'd accumulated since the rape. Mr Marston stated that the embassy was in regular touch with the Libyan government over my case, and that matters would be resolved 'hopefully soon'.

Mrs Hanson had often mentioned during our telephone conversations that the embassy made formal representations to the Libyan Ministry of Foreign Affairs or to the Attorney General's office, but that it might take some time to see any results. At no time was there anything to report from these representations, or on any actions taken by the British authorities on my behalf. Since the rape, I'd made a point of disclosing to the embassy every single event that occurred—from SOC's refusal to meet with my lawyer, to my concerns that it might conveniently lose the DNA sample whose results were still untraceable seven months later, to my lawyer's advice not to file criminal charges against the rapist, to his and most of SOC management's affiliation with the local tribe. I didn't skimp on any detail, however trivial, and candidly bared my entire life since the rape. Upon Mrs Hanson's request to provide the embassy with the name of the rapist, I even included his company registration number, withholding nothing, and doing everything I could to ensure the embassy had every single detail, however minor.

When I mentioned to Mrs Hanson and Mr Marston that I considered approaching the media to progress my case, their eyes locked together for a split second. The glance that passed between them was as quick as a flash, so fleeting as to be almost imperceptible, but I'd caught it. And it made me uneasy. Was I imagining things? I suddenly didn't know who to trust anymore. Was anyone on my side? They advised me to think hard about going to the media as such a move would impact heavily on my life. *I'm sure no more than the rape did,* I thought.

Mr Marston said that a response to my letter to the then Secretary of State, Mr William Hague, was on its way to me, before launching into the usual platitudes promising assistance which, of course, never materialised.

I left for London the next day, eager to put distance between myself, the compound and Libya altogether. It was during this break that I realised that time and distance were, indeed, invaluable tools to instil a clearer perspective into a confusing, complicated situation. It was while I was physically removed from the country that I reviewed all the developments since the rape, seven months earlier. I re-read each and every piece of correspondence I'd exchanged with anyone about the case. I'd been puzzled by the British Embassy's non-committal attitude from the outset, but by the end of this rather depressing reading, something clicked in my head, like the flick of a switch suddenly shining a bright light inside a dark hole. I arrived at the only inescapable conclusion that could be drawn up. My brain sharpened by hindsight and distance, the British Embassy's inertia was finally exposed. I'd relied on its support while it had taken the decision to not provide it. It was a blunt and demoralising eye-opener that hammered home how alone and helpless I'd been in this fight for justice. I'd been politely, but consistently, fobbed off by all parties I'd turned to since the rape. I'd been patted on the head by Mrs Hanson during each of our conversations, which although brimming with sympathy, consistently failed to provide the full backing that my case desperately needed. How could such a mighty institution be so incompetent in dealing with the rape of one of its citizens? Were there no treaties between Britain and Libya to protect British workers' rights in Libya? How could I get my rapist prosecuted in a country that allegedly protected rapists of foreign victims? How could I stand up single-handedly against the seemingly corrupt Libyan system when my own government seemed indifferent to my plight? How could my Libyan lawyer defend my rights when she was frozen out by a subsidiary of a state-owned corporation bent on silencing the rape?

The more I delved into the correspondence and recalled my conversations with Mrs Hanson, the more my already slim expectations of assistance from the British authorities vanished into thin air. Without the embassy's unwavering intervention, a rapist would evade punishment, and a company, linked to the Libyan government, its responsibility in a crime. Why did the British authorities deem my rape unworthy of their intervention? Several times, I appealed to the embassy for assistance to safeguard the DNA evidence. To no avail. Several times, I asked to be put in touch with the Libyan Foreign Ministry since it was the British Embassy's assertion that it was in regular contact with it. Each time, to no avail. The correspondence revealed the embassy's lack of any substantive action to meaningfully support one of its nationals, a victim of a serious crime within its jurisdiction of authority and administration. I understood that, as a general rule, the embassy was under no legal obligation to automatically assist its nationals in need abroad, but was it too outlandish to expect that a crime as serious as rape at knifepoint warranted the embassy's unequivocal involvement? Wasn't the embassy's intervention a priority in a case blatantly undermined by the Libyan authorities? I had naively expected that a rape at knifepoint would not only be taken seriously by the embassy, but that it would benefit from the full force of its limitless powers. How wrong could I be…

Had SOC been a private entity, my expectations of assistance from the British Embassy would have been substantially lessened; conversely, these were heightened by SOC's status as a subsidiary of the mighty NOC—in charge of the entire Libyan oil industry and itself owned by the Libyan government which benefited from millions in yearly financial aid from Britain. Even setting aside the seriousness of the crime against me, these facts alone led me to the logical assumption that the firm involvement of the British Embassy would be forthcoming. But the stark reality was that, other than loads of sympathy and a couple of letters to SOC requesting security measures be put in place, there had been no effective support from the embassy at a time when I was in need of far more than empty sympathy. In truth, nearly a year after the rape, I was choking on sympathy.

I wondered what the role of the embassy was vis-à-vis its nationals in Libya, and, based on my experience, concluded that it amounted to a non-taxing representation of Britain inside that country until it was faced with a serious crime like the rape of one of its nationals, when it proved powerless to live up to its role as an 'anchor of support to its citizens in need abroad'. It was hugely disappointing that, in my case, the embassy had failed dismally to live up to its role. I was living proof of that—how could I possibly feel differently? I'd appealed for help from the embassy while I was at the mercy of the Libyans and their plan to repress my case, but, for some reason, the embassy hadn't considered it part of its business to intervene in the urgent, pressing manner I'd have expected under the circumstances.

As a consequence of the unfortunate passivity displayed by the embassy throughout my case, I was well on the way to being denied my right to justice for the simple reason that the embassy seemed unwilling to challenge the unscrupulous Libyan parties involved.

As I recalled my conversations with Mrs Hanson, I began feeling increasingly foolish to have opened up so freely to her, and to have revealed so much of myself since the rape while she must've been aware that the embassy would offer no significant support. Once I'd seen the light as far as any prospective worthwhile embassy involvement was concerned, I became appalled that I'd been left to face alone the Libyans authorities and their system. I felt that I'd been wronged twice—firstly by the Libyan authorities, then by the British Embassy, that 'anchor of support' to which I'd turned to with so much faith and hope. Instead, I'd been cast aside by both authorities in that sly, deceptive way of pretending to be willing to assist when each knew it would default on its duties. If anything, at least the Libyans had made no secret from the start that my case would get nowhere to safeguard their interests and protect one of their own. Conversely, the British authorities promised assistance from the outset while offering none, leaving me helpless at the hands of the scheming Libyans.

That the case was deemed unworthy of assistance at the highest echelons of the British government was further confirmed as I re-read the British ministers' responses to my letters. Whilst highly sympathetic, all were invariably non-committal and devoid of any plan of action to assist my case. I wondered whether I'd expected too much from both the Libyan and British authorities by wanting my rapist prosecuted and SOC made accountable. It all left a bitter taste in my mouth as my case took on a new dimension—a political one, full of dishonesty and deception. The sub-standard treatment I received at the hands of the embassy was devastating, and, slowly, it fostered in me an increased sense of detachment from the country I'd settled in over thirty years earlier and felt so proud and privileged to call home.

Early in February 2014, I learnt that the British Embassy had arranged for the new SOC chairman, Mr Ali Rahman, to meet with me to discuss my case. I'd previously mentioned to Mrs Hanson my vain attempts over the past months at meeting with him and that I couldn't get past his dogged assistant who was adamant that the chairman refused point blank to discuss what he euphemistically referred to as my 'problem'. It was ironic that it took one single call from the embassy to get the elusive SOC chairman to ask *me* if I wanted to discuss 'my problem' with him. And I wasn't even summoned to his office. No, he was taking the trouble to come to me himself! It was so revealing of how much progress would have been achieved had the embassy been willing to exert the slightest pressure on SOC and the Libyan authorities to resolve the matter, and allow me to draw a line under this depressing chapter once and for all.

Within days of Mrs Hanson's call, Mr Ali Rahman walked into my office, in explicit compliance with the embassy's request. I hadn't met Mr Rahman before and had no idea who the tall, casually dressed man standing nonchalantly by my desk was. He stood there without a word for a few seconds, simply looking around my office before introducing himself.

'Ali Rahman, SOC chairman,' he said. 'I understand you want to talk with me?'

Since Mr Rahman had ignored my own requests for a meeting for two months with the clear instruction to his assistant to keep me and my 'problem' at bay, I had no illusions of any sincerity behind his presence in my office;

I was certain that he was merely obeying the British Embassy's instructions.

He looked quite uncomfortable so I offered him a seat, expecting nothing positive from our meeting that would have any significant impact on my case. He expressed how sorry he was for the rape, and I asked him why SOC had continuously refused Selma, my Libyan lawyer, access into the compound for a meeting.

'Look, the rape happened before I took over as chairman. I really know nothing about your case!'

That wasn't a good start. His response was unacceptable from SOC's most senior executive, but there it was in all its pathetic inadequacy—the chairman pleading ignorance of an ongoing case which his company made no secret of its intention to quash. I handed him a copy of my November 2012 memo to his predecessor, which listed the incidents on Secretary Street over the previous six months, and to which he hadn't bothered responding.

'Again, it was before my time. This is all news to me,' he said as his eyes quickly scanned the document.

Of course, I wasn't buying any of it. He'd taken over as chairman barely two months after the rape, but he was referring to the rape as belonging to a period in the past that had ended with the departure of the previous chairman. As far as he was concerned, my case had nothing to do with him in his current role.

'But surely you must've heard of it, right?' I asked sarcastically.

'Umm, of course, a little…' he replied vaguely.

I informed him that no security measures had been implemented on the street despite several promises to do so from his predecessor. He listened carefully before picking up the telephone on my desk, and dialling the services department's number. He ordered for the works agreed in June 2013 to begin without further delay. I'd heard it all before. These works had been promised eight months earlier so I wasn't holding my breath this time either. I suspected that it was all part of SOC's pacifying stance until I could be removed from the country permanently.

'Call me if the work hasn't started in the next couple of weeks,' he said.

'Only if I can get past that dogged assistant of yours!' I replied cheekily.

Then, out of the blue, he switched the conversation to the rape of an expatriate employee inside the compound in the 1980s. I hadn't expected him to open up—with me of all people—about such a sensitive fact. He recounted how the victim had been repatriated to her home country immediately after the rape. He disclosed her name, although he said he wasn't too sure about its spelling. It was hard to believe that he knew nothing about my own, ongoing case whilst he remembered one that happened over three decades earlier.

I told him that I hoped he'd be more willing than his predecessor to do the right thing and bring closure to my case. He smiled weakly, stood up, shook my hand, and left my office with a non-committal *'Insha'Allah'*.

As expected, not only did the work that Mr Rahman had instructed the services department to carry out 'without further delay' never start, but I was subsequently denied contact with him, either over the telephone or when I showed up at his office. The fact that I'd unsuccessfully tried to contact him for two months before he obeyed the British Embassy's one and only request to meet with me was highly revealing. He hadn't met me out of a real commitment to redress a wrong, but only because he'd been instructed 'from above'. I began feeling that I'd become a thorn in the company's side with my relentless questions about the case, and demands for adequate security. I was making too many waves inside SOC and had to tread carefully or risk losing my job. And this job was vital for the renewal of my visa to remain in Libya until the legalities of my case were finalised.

Aside from the legal conundrum surrounding my case, another troubling issue kept rearing its head inside the compound walls in the form of the local tribe, with its continual claims for more jobs and housing. Bent on causing havoc until its demands were met, it regularly stormed the main administrative building in Area 2, where the company's personnel department was located. These disruptions weren't just an inconvenience for the compound residents and workers, but they had the potential to escalate into serious incidents. They'd already led to the personnel department's manager resigning from his position following threats against his life from the tribe. In the wake of the 2011 conflict, tribes and armed militias had stepped in to fill the political vacuum which was left after the so-called liberation of the country. Emboldened by its self-assigned role as one of the 'guardians of the revolution', the Brega tribe became a real force for disturbance with its almost daily aggressive blockades for jobs and housing inside the compound.

In mid-February 2014, Selma drafted a letter to SOC, in which she emphasised the likelihood of media exposure of my case in Britain, stressing the urgency to negotiate an out-of-court settlement to avoid the 'likely international media focus and impact on both the company and Libya'. She was giving SOC ten days to respond before starting court proceedings. I approved of both the tone and content of her letter, only wishing she'd written it at the time of the rape, not nearly a year later. Most surprisingly, she'd even mentioned the rapist, stating that it was SOC's duty to ensure he was prosecuted since he was employed by the company. She reiterated the detrimental consequences that a non-settlement of my case would have on the company's reputation, and on Libya as a whole. I was so impressed that I couldn't imagine SOC not rushing to the negotiating table immediately upon reading it. But since nothing in the case had been remotely straightforward or logical so far, I reined in my hopes just in case.

That same day, I informed Mrs Hanson of Selma's letter to SOC, and of her intention of starting court proceedings if the company didn't respond within her deadline. I also repeated my own intention of going to the media should SOC's response be either negative or non-existent. I was a little taken aback when Mrs Hanson asked what was the deadline that Selma had in mind before starting court proceedings, but I thought nothing much of it at the time.

Within days, the SOC's lawyer in Benghazi, Mr Suleyman, returned to Selma the package of documents she'd sent him, with the comment that the case wasn't 'his business and to forward the package directly to the courts instead'. No SOC lawyer, whether in Brega or in Benghazi, was prepared to even acknowledge the case, let alone address it. I was now more convinced than ever that SOC was merely stonewalling and using delaying tactics until the opportune time when it could expel me from Libya permanently. And I felt that time fast-approaching. Coincidentally, my work visa was due to expire within weeks, in April 2014. I was terrified that SOC might seize this golden opportunity to achieve its goal of 'closing the file' once and for all. A straightforward non-renewal of my visa would lead to my immediate exit from Libya and an end to my legal plans against SOC and the rapist. The stakes were so high that the fear of being denied a visa was like a massive weight being added onto my already burdened shoulders.

Sticking to its strategy of no engagement in my case, SOC ignored Selma's letter and didn't bother replying. The ten-day deadline given to the company for a response had come and gone. This incessant fruitless to-ing and fro-ing, and the uncertainty of my visa renewal started taking a punishing toll on my psyche and body, and I spent more time at the gym than at home just to stop rehashing the latest setback for a few hours and keep the dreaded depression at bay. It seemed as pointless trying to engage with SOC as it was to prosecute the rapist. I was getting nowhere fast, and could almost hear the countdown of my time in Libya ticking loud and clear. Filing a lawsuit against SOC was the only option left now the company had rejected every opportunity of engaging with Selma, but I dreaded to think what other risks, or complications, this next move would open the doors to.

If my days in Libya were counted, then I had to put into action the one option I'd tried to avoid all along. Before the end of February 2014, I finally instructed Selma to file a lawsuit against SOC. As both an SOC employee and resident inside its compound, I'd initially avoided pursuing the company through the courts for safety reasons, preferring to agree on an out-of-court settlement instead. So far, it had been child's play for SOC to brush aside my case by simply ignoring my lawyer's very existence, but would I be exposing myself to danger by dragging the company to the courts? While I had deep concerns about how this next step would pan out, and its potential impact on my life inside the compound, I was determined to fight for the redress I was owed. Although my expectations of assistance from the British Embassy were at an all-time low, I needed, again for my own safety, to inform Mrs Hanson of my decision to file civil proceedings against SOC just in case I came to any harm as a result. It was my way of putting the ball firmly in the embassy's court in the event I did meet with harm.

Within days, Mrs Hanson asked me to give the embassy a few days' notice before approaching the British media with my story. I was shocked by this request, and wondered cynically whether it was in order for the embassy to cover its back in the rape fiasco. Did it need time to rustle up a convenient story that would legitimise the steady disinterest and ineptitude it displayed in the case, and negate any complaints I might raise against it? I perceived this request as not only a glaring, unspoken admission of the embassy's failure to act, but also as the formal end of any pretence that it was ever willing to assist. It confirmed what I'd been increasingly suspecting—that I'd, indeed, been alone in my struggle. I felt deceived and betrayed. As a governmental mission abroad with absolute authority and influence, the cold fact remained that, in my case, the embassy had been unequal to both its status and to the service expected from it in dealing with my rape. But besides that, the embassy's non-committal attitude was bound to convey the dangerous message that Britain, as eminently powerful as it was perceived to be by Libyans and other nationalities around the world, wasn't at all times willing to protect its nationals abroad. I'd witnessed first-hand, and with mounting embarrassment, the bewilderment from Libyans and foreign colleagues alike as they asked why the British Embassy seemed so detached from my case. Hopefully, this pernicious message wouldn't lead to more neglected British victims of rape in Libya, or elsewhere, and to immunity for their rapists and anyone involved in the crimes against them.

Just as Mr Marston, the deputy consul at the British Embassy, had told me during our meeting, a message from Mr William Hague made its way into my email inbox one morning at the end of January 2014. It was in response to my letter pleading for his assistance. I took the opportunity of repeating in the letter my lame objection to my taxes being handed to the Libyan government as financial aid. For some reason, I'd felt quite confident that Mr Hague would intercede in some way, but I couldn't have been more wrong.

His letter stated that he was 'sorry that on top of that dreadful experience' I was 'struggling to secure justice', and promised to 'monitor the case closely'. My correspondence with government ministers had taught me to read between the lines of their statements, and the implicit message behind Mr Hague's words was that meaningful support in my case would continue to be non-existent. His reply was the usual mix of sympathy and empty promise that 'the embassy in Tripoli would continue to offer consular support', clearly satisfied that I was in good hands with the British Embassy there. The problem was that there had been no 'consular support' from the embassy in Tripoli. While it had written to SOC about security measures, it hadn't questioned the company's improper tactics since the rape to subvert the legal process and evade its responsibility in the crime. That failure to address the crux of the matter was the exact opposite to providing effective 'consular support'.

Mr Hague addressed the financial aid support to Libya by stating that it was partly to support the justice system there, and 'ensure that Libya was better placed to provide support to victims of rape and sexual violence'. While the premise to support and encourage human rights and justice in another country was undoubtedly commendable, it became rather ironic when viewed in the context of my own circumstances. Cleaning up one's own backyard first quickly sprang to my mind. With each letter received from the governmental ministers I'd reached out to, I learnt that politicians were masters of the art of conveying the deceitful impression of being keen to assist when they knew full well they wouldn't raise a finger.

By the end of February 2014, an article in the Libyan Herald newspaper about a Mr John Williams, a London-based barrister-at-law, caught my attention. I immediately contacted him with my story, and he responded with much sensitivity and warmth. Mr Williams acted as counsel to a human rights organisation in Tripoli, and was due to return to Tripoli in early March 2014, so we arranged to meet up at that time. He asked for the case documents to be sent to him in the meantime before confirming his willingness to represent me. I was beyond ecstatic at this unexpected development, and patiently bided my time until I could meet with him. With Selma and Mr Williams by my side, I had lawyers in both Libya and the UK representing me and, for a long time since the rape, felt supremely confident that a resolution of my case was possible. Was Mr Williams that foreign pressure 'from above' to force the Libyan authorities to prosecute the rapist and make SOC face its liability? Could this be the light at the end of that long, dark tunnel? I hoped so with all my heart, but while my morale was raised a millionfold by Mr Williams boarding this fast-sinking ship, I'd known far too many shattering blows to let down my guards too quickly.

Still disgruntled that its demands for jobs and housing had not been met to its satisfaction by SOC, the local tribe started using more extreme measures to achieve its goals. The tribe had so far limited its disruptions to regularly storming the administration offices in Area 2 and ordering their evacuation. To apply more pressure on the company, the tribe increased the frequency of its disturbances before taking steps that upped the game to a whole new, dangerous level.

One early afternoon at the end of February 2014, a group of men brandishing rifles burst into the compound's tiny airport as unsuspecting passengers waited for boarding. The armed men demanded the immediate evacuation of the airport, threatening to shoot down the SOC aircraft if it attempted to take off. To avert a catastrophe, the airport was swiftly evacuated and, needless to say, no one made the flight to Tripoli that afternoon. By the next day, the tribe had extended its threats to preventing the SOC coaches bound for Ajdabiya and Benghazi from leaving the compound. The end of the war might have been officially declared a couple of years ago, but its chaotic fallout was alive and well inside the compound. The airport stand-off lasted two long days during which I worried that I'd be prevented from flying to Tripoli for my first meeting with Mr Williams.

Apart from the tribe's aggravating disruptions, life inside the compound ticked along in relative calm when compared with the growing chaos spreading elsewhere in the country.

While I felt that my safety inside the compound was tenuous most of the time, I knew that this was mainly due to my fears that the rapist would return to harm me. This thought was constantly on my mind, hovering over me like a dark, menacing cloud. To exacerbate my vulnerabilities even further, the compound began experiencing frequent blackouts, mainly in the evenings, while access to the internet, available during office hours only, was down for long periods of time, creating a disturbing feeling of being cut off from the outside world. Unlike the early days of the 2011 conflict, when the locals had been reluctant to discuss the deteriorating situation in their country, this time they openly voiced their fears that a civil war might well be on the cards. The 'liberation' of their country had so far failed dismally to bring the peace and security promised by their foreign liberators. Instead, Libya was forced into an abyss of political and social mayhem, and no one knew when it would emerge from it.

I was barricaded at home one evening in early March 2014, watching the BBC News, when the lights suddenly went out, plunging the whole house into total darkness. These blackouts weren't rare occurrences and never lasted too long, but, in my circumstances, they were at the top of my list of worst nightmares. Legs shaking, I toddled across the floor towards the kitchen window, and looked through the gaps in the steel shutters. It was eerily silent. The night had closed in, blocking my view of the kids' playground opposite, and engulfing the whole street and beyond under an ominous black shroud. Even the moon and stars hid behind it. I could feel my anxiety steadily rising while I grabbed handfuls of candles from the kitchen cupboard. I dreaded these power cuts so much that I'd built a massive stock of candles that

I was sure could light up the whole house continuously for a few weeks straight. I placed dozens of them along the hallway and inside my bedroom, and tried to convince myself that this was just another random power cut that would soon be over. The glow from the candles created a cosy, but deceptively false ambience of imminent celebration.

I lifted the phone receiver to call Mary, who lived right at the back of my new house. The line was dead. I reached out for my cell phone. No network. That was the moment that sheer panic erupted inside me. I was completely cut off, totally unable to reach out to anyone. In a split second, all my fears about the rapist returning resurfaced with a vengeance. I was convinced that I was the reason behind this power cut, and that the rapist was on his way to my house. I became so distraught that I berated myself for not keeping the gun Eissa had offered me for protection. I tried to reason that the whole street being in darkness proved that I wasn't being personally targeted, but it was all pointless. A sense of foreboding took over my whole being as my unbridled panic opened the gates wide to the most irrational and terrifying scenarios, with the rapist in the starring role. Mary's house was less than a hundred metres away, but I was too petrified to even consider stepping outside my own doorstep, let alone dashing towards hers in the pitch dark—I knew my limitations and certainly respected them.

The eerie darkness, the deadly silence outside, the vacant plot on my doorstep, and my isolation from my immediate neighbours all provided the perfect setting for the rapist's return. I told myself that there had to be a sinister plan behind the simultaneous power cut and the dead phone lines, that the scene was set for some ghastly event in which I'd be the hapless casualty. I was locked inside a vicious circle of fear, with no way of escaping from whatever was in store—at best, another sleepless night, but, at worst, I'd be in the hands of the rapist and his evil intentions. I shut my eyes, breathing deeply to snap out of these debilitating thoughts. I circled around the brightly lit living room repeating loudly, 'Everything's going to be fine.'

I was in the midst of this mind-calming exercise when I heard a car stop outside my house. My heart missed several beats as I wondered who it could be. The rapist? Someone from his tribe? Or just a concerned friend checking up on me? I stood by the window, shaking like a leaf, and listened. I could make out several male voices talking right outside my garden gate. The horizontal steel shutters severely restricted my view and the garden wall was too high to see anything, but I could make out the flickering blue light of a security patrol car and hear the men's radio devices. I opened the window and asked what was going on.

'This is SOC Security. There's a power cut throughout Area 1. Everything's down, but we're working on it...'

I hesitated for a brief second whether I should ask them to drive me to Mary's house, but a gut instinct told me they might not be genuine SOC security guards. Paralysed with terror and suspicion, I chose to stay barricaded inside my candlelit house instead. After a few minutes, the men drove away, leaving only darkness and deadly silence behind. I was alone with my fears again, in desperate need of a comforting, human presence. At least I was thankful that I'd had such a large stock of candles, with many more waiting to be burnt, if necessary. I lay down on the sofa, praying to be overpowered by the deepest sleep until daylight.

It was after two in the morning when I heard the sound of gravel crunching beneath car tyres. I immediately sat up. A car had driven past my house and onto the adjoining vacant plot of land. My heart began thumping in my chest, and my fears crept up all over again. I dashed to the kitchen window, and stood precariously on a high stool to see over the garden wall. It was hours before dawn and darkness still engulfed the street, but I could make out the sweep of car headlights by the women's gym. Only this time, it wasn't a security patrol car. Car doors slammed and animated male voices cut through the silent night. What were these men doing outside the women's gym in the dead of night? All my senses were on high alert at the thought of the rapist being amongst them. This power cut gave him the perfect opportunity to return, just as he'd said before fleeing after the rape. My anxiety levels skyrocketed, taking me close to breaking point.

I lifted the telephone receiver, but the line was as dead as ever, and so was my cell phone. Then the loud banging on metal began outside. I was tempted for a brief second to venture quietly into the front garden to investigate, but quickly came to my senses—thankfully, my bravado, just like the recurrent power cuts inside the compound, never lasted too long. The banging lasted for nearly an hour then abruptly stopped. I stood on the high kitchen stool again, but could see nothing. Then the car doors slammed again and the men drove away. The electrical power was restored just before four in the morning. A wave of tremendous relief swept through me as my anxiety gradually subsided to make way for a calmer, more rational mind.

I watched the first light of dawn filter gently through the gaps in the shutters, and reflected the truth of the darkest hour being just before dawn, and of the darkest of nights always giving way to the brightest of mornings. I felt invigorated that I'd come to no harm despite the night's events, but with yet another sleepless night under my belt, I wondered how much longer I could bear the stresses of similar moments. I readied myself for work as quickly as I possibly could, before walking out of the house into the morning light, and the safety of the presence of people.

As soon as I stepped out of the small front garden, I noticed the shocking sight of the burnt-out façade of the women's gym. It was obvious that an attempt had been made, during the night, to break into the building and set it alight. This was the loud banging I'd heard as the men tried to smash the gym's large metal door and the bars fitted to its windows. They'd been unable to break in and hadn't caused serious damage, but my heart sank at this mindless act of vandalism. Would the men return to finish the job? My daily gym workouts were indispensable to deal with the stresses I lived under since the rape, but life inside the compound had taken such a turn for the worse that I feared my workouts would soon become a thing of the past. Throughout that day at work, I fished for information about the attempted break-in at the gym, but no one knew anything, or seemed even remotely interested in it. For the compound residents, it had been just another ordinary night, but a terrifying one for me thanks to the stresses and fears that lived in me since the rape.

That latest blackout made me realise that I'd reached a stage where I anticipated danger everywhere around me, with my senses on permanent alert for imaginary threats. I was so fearful of what might happen next that my mind plotted frightening scenarios that haunted me mercilessly, and kept me awake at night. Each day on my return home from the office, I half-expected the rapist to be lurking inside my garden, waiting for me, and I knew that, if left unchecked, these fears would not only run my life, but ruin it. I was so relieved that nothing had happened during this last blackout that I resolved to focus purely on the fact that no one had come to harm me at a time when they so easily could have, and that I was, indeed, happy to be alive!

I'd developed such a warped sense of my reality since the rape that, for my own sanity, and whilst I still could rationalise them, I had to stop these thoughts taking over my life and leading me into uncontrollable emotional excess. My new, distorted reality had been created by my rape experience, and I was so terrified that the rapist would return that I seemed unable to keep my unruly imagination from running away from me. My brain reacted to the most innocuous sound, perceiving it as a potential threat. I recognised that I'd been twisting my reality into a warped version of itself that wasn't real, but that made my life a waking nightmare. The latest blackout shed light on all the amount of mental energy I'd expended on disruptive thoughts, and I was determined to stop imagining danger shadowing me at every turn. My morale was massively lifted that no one had come to harm me, and I could only smile at the irony of a lightbulb moment being born out of a blackout.

While I was happy to have finally seen the light in respect of my imaginary fears, I didn't kid myself that I wasn't an excellent candidate for psychotherapy. I knew that all the bicep curls and leg raises I could muster at the gym could never dispel the debilitating thoughts that created mental dramas where there were none. Every aspect of my life had become more complicated since the rape, and I couldn't allow these irrational perceptions to compound my wellbeing further. However, these irrational fears weren't *that* irrational—they stemmed directly from the rape and my frustrating dealings with those I'd expected support from. These fears were an inescapable part of my emotional journey towards recovery, healing and, hopefully one day, even justice.

Mr Williams and I had arranged to meet during the first week in March at the Tripoli offices of the Libyan National Council for Civil Liberties and Human Rights (NCCLHR). Luckily, the airport stand-off by the Brega tribe had ended in time to allow me to make my flight to Tripoli. Mr Williams was counsel to the NCCLHR, a Libyan human rights organisation committed to the fight against social injustice in the country. He was a gregarious, personable man in his early forties who exuded the type of positive energy and confidence that made me feel instantly in good hands. He introduced me to the NCCLHR's chain-smoking leader, Mr Hamdi Farouj, and to other members of the NCCLHR's staff. They'd discussed my case beforehand before agreeing to take it on. My heart leapt with joy at this spectacular development. As a first step, the NCCLHR proposed contacting SOC to confirm its involvement in the case, before carrying out its own investigation, and liaising with the Attorney General in Tripoli. With both Mr Williams and now the NCCLHR in my corner, this could well prove to be the breakthrough I'd hoped for, the ray of light in the dark hole I'd been trapped in for the past nine months. I was already flying high as I boarded the SOC aircraft for my return to the compound later that afternoon.

In the middle of March 2014, I received the NCCLHR letter addressed to the SOC chairman, which I was to deliver to him personally. First thing the next morning, I marched towards the chairman's office with the letter in my hand and a decidedly bouncy spring in my steps.

'The chairman? He's not in yet,' said his male assistant, Mr Zayn Omar. 'In fact, I don't think he'll be in today at all...'

I wasn't surprised at Mr Omar's evasiveness. He was, after all, under strict instructions to keep me and my 'problem' as far away from the chairman as possible. But I was on a mission to personally deliver an urgent document to him so I stubbornly took a seat to await the chairman's arrival. After two long hours of what I suspected to be a cat-and-mouse game, I handed the NCCLHR letter to Mr Omar.

'Please make sure he gets this as soon as he arrives. It's very important.'

He looked at me over the top of his spectacles then smirked. 'Well, what's important to you might not be to the chairman...'

I didn't expect that mean-spirited, uncalled-for jibe from someone who'd spontaneously expressed his sadness at the rape as I entered his office two hours earlier.

Later that day, a rather short-tempered Selma called to ask me to chase the chairman for a response to her letter of over a month ago, to which she'd given a ten-day deadline for a reply. Whilst I was aware of the difficulties that SOC had placed in her way by persistently ignoring her, I couldn't see how I could 'chase' the chairman when I was handed the same dismissive treatment by the company.

'I know SOC has made things difficult for you, but things are hard for me too. As my lawyer, you should chase the chairman yourself. But I'll speak with my manager,' I said.

All I could get out of Mr El-Abadi was his usual 'I'll find out and get back to you'.

While I struggled in Libya in a hopeless quagmire of incompetence and deceit, in London, Mr Williams worked tirelessly to achieve progress, meeting with the Foreign Office and liaising with the British Embassy in Tripoli. At his meeting with the Foreign Office, the British ambassador promised to write to the SOC chairman with a request for 'improved security for the expatriate employees'. I appreciated the ambassador's efforts, but my case didn't need yet another letter about security; it needed the explicit demand that my open-and-shut case be resolved with no further time wasting from the Libyan authorities. I found it incredibly frustrating that the Foreign Office, in similar fashion to the embassy in Tripoli, merely focused on the provision of security whilst it ignored the wider picture. Of course, the issue of security was undoubtedly crucial, but it had already been the subject of a couple of letters sent by the embassy to the SOC chairman, which, incidentally, had all been ignored by the company, with no questions asked from the embassy. The premise of yet another letter on the same subject would only be part of the same dead-end game played for nearly a year by the authorities, and would be missing the main critical points to address—the undermining of the rape case of a British citizen by a subsidiary of a Libyan state-owned corporation, its accountability in the rape as well as the unchallenged impunity granted by the Libyan authorities to the rapist.

SOC had succeeded in erecting a wall of silence around the case, but in virtue of its ownership by the NOC, itself property of the Libyan government, it was my contention that SOC's outrageous attitude deserved to be challenged at the highest echelons of the British government. These were the important points that needed to be raised by the British authorities with the Libyan authorities, but which they consistently evaded, focusing instead strictly on the provision of security. It was understandable that, as a general rule, Britain couldn't interfere with the legal system of another sovereign state, but when the local authorities were unwilling to carry out their duties without pressure 'from above', and the status quo meant that serious crimes against British citizens were left unpunished, then it was surely high time to attach revised conditions to that general rule in order to protect those citizens.

Soon after Mr Williams contacted the embassy in Tripoli in March 2014, it sent a letter to the SOC chairman, requesting appropriate security, a letter which SOC paid no attention to. The embassy's quick reaction re-enforced my suspicions that it had been satisfied standing on the sideline until it was jolted into some form of action by a communication from an attorney at the prestigious Bedford Chambers in London. The rape happened nearly a year earlier and, as far as I was concerned, the embassy's letter was way too little, too late. The inescapable reality was that my case had held no interest for the embassy from the start—at least not enough to warrant its active input.

Powerless to challenge SOC's unflinching stance of 'strictly zero involvement', Selma showed all the signs of being close to throwing in the towel, and appeared as helpless as I was. It looked like SOC had succeeded in wearing her down. She stopped responding to my emails, and I was forever chasing her for news that never came. After being so contemptuously marginalised and given the run around by SOC for so long,

I could understand if her commitment to the case had waned and she'd finally hit a brick wall. Although I'd instructed her to file a court case against SOC in February 2014, I still had no idea whether she had done so. I was rather surprised, to say the least, when she called me one evening in mid-April.

'SOC has refused to talk to me or meet with me,' she said in one breath before launching into listing each stumbling block SOC had put her way. Something in her voice told me she wasn't the bearer of good tidings.

'Yes, I know...' I slowly agreed, concerned at what was coming next.

'I wasn't even allowed into the compound! I've waited for a sign from SOC for nearly a year... Their Benghazi lawyer has refused to accept the case documents... I've been going round in circles... I can't work like this,' she added as she poured out her grievances against the company in one dispiriting tirade.

I closed my eyes and sighed heavily. Her words sounded like the prologue to worse news to come, and I dreaded to think what other setbacks she was laying the ground for.

'Frankly, I don't know what else I could do for you. But since you're in the compound and they've denied me access, you'll have to chase the company yourself!'

She'd asked me once before to do just that and I'd taken quite a risk compiling the photographic evidence she'd requested. While I recognised that SOC had made it impossible for her to do her job, I wasn't comfortable one bit with the idea of 'chasing' the company myself.

'Selma, no one in management will talk to me about the case, apart from my own manager who never knows anything anymore,' I replied. 'As my lawyer, you're bound to have more authority with SOC than I could ever have. There must be—'

'OK!' she interrupted. 'This is what I'm going to do. I'll file a civil case against SOC with the court in Ajdabiya...'

I was more than happy with that, especially since it was exactly what I'd instructed her to do two months earlier.

'But it's the last thing I'll do for you as I won't be able to attend court in Ajdabiya since I'm based in Benghazi.'

Her words were like a massive hammer blow to my unsuspecting head. And I was confused too—she'd always known that the court was in Ajdabiya, and it hadn't troubled her until now. After all the difficulties in finding a Libyan lawyer to represent me, I was devastated that Selma was prepared to drop me high and dry. But, despite it all, part of me understood her position and felt sorry for her. Her hands had been tied from day one by SOC's refusal to communicate with her. She was a highly respected lawyer dealing with a powerful opponent determined not to play fair. She hadn't anticipated the obstacles that SOC put in her way, and, initially, had been hugely confident that she'd win my slam-dunk case. The fact that she'd been unceremoniously sidelined had taken its toll, and she was now ready to jump ship. I didn't like her decision, but I understood the reasons behind it. It was maddening that, by merely shutting her out, SOC hadn't even aggressively obstructed the legal process; it had simply proceeded to freeze her out until she was forced into such an untenable situation that she gave up the fight, and all the while the company waited for the opportune moment to remove me from the country. It had ignored Selma, her calls and her correspondence, all in line with its plan of 'strictly zero involvement' about the case. I understood her position, but the daunting task of locating another Libyan lawyer willing to take on my case loomed like another gigantic mountain to climb.

The chaotic political climate around the country was steadily worsening and, before long, alarming news of fighting between militias in the nearby town of Ajdabiya reached the compound on a regular basis. Further afield, rockets were launched on the capital, Tripoli, in yet another sign that the conflict was escalating dramatically. It was anyone's guess whether it would get so out of hand that the company would be forced to evacuate its workers again. I dreaded leaving Libya whilst the legalities of my case were still so up in the air, and was convinced that, should the SOC expatriates be repatriated this time, then my chances of being allowed back in the country would be non-existent. More than ever, time was of the essence for the civil lawsuit against SOC to be filed at the Ajdabiya courts.

The day following Selma's call, I approached my manager, Mr El-Abadi, about SOC's response to her letter of February, but, as I'd anticipated, he merely repeated that he had no idea about the company's intentions, but that he would find out. Shortly thereafter, he informed me that the legal department's manager, Mr Tahar, was in possession of the package of documents which Selma had forwarded to him after being refused by the company's lawyer in Benghazi. Now that SOC had all the documents in hand, all photographic and video evidence of neglect on Secretary Street, it would be interesting to see what the company's next move would be. Although I wasn't too optimistic that SOC would change its position any time soon, I still hoped against hope for a turnaround in the case.

Then Selma called with the latest setback. She usually began her conversations with small talk, but not this time. No, this time there was an unfamiliar agitation in her voice as she announced that the courts in Ajdabiya would be closed until September 2014 at the earliest, and that, therefore, the lawsuit against SOC couldn't be filed until then. With the deteriorating situation around the country, this delay was a massive blow to my legal plans as my days in Libya were undoubtedly numbered.

'September 2014? I might not even be in Libya by then!' I said.

'Look!' she snapped, 'You need your embassy! Now more than ever. There's no other way for you to get progress in Libya. Tell them to put pressure on both SOC and NOC. That's the only way you'll get anywhere!'

Like all those privy to my long-running rape saga, Selma was at a loss to understand the British Embassy's failure to intervene in a crime against one of its nationals.

'I no longer expect anything from the embassy. I've been begging for its help since the rape happened! I can't believe any more than you do that it's been so ineffective, but it's the reality…'

'Bulls**t!' she exploded. 'It's their job to help you!'

Wow. Did she really just say that? I thought. I knew her English was good, but I hadn't realised it extended to choice expletives. And she was, indeed, right—it was their job! I wished that, as my lawyer, and a prominent one at that, she would tell them that herself.

'I'll file the case at the court in September, but that's all I can do for you. Only your embassy can change things for you.'

Again, there was no mention of any proceedings against the rapist. As far as she was concerned, he was totally out of the picture. That conversation left me feeling utterly defenceless and, if at all possible, more despondent than ever.

Selma and all her thwarted efforts had reached the end of the road, and she could do no more for me in my frustrating circumstances. She'd insisted all along that only the British Embassy's involvement would get the case out of the deadlock it'd been languishing in. I'd felt unsure about her the very first day we met in London, when she commented that there was 'no point' in pursuing the rapist, and any lingering faith in her had eroded with her statement that compensating me because I was a 'foreign woman' would be 'unfair to Libyan women'. Indeed, it would be tragically unfair, but the solution wasn't to ensure that all victims were mistreated equally. The solution was the legislation and application of the appropriate laws to change this sorry state of affairs. As a prominent female lawyer, I wondered why she wasn't fighting for the systematic application of her country's existing rape laws, regardless of the difficulty of the task in a patriarchal society like Libya.

As soon as I got to my office the next morning, I contacted Mrs Hanson with Selma's request for the embassy to apply pressure on both SOC and NOC, and repeated my request for a meeting with the Foreign Ministry.

A few weeks before the end of April 2014, a bombshell of an email from the Foreign Office in London landed in my mailbox to inflict even more misery on my demoralised spirits. The message, nearly a year after the rape, stated that the Foreign Office 'could not possibly get involved in making representations to the Libyan Foreign Ministry to get them to pressure the National Oil Corporation', but, worse still, that the 'embassy could not become involved in individual disputes'. There it was, in black and white, stark and unembellished, the cold truth and the reason why my rape had elicited so little interest from the British authorities. The missing pieces of the puzzle had finally fallen into place to explain the embassy's long-running apathy. My rape had been declared, from the outset, a private 'individual dispute' between SOC and I, just as SOC had conveniently viewed it as a 'personal matter' between the rapist and I, in order to protect its interests. I was numb with shock. And why did it take the embassy or the Foreign Office a whole year to clarify their position?

For a year, I was kept in the dark while I struggled to make sense of the embassy's inaction, completely unaware of the pass-the-buck game going on behind the scenes within both SOC and the British Embassy. I was incensed that the Foreign Office could come up with such an offensive statement so long after the rape to justify the non-involvement of the only institution that could have had a significant impact in my case. No wonder I got nowhere! And, of course, the British authorities' failure to provide tangible assistance was bound to have huge consequences for the future of my case. I was incensed that the British authorities could consider a violent rape an 'individual dispute' within the scope of an employer and employee relation. I hadn't asked for the embassy's help in a pay dispute with my employer, but in a rape at knifepoint! The Foreign Office's outrageous statement was an affront to my dignity as a woman. As the email bluntly disclosed the offensive reason behind the embassy's lack of involvement, its logical implication was that nothing could be expected from it in the future. For the Foreign Office to concoct such a pathetic excuse a year after the rape was not only supremely insulting, but the ultimate blow to any hope I still had that justice would be served in the end. The email ended with the habitual platitudes that the Foreign Office would 'continue to follow the case very closely… and continue to make representations to the authorities for justice on your behalf', which directly contradicted its earlier statement of being unable to make representations to the Libyan authorities.

My British attorney, Mr Williams, was as outraged as I was by the Foreign Office's latest comments, and responded by requesting the British authorities directly re-engage with the Libyan authorities 'to set the conditions for an effective legal finish'. Despite all the obstacles I'd stumbled upon since the rape, I'd always held on to hope and optimism, but once the Foreign Office revealed the official reason for its failure to intervene, my mood grew darker, and, wherever I looked, I saw nothing but gloom and doom on the horizon—from the fast-deteriorating situation in Libya that might force the evacuation of SOC's foreign employees which I was sure would lead to my permanent expulsion from Libya, to the lengthy delay before my case could be filed at the Ajdabiya court, to my case being viewed as an 'individual dispute' by the Foreign Office, to the imminent expiry of my work visa which might well provide SOC with the perfect opportunity to terminate my employment contract… It all seemed so hopeless. I was slowly being brought down to my knees and feared that justice might well prove unattainable, even in my open-and-shut case.

While I grappled with the helplessness of my situation and the precarious safety inside the compound, I began catching the SOC bus to work each morning despite the short distance to my office. I left my house for work one morning on a beautiful spring day at the end of April 2014, to be faced with two men sitting in a grey Mazda type car with darkened rear windows, its engine running. The car was parked right outside my house. Alarm bells immediately rang out in my head. There were eight houses on the tiny stretch of road I lived on, all occupied by foreign medical staff, and this car was totally out of place being parked there.

Within seconds, an internal drama played out in my mind as I imagined being bungled inside the car and driven away. I quickened my steps towards the nearby bus stop, feeling the men's eyes on me as the car crawled past before gathering speed and disappearing, leaving me badly shaken. Was this just another segment of my fertile imagination, or was it a sign that real danger lurked around me? Whatever it was, this incident brought to mind an earlier one which happened just weeks before when a car had followed me on my way towards the supermarket. I hadn't thought much about it, but I was so unnerved by this latest incident that I decided to report both to SOC and to the embassy. No one responded. Despite my determination to stop imagining danger at every corner, I couldn't put these two incidents down to pure coincidence, and became more convinced than ever that there were malevolent eyes out there watching me. Unfortunately, there seemed to be no one in authority remotely interested in hearing my plight, let alone addressing it.

While careful not to make any waves with SOC to risk losing my job and being evicted from Libya, I feared that I'd become such an enormous headache for the company that it would surely deny the renewal of my work visa which was due imminently. Every second of my time in Libya depended on its renewal to give me another year to consolidate my legal plans. I was filled with dread at the thought that SOC would grasp this perfect opportunity to remove me from the country.

But to my surprise and endless relief, my visa was duly renewed. I decided rather cynically that SOC terminating my employment by conveniently refusing to renew my visa would have been a far too conspicuous sign of its intention to get rid of me before a civil lawsuit against it was filed in the courts. I suspected that SOC still believed that it was on the British Embassy's radar, and, therefore, had to be seen to be acting in good faith towards a British national in the company's employ. SOC would just have to wait a little longer for a better occasion to achieve its goal, but I knew it was coming, and in the battle of who could bide their time the longest, SOC had to be the undisputed winner. I still had, technically, over four years of employment before retiring from SOC—enough time to have my day in the Libyan courts. However, my visa had to be renewed each year and, under my complicated circumstances, there was no guarantee it would be next year or the year after. But, until then, I was thankful for its renewal this time, and the chance of a whole year before me to get the legal ball rolling.

On a warm day in May 2014, as had become its regular custom, the local tribe stormed the administrative building in Area 2, ordering its immediate evacuation. I was at my desk in my Area 1 office when I received a nervous call from Hannah, a colleague in the besieged Area 2 building, warning that a group of tribal members were on their way towards my area to demand the evacuation of the buildings there too. Hannah's words had barely sunk in when my office door flew open and Ayman burst in.

'Quick! They're coming! We must leave right now! I'll drive you home!' he blurted out, the look of sheer panic on his face in sharp contrast to his impressive height and burly frame.

Each time it intended on disrupting the day-to-day activities of a particular office building, the tribe descended upon the area, rifles at the ready, threatening the armed security guards manning the checkpoints before taking control of the targeted buildings. Thanks to Ayman, I was home before the tribe arrived at my building, but, for the next two days, it lay siege to the area, preventing employees from gaining access to their offices. When the tribe finally retreated, I arrived at work to find only a handful of workers and no sign of my manager anywhere. I had two options—head back home or spend the day working in an empty office. Being shut off at home didn't appeal to me one bit so I double-locked myself inside my office, and caught up on my work. There were no more disruptions that day, but the tribe's menacing spectre now loomed constantly over the compound, ready to manifest itself in yet more upheaval at any moment. These aggressive interruptions created such an unstable environment around the compound that it was surely only a matter of time before things came to a head with disastrous consequences.

While she'd announced that she could no longer represent me, Selma had a change of heart, deciding to continue to do so, but with the assistance of another lawyer attending the courts in Ajdabiya in her place. However, I'd already contacted the NCCLHR in Tripoli for its recommendation for a replacement, and it had swiftly suggested the names of two lawyers based in Ajdabiya, whom I'd immediately arranged to meet.

I met with Mr Ali Hamdi and Mr Adam Nadir at their office in Ajdabiya in May 2014. Both men were in their early forties, friendly and affable, and spoke good English. They told me of their shock at hearing of the rape nearly a year earlier. I was taken aback that they'd heard about it at all.

'The *whole* of Libya's heard about it!' said Mr Nadir. 'These things are unheard of in our country...'

The whole of Libya? Wow, lucky me, I thought with a heavy heart. I couldn't believe that I was the woman whose rape the 'whole of Libya' had heard about; it was a crushing realisation. If it were indeed true that 'these things' were unheard of in Libya, then what had been the odds of my being raped? Had I just been unlucky? Or were they 'unheard of' for the simple reason they weren't reported in Libya? I knew what the answer was.

Both men listened intently to my account of the events since the rape.

'We need time to look into your case in detail, of course, but it sounds quite straightforward,' said Mr Hamdi. 'I'm surprised that nothing's happened if the rapist has been identified, there's DNA available, an eye witness... The company's negligence must be established before it becomes liable for damages. And the rapist must be prosecuted. I'm confident we can represent you successfully on both counts.'

'Really? On *both*?' I asked, beaming from ear to ear.

It was hugely frustrating that it took a whole year for me to come across these two lawyers who, to compound my exasperation even further, were located so near to the compound. But I'd found them, and I had an auspicious feeling that they would succeed in turning my situation around. They proposed filing a civil lawsuit against SOC, and a criminal case against the rapist. My heart danced with joy inside my chest, not only at the lawyers' willingness to represent me, but at hearing that the rapist could, indeed, be

246

prosecuted—even in Libya! But like all those who'd advised on the case before them, they stressed the need for that one missing, vital ingredient that had kept my case in limbo—pressure from the British Embassy.

'It's essential in Libya,' insisted Mr Nadir. 'Nothing will happen without it...'

I had no illusions whatsoever about any worthwhile assistance from the embassy, but I trusted these two legal professionals to, somehow, bring it about. This whole rape business had drained me of all energy, and I longed for the moment I could dump the entire case onto some capable Libyan hands to take over, and spare me any further mental anguish. An interesting discussion followed about sexual violence in Libya, and the way it was dealt with. Both men agreed that urgent changes were needed both on a judicial and a societal level before victims could feel safe enough to report the crimes against them in a staunchly patriarchal environment pressuring them into silence. Only then would sexual violence crimes be prosecuted for the crimes they really were, and the burden of 'shame' that society conveniently heaped onto the victims be lifted.

'Yes, things must change in Libya,' said Mr Hamdi, 'But, unfortunately, change won't happen overnight...'

Amen. Their words were music to my ears. I felt on the same wavelength as these two men, and so invigorated by their way of thinking that I dared hope with all my heart that I could play a part in the drastic societal change they were calling for.

Mr Hamdi promised to contact me as soon as the Ajdabiya courts reopened sometime in September, whilst Mr Nadir, involved in the drafting of the new Libyan Constitution, offered his services on a consultancy basis. I couldn't have asked for more. By suggesting tangible, explicit steps to move my case forward, and displaying such a strong commitment to obtaining justice on my behalf, they lifted up my bruised spirits no end, and I couldn't wait for them to officially start the ball rolling in September. I had an overwhelming feeling that I'd finally found the perfect Libyan team to stand with me and fight my corner. That they were prepared to pursue the rapist in the courts was like a huge barrier had just been smashed down by the unstoppable, incorruptible force of the law. I couldn't fathom why Selma had deemed it 'pointless' to prosecute the rapist while these men were ready to do so as part of the normal Libyan judicial process. I was euphoric at this stupendous development, and all I had to do was wait patiently until Mr Hamdi contacted me in September. And if there was one thing that my case had taught me, it was patience! In the meantime, I looked forward to my annual leave in London in a few weeks, and putting this miserable saga aside for a while with the knowledge that valuable help would be waiting on my return.

It became impossible to approach my manager for any update on the case, and I even got the impression that he felt harassed by my relentless quizzing, and, since he never had anything to report anyway, he took to avoiding me altogether. A cat-and-mouse game played out between us which was not only frustrating, but highly embarrassing as we occupied adjoining offices. I had so many legitimate questions that needed answers, but told myself that I could wait until September when I'd gladly hand over the entire fact-finding mission to the two brilliant lawyers in Ajdabiya.

In June 2014, I left the compound on my annual vacation, and wasn't due to return until the first week in August—several weeks away from the compound and my depressing predicament. The situation in Libya had been going steadily downhill, and I left the country with a mix of relief to be escaping for a while, but also deep concern that I had no legal case filed at the Ajdabiya courts yet. Despite the renewal of my work visa, I dreaded leaving Libya whilst I feared that SOC would terminate my work contract at any time. Although I desperately needed a break, I'd barely landed in London when I regretted not postponing my leave until after Mr Hamdi had started the legal process. But while I distrusted SOC with all my might, I didn't believe that it would sink so low and be so sneaky as to terminate my contract while I was on leave out of Libya. I started counting the days until my return, confident that my two Ajdabiya lawyers would deliver a substantially better job than Selma had been allowed to do by SOC. And I even suspected—rightly or wrongly—that, as male lawyers, they might even be taken seriously by SOC and granted the respect denied to Selma as a woman.

Upon my return to London, Mr Williams and I met with Mrs Lynda Johnson, the Amnesty International's representative, at their offices in Central London. It was depressing to hear her opinion that it would be quasi-impossible to achieve any traction in Libya, especially in the aftermath of the recent war. A meeting with my local member of parliament, Mr Steve Reed, followed, during which he promised to raise my case at parliament. Now that was a huge positive development! It was during this meeting with Mr Reed that I gained an insight into Mr Williams' formidable expertise as I observed him skilfully discussing my case and pushing to secure the involvement of the British authorities. I felt supremely confident that with Mr Williams and my two Ajdabiya lawyers by my side, my legal woes would soon be making a radical sharp turn for the better.

Before I left Brega, Mr Williams brought to my attention that a conference—the Global Summit on Sexual Violence in Conflict Areas, organised by the British government—was scheduled to take place at the Excel Centre in London over three days in mid-June of 2014. I made a mental note to attend seeing that I felt so regrettably closely connected to the topic. The summit was hosted by Mr William Hague, Secretary of State at the time, and Angelina Jolie, the Hollywood actress. On the day I visited, even her then husband and fellow actor, Brad Pitt, made an appearance. There was nothing glamorous about the topic, and I couldn't help feeling a little uneasy at this étalage of show business glamour at an event highlighting the scourge of sexual violence that blighted the lives of millions of women around the world. The summit was attended by representatives from over one hundred countries, hundreds of foreign ministers and NGOs, experts from the health, legal, military and academic fields, as well as survivors of sexual violence crimes. A mock trial was scheduled with the participation of well-known lawyers such as Cherie Blair, and, incidentally, my own attorney, Mr Williams.

Behind the scenes, Mr Williams had requested that I be allowed to participate in my sad capacity as a rape victim, but his request was denied. I was disappointed, but no doubt there were already enough victims under one roof willing to testify. During the mock trial, about half a dozen representatives from different countries commented, amongst other things, on the number of sexual violence crimes in their respective countries. As luck would have it, there was a Libyan spokesperson whose input I awaited with particular interest. I was totally unprepared for the shock I was about to experience.

'Since the end of the 2011 revolution, there hasn't been *one single* report of rape in Libya,' the young woman declared with brazen confidence.

Her words felt like a dagger being plunged deep in my heart. They were identical to those spoken by the Tripoli prosecutor at the October 2013 conference in Tripoli, which had, in all certainly, been attended by the British Embassy. This was, in a nutshell, my problem—the Libyan authorities refusing to acknowledge the crime against me, with tacit compliance from the British authorities. This was the reason my easy open-and-shut case got nowhere. But the Libyan representative's statement had been made at a conference organised by the British government itself, on British home soil, and yet, it was allowed to be made without any challenge. I wasn't even a statistic—I simply didn't exist in the eyes of either the Libyan or the British authorities. I'd been completely written off. Seething, I raised my hand to correct this downright lie.

'That's not true! No rape in Libya since the end of the 2011 revolution? Really? I was raped in Libya in 2013, two years after your revolution ended!'

Silence fell like a ton of bricks over the proceedings, and all eyes turned towards me. The Libyan representative looked at me, but said nothing. The whole panel of lawyers and judges looked at me, but said nothing. There was no reaction, other than stunned silence. After an awkward moment for everyone in the room, the trial continued—perhaps claiming even more untruths. I've had many opportunities to remember that moment, and to regret not being more aggressive in my reaction to that false statement. At the end of the mock trial, I approached a United Nations representative who had sat on the panel, and briefly outlined to her my experience and frustrations at the lack of involvement by the British authorities.

'Oh dear. I'm so sorry, but I'm not surprised at all,' she said with a slight chuckle. 'But, anyway... good luck!' she added after a brief, awkward moment.

She then scurried away, leaving me standing there, at a loss to understand her words or her inappropriate giggle. I'd shared only the most fleeting moment with this UN representative, but her comment and out-of-place chuckle were enough to demonstrate that even at the highest levels, and despite the lip service being paid to the issue, the treatment meted out to victims of sexual violence crimes would continue to be sub-standard as long as the powerful institutions whose role it was to confront and deal with this social evil didn't show full, serious commitment to the task.

So far, my impressions of the conference weren't exactly glowing, but I looked forward to the speech Mr William Hague was scheduled to give later on that afternoon. When the time came, his speech only emphasised the sharp contrast between my experience and the dedication and commitment expressed in the words of a 'Britain at the forefront of the fight to eradicate and punish the crime of rape in other countries'. Again, cleaning up one's own backyard first sprang to my mind. The sad reality, based on the fiasco that resumed my case, was that the same Britain he spoke about so glowingly had been unwilling to come up with a protocol that could have helped me. It hadn't been a case of simply being 'unable' to assist, but rather of being 'definitely unwilling'. How could it ever be acceptable that I struggled to keep the plight of my rape alive single-handedly whilst the British authorities turned a blind eye to it? Their unwillingness to disrupt the status quo of their renewed diplomatic relations with Libya only demonstrated that I, a British citizen, wasn't deemed worth standing up for by my country's authorities. There was no other logical conclusion to arrive at.

When an institution as powerful and as respected around the world as the British government allowed crimes against its citizens abroad to go unpunished, then its citizens weren't governed at all times by a government of law, but by a government of passive and, by extension, corruptible men. If I, as a citizen of one of the most powerful nations in the world, could be so disdainfully cast aside at such a time of dire need, I wondered what chances a rape victim had in some obscure, remote country.

The Libyan justice department was under the direct responsibility of the Libyan government, owner of NOC— SOC's boss. Despite their insulting position of considering my rape a private 'individual dispute' with my employer, the British authorities were made aware of SOC's efforts to repress the case, but still didn't think it necessary to follow up the Libyan authorities' investigation to ensure that the rights of a wronged British citizen weren't denied. This failure amounted to the most elementary dereliction of duty. When the British Embassy could attend a conference and hear the Tripoli public prosecutor making a false statement about no rape crimes in Libya since the end of the 2011 conflict, and not challenge this absolute lie, then some appalling, unacceptable *laissez-faire* had been deliberately allowed to sabotage my case.

As events slowly unfolded since the rape, I'd come to suspect the inevitable—that the Libyan authorities would eventually expel me from the country—but I never expected that my rape would be waved aside by my own governmental authorities. While this wasn't a comforting or empowering realisation to come to grips with, it was the stark reality of my case. While it took the British authorities a whole year to finally reveal the official reason behind their lack of involvement—that they 'could not become involved in individual disputes'—I certainly wasn't buying any of it and I remained convinced that the debacle of my case was rather the direct result of the British authorities allowing their diplomatic relations with a recently 'liberated' Libya to supersede one of their citizen's right to justice.

The bitter realisation that there would be no political pressure from the British authorities on the Libyans to resolve my case dealt a heavy blow to any hopes I still clung to that justice would prevail one day. My only option, as long as SOC granted me a work visa, was to turn to the Libyan courts and prepare for the long haul of a legal struggle inside an environment bent on silencing me.

The political situation in Libya deteriorated so significantly during the summer of 2014 that the British Embassy was forced to cease its operations in Tripoli and move to neighbouring Tunisia. By then, my earlier confidence in the embassy's ability to assist me had been in free fall anyway, but once the reason for its lack of intervention had been disclosed, the embassy's geographical relocation became of no interest or consequence to me whatsoever. As far as I was concerned, it could move to another planet altogether. It was soul-crushing that a heinous crime against me could be dismissed by an institution I'd turned to with wide-eyed, unbounded faith. I decided to quit relying on the embassy, and instead placed all my hopes for justice firmly in the expert hands of my British attorney, Mr Williams, and my two new lawyers in Ajdabiya, Mr Hamdi and Mr Nadir. They were the only light on my murky horizon, and I couldn't wait to return to Libya to start the legal ball rolling. With such a team by my side, I felt to my core that nothing would go wrong this time.

Days before I was due to fly back to Libya, there came the shattering news that Tripoli international airport had been badly damaged in a bomb blast. This incident couldn't have happened at a worse time to hamper my legal plans. The airport was shut down, and I could only speculate on when it would reopen. While I hated delaying my return, I had to admit that I was extremely concerned about the chaos spreading across Libya. I informed my manager, Mr El-Abadi, that I'd be unable to fly back as scheduled, and started researching alternative routes. He quickly emailed back that 'it would be best to remain in London until further notice due to the situation in the country'. I was desperate to return, but relieved for his permission not to travel at such a tumultuous time.

I accepted Mr El-Abadi's suggestion at face value, not suspecting for a second that SOC could use the bomb incident to keep me out of Libya permanently. Tripoli airport had, indeed, been hit, and that reality blinded me to the possibility of any underlying motive behind my manager's advice to extend my leave. I candidly expected to be recalled at the earliest opportunity, and patiently waited for that time. But my patience soon turned to concern when SOC didn't respond to emails about my return. It wasn't until weeks turned into months, and friends writing that I was the only expatriate kept out of Libya by the company that I finally saw the cold truth behind my manager's suggestion. The bomb blast at Tripoli airport had presented SOC with the perfect excuse to achieve its goal of terminating my employment, and removing me from Libya.

Ever since the rape, I'd suspected SOC would seize the first chance to expel me from Libya, and yet, I hadn't seen it coming when it finally did happen. With all the evidence before me of SOC's sneaky methods, I still hadn't expected my employment to be terminated whilst I was out of the country—such a brazen move would've been too treacherous, too underhanded. Instead, I'd foolishly trusted the company to call me back as soon as Tripoli's airport reopened. My inability to return was the worst possible blow to the filing of my court case, for which my physical presence in Libya was a prerequisite. I began contacting various government ministers in my search for urgent assistance, but, again, got nowhere.

Over time, even my regular contact with Hiba and Mary dwindled until they too stopped responding. I was baffled and deeply hurt by their silence. They weren't just friends with whom I'd shared some unforgettable moments, they'd become my indispensable lifeline to Libya. I was mortified that circumstances beyond my control had severed our friendship, but I could somehow rationalise their detachment as any communication with me about the company or the compound could jeopardise their employment with SOC. All the doors I'd knocked on for help since the rape had firmly slammed in my face, and it was heartbreaking that even close friends kept their distance too.

The rapist continued with his life, untroubled by the Libyan authorities, while I faced mounting obstacles on my road towards the redress that the law insisted I was entitled to, but refused to grant me. I felt, at times, like a career criminal searching for a way out of a ghastly bind, and had to remind myself that I wasn't the criminal, but the victim! Although I was massively disillusioned by the circumstances of my case, I refused with all my might to let my determination to continue pressing ahead waver. Despite having been let down by all those I'd expected support from, the eternal optimist in me still clung desperately to the belief that justice would prevail one day, no matter how fast that day faded into the distance.

In July 2015, I received an encouraging response to a letter I'd written to the Foreign Office in London. In essence, it promised that the British authorities were 'determined to pursue this case until justice was forthcoming'. This was uplifting and encouraging news, but in direct contradiction to the Foreign Office's earlier stance that 'the embassy cannot become involved in individual disputes'. I decided that 'until justice was forthcoming', I'd continue writing to government ministers and anyone who might listen until, hopefully, one paid attention.

Many of the ministers I'd contacted didn't bother replying, which only further confirmed that my case was of no interest whatsoever to the authorities. All the respect I'd held towards the political and judicial systems before the rape was unravelling at high speed to make way for cynicism and distrust. And not an ounce of respect would be restored until

I was allowed to stand and be counted, and was granted the justice I was entitled to.

In July 2016, exactly two years following my manager's permission to remain in London until 'further notice', a money transfer from SOC made its way into my bank account. I recognised the significance behind this transfer at once. While there was no message attached to the transfer, the amount corresponded exactly to that owed to me for accrued leave, but, most importantly, it was the type of payment made only at the termination of a contract. With this monetary transfer, SOC was finally giving me official confirmation that it had terminated my employment, without my prior knowledge, but with plenty of deceit and cunning. Of course, I'd suspected long before this bank transfer that the company had achieved its aim of removing me from Libya by using the Tripoli airport bombing, but to receive confirmation of SOC's devious scheming without a single word of explanation was a particularly bitter pill to swallow. I immediately contacted Mr Ali Slimane at the personnel department.

'It's the final amount owed to you by SOC,' he said calmly.

'And why am I receiving this "final amount" now?' I asked, my heart thumping in my chest at the inevitable blow he was about to deliver.

'Because your contract was terminated…'

'When? And without giving me prior notice?'

'In August 2014…'

'What? Two years ago? So, you gave me permission to stay in the UK until "further notice" then quickly terminated my contract! And you're letting me know in 2016?' I said, my voice shaking with anger. 'But I'm not surprised one bit… You and I know why SOC acted in such a deceitful way.'

What I'd dreaded the most while I was in the compound finally happened while I was outside of it. I hadn't just been dismissed and my contract unceremoniously terminated in violation of its terms, but it was all done without my knowledge! But that was a moot point. If SOC didn't hesitate flouting the law over a crime it was partly responsible for, then I didn't suppose it would trouble itself one bit about abiding by the terms of a foreign employee's contract who'd become a headache to the company. I was fuming. SOC's dishonesty and shameless duplicity were truly breathtaking. And by terminating my contract immediately following my manager's authorisation to stay in London 'until further notice', SOC had simply ended its legal obligation to pay me a salary while I remained in London, waiting to be recalled by the company. But since SOC had no intention of recalling me to work, it was in its interest to sever all ties with me immediately by terminating my employment. It had taken some time, but it all clicked into place. I thought of all the emails I'd sent the company, enquiring about my return, unaware that my contract had long been terminated, and felt incredibly foolish. No wonder my friends and colleagues had chosen to keep their distance—nobody wanted to be the bearer of bad tidings by announcing the news of my sacking!

I requested from SOC the return of all my personal belongings, as per the terms of my contract, but, again, received no response. The bomb incident at Tripoli airport had handed SOC the perfect opportunity to keep me at arm's length permanently, and it had taken full advantage of it. I was repulsed by the company's reprehensible actions, but I was furious and incredibly embarrassed at my own naivety. Now that SOC had succeeded in its perfidious plan to expel me from Libya, and since a visa was required to enter the country, it was safe to assume that there would be no chance in hell that such a permit would ever be granted to the *persona non grata* I'd become as a result of the rape.

SOC's unconscionable conduct only fuelled my resolve that this wouldn't be the end of the story, and increased my resentment towards the British authorities whose sustained *laissez aller* had allowed SOC to flout its responsibilities towards a British citizen. By sneakily ending my employment, SOC had also ended any prospect of redress in Libya, whilst allowing a rapist to evade prosecution and become a potential threat to other women. I simply couldn't believe the injustice of it all.

I was fast-nearing retirement age and experiencing, for the first time in my long working life, the full force of an employer's downright underhanded manipulations. I'd worked most of my life, and showed at all times the utmost integrity and loyalty to my employers. I was broken-hearted that my working days had been ended by a sordid rape, and that I'd been treated in such a despicable manner by those whose duty it was to support me. I'd been cast out, thrown on the scrap heap before being ready or willing to retire. I'd been banished into early retirement because SOC was bent on evading its responsibility in my rape. For the sake of my sanity, I again turned to the incurable optimist in me to find the strength to continue clinging to the notion that, as long as my case was kept alive, then justice—however painfully trying it'd been so far—couldn't be denied forever.

Since taking on my case, Mr Williams had contacted several British government ministers, but this exercise produced nothing more substantial than the usual inconsequential responses. All efforts to achieve an engagement from the British authorities had led absolutely nowhere. In the midst of this legal no-man's land, came another shattering blow to my fast-fading hopes. Mr Williams was leaving his position at the prestigious Bedford Row Chambers, and could no longer represent me. I was crushed. His departure was bound to have a tremendously negative impact on whatever I had to face in the future. From the outset, Mr Williams had been my staunchest ally, and the most formidable spokesman by my side. If there was one person able to bring about a solution to my case, it was Mr Williams. The loss of his support was devastating. Mr Williams had once told me that the problem with progressing my case in the UK would be my 'lack of funds' as the cost of the litigation involved was likely to be prohibitive. Now that I'd been officially dismissed by SOC, this 'lack of funds' would only become an even greater hurdle. Indeed, Joe Public didn't figure on the clients' lists of renowned law practices. As the victim of a crime, this case had already cost me upwards of forty thousand British pounds, with nothing to show for it—nothing other than the hard-learnt lesson that justice was an onerous privilege that seemed designed only for those with unlimited funds, or those benefitting from the western equivalent of the Libyan *wasta*; and I had neither.

Before leaving me to my fate, Mr Williams searched tirelessly for law practices willing to accept my case on a pro bono basis. None would represent me on that basis, expecting instead payment of their eye-watering fees upfront. It was frustrating, but I understood the logic behind this as my cross-border rape case granted SOC the scandalous privilege of being under no legal obligation to respond to any foreign summons, and, therefore, any law practice in Britain representing me on a pro bono basis had no guarantee whatsoever of recouping its presumably considerable costs. Just as SOC had so easily sidelined Selma, inadequacies in international law would allow the company to play the same game with the British courts, and get away with it. The judicial system was disgracefully handing SOC a free pass to evade its responsibilities, and granting immunity to a rapist to maybe rape again. I was losing on both counts, and there was nothing I, or anyone else, could do about it.

Being a homeowner precluded me from receiving legal aid and I had no intention of risking my family home as I'd once been advised to do by counsel. Clearly, law practices aren't in the charity business and they have to evaluate the financial risks of the cases they take on. However, the fact that crime victims could be denied redress because the judicial process became a prohibitive option was testament that the long arm of the law didn't reach far and wide enough to protect all victims, irrespective of their financial status. I was both incensed and highly resentful each time I watched the legal apparatus being rolled out and put at the service of foreign criminals—especially Libyan ones—granting them legal aid to fight their cases in the UK whilst I—as a victim—was expected to pay thousands of pounds and still get nowhere; or when, still courtesy of the public purse, criminals avoided deportation to preserve their human rights whilst my own had been deliberately and mercilessly trampled over by two governments, including my own. Even in the zillion to one chance that a civil case against SOC could be tried in London and a by-default judgment pronounced in my favour, international law would still be powerless to enforce the ruling against a defaulting foreign entity on its home soil. Whatever the outcome, SOC would remain legally untouchable. I was sickened by the unfairness of it all, and by a system in which justice didn't serve everyone equally and became just another empty word.

Shortly following official confirmation of my dismissal from SOC, I received the astonishing news from a Libyan colleague that the rapist had resumed his work with SOC. I had no way of verifying this, but I trusted my colleague implicitly and had no reason to doubt the veracity of his claim. The reinstatement of the rapist by SOC only reaffirmed the company's plan of removing me from Libya, and that it clearly had had no intention whatsoever of calling me back to work following my manager's advice to stay in London 'until further notice'. It also emphasised the system's devious scheming when tribal loyalty interfered to inhibit and stifle the truth. It was business as usual for the rapist as he benefitted from sustained protection not only from his country's authorities, but also, indirectly, from that of the British authorities.

While I searched for a way out of my legal abyss, Mr Williams contacted me with the exhilarating news that one renowned law firm in Central London had agreed to meet with me with the aim of taking on my case on a pro bono basis. All my hopes for redress, which had been on a knife edge for years, resurfaced again, cautiously, but as strong as ever. A meeting was promptly arranged, and I met with three of the firm's lawyers at their Westminster Road offices in Central London. The practice was involved in the legal case of one of the most powerful leaders in the world, which I found extremely impressive. Everything about the firm reflected its professional high ranking and eminence—from its plush offices in a prime location to the imposing, formal demeanour of its lawyers.

Following a lengthy meeting during which each of the three lawyers probed for the most minute detail of the case, they confirmed their willingness to take on my case on a pro bono basis. I was sure that was the closest I'd ever got to a miracle! I was elated beyond belief that my luck was taking such an unbelievable turn. All my hopes revived to make me feel that the closure of my rape saga was close at hand. But my elation was about to be crushed.

Within days, I was invited to a second meeting with the same three lawyers. But this time, they looked uncomfortable, and something inside told me to expect the worst. I wasn't wrong. Following review of my case, the lawyers had decided that the costs involved to bring it to the London courts would be far too high when they had no guarantee of recouping them. They explained what I only knew too well—how SOC could default on a trial outside of Libya, leaving them with no legal recourse of enforcing a court judgment against the company. My case was, therefore, deemed a considerable gamble for them to take on, and they concluded that representing me on a pro bono basis was a massive financial risk not worth getting involved in.

'Had the rape happened in the UK, or anywhere in Europe, your case would've been an easy one to settle in your favour.'

These words held no consolation for me whatsoever. Their last-minute decision not to represent me broke my heart. I wished they'd never contacted me in the first place, raising my hopes sky high to only shatter them into a million pieces. I was devastated and enraged that justice could be corrupted by pernicious flaws within international law that none of these supremely accomplished professionals could challenge to bring about a fairer state of affairs for victims like me.

As my case wasn't the first rape in the compound—and might not be the last as long as the Libyan system granted impunity to the rapists—this grim reality signified that SOC, protected by its status as a subsidiary of a mighty state-owned corporation, would simply terminate the employment of the next rape victims, and expel them from Libya to get rid of the legal problems the victims represented. Just as my Libyan female co-workers had revealed that there was no day in court to be had for rape victims in their country, there would be none for me in Britain either, that supposedly fairer and better equipped nation at delivering justice to its citizens. I'd been so exhilarated by the prospect of such a prominent law firm representing me that its change of heart hit me like a ton of bricks. Was I destined to remain imprisoned inside that dark, ever-expanding maze that I could find no way out of? I seriously worried that the constant see-sawing between hope and despair would compromise my sanity forever.

At times, just like in the movies, I'd catch myself daydreaming of a maverick lawyer suddenly appearing when I least expected it to fight my corner, purely in the name of doing the right and honourable thing. Although I'd quickly snap out of these reveries, they were a welcome distraction from my bleak reality. Unfortunately, my plight wasn't a fiction that could be moulded into conveniently happy endings; it was real life with its unfair trials and tribulations, and I stood pitifully alone to face them.

Despite no longer handling my case, Mr Williams hadn't given up searching for anyone willing to assist me, and I'll forever be grateful to him for this. He soon put me in touch with Mr Nasser Hassan, an ex-member of the National Council of Civil Liberties and Human Rights (NCCLHR), whom I'd met in 2014, during my first meeting with Mr Williams in Tripoli. Mr Hassan fled Libya after the 2011 war, and was seeking asylum in the UK. I arranged to meet with him at a venue in Central London. Over coffee, he recounted how he came to be in his current ghastly situation as a direct consequence of the Libyan conflict. The war of 'liberation' recently inflicted upon Libya was causing untold human suffering to its population. In different ways, Mr Hassan and I were victims of that same tragic event which had brought nothing but mayhem and insecurity to the whole of the country. It was heartbreaking that this once prominent professional man was reduced to begging for asylum in an unfamiliar country whose language he barely spoke.

As tragic victims of the ravages of war, he and his family were forced to start a new life from scratch in a country they had no ties to. It was disastrous that a country's elite had to flee towards a life of uncertainty in a foreign land simply because of man-made wars motivated by political interests and greed. I felt tremendously sorry for Mr Hassan who, despite his own troubles, promised to advise me on my Libyan dilemma.

The recent SOC confirmation that I was out of a job compelled me to reassess my future living plans. I was over sixty years old, and only too aware that my age rendered me quasi-redundant for the job market. Admittedly, I was reluctant to look for work at my age if it meant rejoining the hustle and bustle of a busy city like London. I'd been part of the London rat race for over thirty long years, and it had been more than enough to extinguish any desire to jump on that wagon again at my age. I was lucky to have repaid the mortgage on my house during my years in Libya, but I had no significant income to sustain me until I received a state pension a few years down the line. All the time I foolishly waited for SOC to call me back to work, I'd felt technically still employed, and, therefore, that I still had a purpose and goals to achieve in life. But all my plans for a comfortable retirement in a few years' time had been significantly scuppered by my rape and its aftermath. To be brutally flung into retirement without notice had caught me unawares in spite of my suspicions that SOC would seize the first occasion to end my employment.

I was at a complete loose end, and was seriously apprehensive about my imposed reality as a retiree while I still grappled with the unresolved circumstances of my rape. What would I do with the rest of my life now that my job prospects were non-existent at my advancing age? I'd worked all of my life, and couldn't imagine not going to the office again. All of my life, work had been a pivotal force, an essential part of it like breathing, eating or sleeping.

Retirement felt like a frightening finality that scared me no end. For a while, the thought of being unemployable purely on the basis of age made me feel like I'd suddenly become of no use to society, which filled me with profound anguish. I told myself repeatedly that I'd retired from work, not from life itself, but for a long time, these words were of no consolation. I had to find a way to adjust to this colossal change—which I'd neither sought nor initiated—and create another reality for myself with other routines and aims.

As a result of the inadequate manner my case was dealt with by the British authorities, I became aware of a burning sense of resentment, even abandonment, stirring inside me. I found it increasingly difficult to come to terms with the authorities' unwillingness to support me during the most harrowing time in my entire life, and deal with the bitter indignities that came with feeling unworthy of assistance from my own government. I'd felt deeply insulted in my dignity as a woman as they simply fobbed me off with platitudes and empty statements. In spite of my best efforts, I couldn't shake the feeling of betrayal and alienation from the country that had once been my dream to settle in. I had to face the daunting prospect that I could no longer continue living in Britain and be at peace. I decided to seek solace somewhere that wouldn't be a permanent reminder of my rape fiasco, a place where I could find refuge as far away as possible from those who'd denied me redress.

Leaving Britain was going to be an agonisingly difficult move to make, but it was one that I had to make for my own peace of mind. I needed to put aside, at least for a while, the whole sorry saga of the rape and its disgraceful aftermath.

The thought of selling my house and uprooting myself at my age was terrifying to contemplate, but I was ready to follow my instincts. My desperation for leaving was so urgent that I listed my house for sale while I still had no idea where to move to. Ever the pragmatist, the main criterion for a destination was somewhere where house prices were cheaper than Britain to leave me enough funds to live on comfortably until my state pension became due. Not surprisingly, since I grew up there, France topped the list of potential destinations. I had no doubt that this move represented another challenge, but

I was undeterred, reflecting that it would be as stressful, or as exciting, as I allowed it to be.

Just as I'd felt the time was right to embark on a new stage in life by moving to Libya more than a decade earlier, I was now guided by that same urge to start again on different shores, albeit for different reasons. With no job or legal prospects in the pipeline, the time was ripe for my departure towards new horizons. To complicate matters even further, I toyed with the idea of moving to a country whose language I'd have to learn, deciding that an extra challenge would be the perfect solution to take my mind off all the problems surrounding the rape. But while I was ready to turn another page of the book of my life, I was as determined as ever to keep the rape chapter wide open as long as the crime remained unpunished.

My house in London sold quickly, in fact too quickly since I still hadn't decided on which country to move to. Italy? Malta? Cyprus? Greece? My mind hopped excitedly between each Mediterranean island, but remained undecided. The choice was wide, and I urgently researched each option, delighted that each country met my criteria of cheaper properties, sunny climate and laid-back inhabitants. But, against all logic, I opted for the hands-down outsider: Spain, a country I'd never had the slightest desire of visiting before, but yet, inexplicably, was suddenly prepared to make my home. It was most bizarre indeed as, until that moment, I'd reserved impulse buying strictly to items of clothing and shoes. And so I travelled to Spain in search of the retreat that would help me overcome all the pain and frustrations I'd accumulated since the rape.

I purchased my quaint Spanish house within four weeks of arriving in the country, after barely ten minutes of viewing it. As soon as I saw it, I fell in love with its white-washed walls, terracotta tiles and arched doorways, whilst the exquisite, picturesque village it was located in, nestled at the feet of the Sierra Segaria mountains, sealed the deal. The sleepy village of a few hundred inhabitants was exactly what I needed—a shelter from all the heartbreak of the past years. Even my choice of a country whose language I didn't understand or speak had been part of my desperate need to alienate myself from a system that had let me down so badly.

Early one morning in February 2015, I flew out, filled with bittersweet emotions, out of London and towards a fresh start on Spanish shores. My new garden might have lacked the exotic palm trees I'd so cherished at my Brega house, but my new home was surrounded by endless rows of fragrant orange groves, and gigantic mountains standing majestically almost within arm's reach. The scenery was breathtaking. Wherever I looked, the mighty silhouettes of the mountains dominated the horizon like protective giants, making me feel so safe. They reminded me of the power of the Higher Being, just as the sun setting over the Brega beach in hues of fiery reds had reminded me of Him. Oleander trees with hot pink blooms were everywhere in the village, taking me back, with much nostalgia, to my home in the compound and the relaxing moments I spent trimming their invading branches as they cascaded over Mary's garden wall onto mine. In a strange way, many things within my new surroundings reminded me of the best that Brega had given me, and which I'd been so grateful for: the glorious hot weather, the tranquil, slow-paced life and the friendly, easy-going inhabitants. I'd chosen this isolated Spanish village to escape memories of Brega, but

I now realised that there were many happy memories of the compound that I hoped would live inside me forever.

I soon found out that life inside a sleepy Spanish village was a massive change from life in hectic London, or even from the Brega compound, but my exhausted, over-burdened mind basked in the remoteness and tranquillity of it all. Each morning, I'd step inside the maze of orange groves arranged neatly into lines that faded far into the distance, and wallowed in their sweet, intoxicating scent. Dwarfed by the towering bulk of the mountains around me, I prayed to never take this magnificent scenery for granted, and to always feel a sense of wonder at the breathtaking beauty on my doorstep. These stunning surroundings made me feel the power of the Higher Being to my deepest core, and reassured me that one day He would be the ultimate judge of my rape disaster, when all those involved would have to account for their actions. In my so far fruitless pursuit of justice, I found solace in this comforting belief.

As time slowly ticked by in my new Spanish surroundings, it showed me that leaving London had been the right thing to do. The typically rural Spanish village was smaller than Area 1 of the Brega compound, and I enjoyed its rustic charm and relaxed ambience—the *plaza mayor* around which village life centred, its one restaurant bar and one grocery store. I rediscovered the security of living amongst a tiny community, just as I'd done at the compound, and spent my days exploring my surroundings, feeling incredibly lucky to have been guided to this part of the world. The house needed some light cosmetic work, so I threw myself wholeheartedly at the task. It was easy to push aside any thoughts of the legal abyss I was in as I busied myself with decorating chores around my home. I'd given up all hope of finding a lawyer willing to take on my case, and increasingly felt like a seasoned criminal seeking a defence lawyer to plead their hopeless case. It made no sense to me, but for now, for my own sanity, I had to bury my last years in Brega into the most inaccessible corners of my mind, and concentrate instead on the exciting challenges of my new chapter in Spain.

For a whole year following my arrival in Spain, I entertained no other plans other than taking life one day at a time, enjoying my new home and fitting into village life. Until one morning in May 2016.

Mr Hassan, the ex-NCCLHR lawyer seeking asylum in the UK, called unexpectedly with details of a London lawyer, a Mr John Adams, who was willing to help with my case. After all the disappointments I'd gone through since the rape, I surprised myself at feeling any excitement at the news. The experience with Mr Adams turned out to be the worst of them all, and was nothing but another costly opportunity to observe, first-hand, how unethical some law professionals could be.

In Libya, Selma had achieved close to nothing because SOC, empowered by its status as a subsidiary of a government entity, had been allowed by the system to use less than honourable methods to sideline her. But while Selma had appeared, at times, frustratingly out of her depth due to the circumstances forced upon her, at no time did I detect in my dealings with her the lack of integrity or honesty that I experienced with Mr Adams.

Not wishing to point an accusatory finger at one specific individual, I would instead deplore a whole system for allowing some professionals to practise law whilst being primarily motivated by financial gain alone, above any consideration for basic decency, ethics or the rights of the victim. Nothing positive came out from this latest collaboration other than a great deal of stress, more monies paid, and more disillusion to add to the large stockpile I'd accumulated since the rape. Following that latest shambolic association, I decided to focus solely on writing to government ministers, newspaper editors, anyone who might listen, and to no longer put my trust in lawyers making exorbitant financial demands whilst still getting me nowhere.

After three years of a hugely frustrating cooperation, I severed all ties with Mr Adams, and began writing to newspaper editors in the hope one would be interested enough in my story. Despite the undoubted professional reputation of those I'd approached, no one responded, not even out of basic courtesy. It was at this time of complete legal limbo that the idea of putting pen to paper to write my story crossed my mind.

TODAY

Any violent criminal act is bound to leave a traumatic psychological impact on its victim, and it took years before I realised just how much my rape experience had affected me. Determined not to let the memory of my ordeal ruin the rest of my days, I strived desperately to neutralise its toxic effects by reliving the full gamut of painful, crippling emotions until I could remember the rape simply as a dark moment in my life that no longer had any power to disrupt my present, my wellbeing or my peace of mind. But it's equally painful remembering the indifference and disregard I was subjected to by those I'd turned to for assistance. It's still difficult coming to terms with the British authorities' decision not to intervene despite being aware that their input was critical to my case.

Two months after the rape, an officer at the Brega police station had declared—in a brazen example of corruption at play—that nothing would happen unless pressure 'from above' was exerted on the Libyan authorities. In a nutshell, my case was hindered from the start by the passivity of the British authorities and their refusal to apply any pressure on their Libyan counterparts to do their job. I'd been wronged while I'd rightly expected a retribution that never came. It is an innate expectation for a crime victim to be given his or her due process rights, especially in our so-called enlightened, sophisticated world. Peace and closure only follow after justice is served; when justice isn't forthcoming, then the judicial system has failed abysmally in its duties to uphold the law and protect victims.

The notion that a rape case could be deliberately waved aside by the authorities responsible for law enforcement is deeply disturbing, and the significance of such a callous state of affairs should not be understated. How could it ever be acceptable for any governmental authority to be aware of a citizen's struggle following a rape within a foreign, hostile environment and not step in? What justified granting a rapist freedom from prosecution when his identity and whereabouts were known to authorities, when he'd admitted to his crime, when DNA and an eye witness were available? Why would both the Libyan and British authorities allow such an unjust situation to unfold? Why such blatant dereliction of duty on both sides? Why would the British authorities allow a state-owned entity of a country it paid millions in yearly financial aid to, to evade its responsibility in the violent rape of one of its nationals? Was the fiasco of my rape an isolated case or standard occurrence in cross-border crimes? These are some of the legitimate questions that still beg for answers.

Bearing in mind the rape happened less than two years after the end of the 2011 Libyan conflict in which Britain was militarily involved, it wasn't far-fetched to connect it to that politically sensitive event, and conclude that my rape had stood in the way of post-conflict relations between the two countries. Both authorities' apparent unwillingness to assist was testament to that and, for that reason, the case was conveniently brushed under the proverbial carpet. Are the powers that be too arrogant to realise that when they fail—either by design or ineptitude—to step up to the plate, their incompetence only opens the doors to endless human suffering? All I'd wanted was the legitimate enforcement of the law in response to the crime against me. Was that too much to ask? All these enduring questions surrounding the debacle of my case could have compromised my mental health forever, and it took sustained, gruelling efforts to keep dark depression at bay.

For several long years after the rape, I seemed to have lost control of my life as it passed from the hands of the rapist into the hands of parties falsely promising assistance while they were committed to offering none. There'll be no lasting peace as long as the rapist remains out there, unpunished and, worse still, free to rape again. When a crime is left deliberately unpunished by those whose duty and obligation it is to prosecute, then the entire justice system fails not only the victim, but the whole society at large. It's a sad indictment of our judicial system that, due to the actions of some actors within it, justice isn't grounded at all times in the spirit of fairness, morality and decency that citizens not only expect, but are entitled to.

There hasn't been any meaningful contact with the Foreign Office or the British Embassy since I left Libya in 2014, although the Foreign Office reiterated, in a letter of May 2020, that it 'continued to take the case seriously but that there was no more it could do at this stage to help'. It also stated that it appreciated my 'frustrations' at the 'lack of movement by the Libyan authorities over the last few years...' Wrong! My 'frustrations' were caused principally by the 'lack of movement' from the British authorities themselves! Clearly, it's far more convenient for the Foreign Office to play a pass-the-buck game and blame the Libyans for the whole debacle instead of admitting to its own blatant failure to act effectively.

My response to that letter received no reply. Despite that last statement from the Foreign Office that it 'continued to take my case seriously', my case is as dead as ever, and I have no illusions whatsoever that anyone within that institution would be interested in giving it the kiss of life any time soon. I've had plenty of time on my hands to ponder the British authorities' shortcomings in their handling of my case. I was aware that their assistance wasn't an automatic entitlement, but I'd expected that the brutal rape of one of their nationals would warrant their close involvement. In fact, I never doubted that the British Embassy in Tripoli would step up, especially after requesting, from the outset, every relevant, specific detail and document relating to the rape—all names, dates, addresses of medical centres, hospitals, police stations, etc.—and keeping regular contact with me. I'd been ignorant at the time of the precise support to expect from the embassy, or of the process involved in a case such as mine, but who could the embassy assist if it turned down a rape victim? I'd needed concrete help tailored to my specific circumstances, but received none.

While the reason for the embassy's passivity was made clear a year later with its astonishing statement that it 'didn't get involved in individual cases', the tragic reality remains that the embassy's lack of intervention opened the door wide to the Libyan authorities' own dereliction of duty. Again, I won't point the finger at any individual in particular, but at a wider system that shamelessly allows cases such as mine to be denied redress for any reason. I unapologetically maintain that the covert dealings between two governments robbed me of my right to justice. Besides both countries' unwillingness to assist, I'd also been warned several times that my case required exorbitant amounts of funds to be put in front of the British courts. This, in itself, highlights the unequal state of our justice system, while many aspects of the law, as they stand, aren't in line with the values of fairness and equality that our society is supposed to uphold. I'd always believed that justice was a right, not a privilege and yet, I found myself trapped inside a crooked system bent on withholding it from me. At this stage, even though there appears to be not the slightest chance for redress, the eternal optimist in me still clings to the hope that someday, somehow, justice will prevail. And until that day, I shall seize every opportunity to expose the unethical dealings I encountered as a result of the rape. Many times over the last few years, I've felt lost inside a convoluted maze, unable to find a way out of my ordeal; until the rapist is prosecuted and SOC made to face its responsibility, then a small part of me will, somehow, remain trapped inside that maze.

Most of the women's rights organisations I contacted following the rape—including the 'MeToo' movement—didn't respond; those who did expressed sympathy, but could offer nothing else due to the complexities of my case which, although it had all the elements of an open-and-shut case, made it hopelessly complicated to deal with outside of Libya: the flawed cross-border legislation, the country's typically unreliable system, the recent war, SOC's privileged position as a subsidiary of a major state-owned corporation...

Having absolutely nothing to lose, I wrote to a handful of top human rights lawyers, who also didn't respond. There was something particularly galling about turning to a prominent professional, and not being granted the courtesy of a response. Regardless of the lip service paid to sexual violence, the fiasco of my case showed me that the issue is far from being dealt with seriously, and that prejudiced attitudes prevail not only within society at large, but within the legal system itself.

In the summer of 2015, during a meeting with a small group of lawyers at a prestigious London venue, one commented that damages granted by the courts couldn't be expected 'to be as high for a sixty-year-old woman as for a younger woman'. As if this wasn't shocking enough, another chimed in with his belief that the ordeal suffered by an older rape victim 'couldn't be comparable to that of a younger victim'. Each outrageous statement was delivered with conviction and met with nods of agreement from the group. I couldn't believe my ears. How could such offensive words be uttered by highly educated, forward-thinking professional men, in one of the most progressive countries in the world?

I was reminded of Selma's comment that it wouldn't be 'fair' for me to be compensated just because I was a 'foreigner'. Her words had exposed a prejudice based on nationality, but I was a million miles from expecting one based on age from the legal system itself, but there it was. Wrong country to be raped in, wrong nationality, and now wrong age—I wondered what was the right criteria for a rape victim to qualify for justice!

I'd learnt through my research on societies' attitudes towards sexual violence crimes over the centuries that, in medieval Europe, the rape cases of wives, widows or women considered as 'lower class' were deemed not worth pursuing in the courts, their rapists being simply released on the payment of a small fine or, in some cases, marriage to their victims. In my case, in our enlightened twenty-first century, the rapist was released without even the payment of a small fine! It would be downright laughable if it wasn't so tragic. My whole experience demonstrated not only the lack of consideration and commitment to cases like mine, but also the prejudices that invariably raise their ugly heads to complicate the issue, and create highly prejudicial obstacles to the sound, orderly functioning of societies. In a world where women's lifestyles or attire could, at times, still be perceived as partly to blame for their rape, then these prejudices have to be fought tooth and nail. Archaic attitudes attached to sexual violence crimes need to be eliminated so victims are granted their rights to justice inside a healthy, dignified environment.

Despite rape laws in place, lip service paid to the issue and powerful women movements in place, women are still being raped and, in many cases, not taken seriously by the system, as evidenced by the lenient sentences meted out to their rapists. The situation is clearly far worse in countries like Libya, where sexual crimes are reduced to a convenient taboo crippling the victims' lives. Although Libya's penal code criminalises sexual violence and provides for the prosecution of perpetrators, it also provides that, in some specific circumstances, the offence and its penal consequences may be invalidated if the perpetrator agrees to marry his victim. For the judicial system itself to suggest a victim be married to her rapist shows not only a dangerous lack of awareness of the traumas inflicted on a rape victim by her rapist, but it trivialises the crime itself and compounds the victim's ordeal by punishing her further. By dismissing the rapist's crime upon marriage to his victim, the legal system legitimises the crime after the fact, effectively breaching the victim's right to justice and granting immunity from prosecution to the rapist. There could never be any deals between a rape victim and her rapist. It's high time to put an end to this legacy of amoral disregard of the victim's basic rights, and to the amnesty of the rapist.

As an abominable human rights violation, the only redress to sexual violence crimes is the systematic enforcement of the appropriate laws to bring about the only acceptable outcome—justice for the victim and punishment for the rapist. Justice could never be served by subjecting the victim to a marriage to her rapist, and to the added psychological trauma, and perhaps even physical violence, associated with such an arrangement. Real justice for the victim doesn't include marriage to her rapist. Justice for victims in countries like Libya will only begin when these societies face up to the reality that sexual crimes happen within their societies too, and that hiding them under a convenient taboo only serves to compound the victims' ordeal further, and to grant impunity to criminals. The 'shame' which is automatically heaped on the victims needs to be directed squarely towards the perpetrators, and on all those in authority who, at times, prefer to look the other way. Early education is the only solution to break free from these societal taboos as keeping the issue of sexual crimes silent will only make this evil fester and spread its malignant tentacles into the next generations.

Even though justice has been non-existent in my case, I decided years ago to always be hopeful that it could still happen one day; it's my way of keeping mentally sound and motivated to continue on with my life. With hindsight, I understand that there were far too many obstacles—some deliberate—that turned my quest for justice into a long uphill struggle that was doomed from the start. Doomed because of the unscrupulous actors behind the scenes within the Libyan and British systems paying empty lip service to resolving a crime they had no intention of resolving. The resounding outcome of these parties' unwillingness to carry out their duties is that a Libyan rapist has evaded prosecution, remaining a potential danger to other women in Libya, whilst a subsidiary of a government corporation has arrogantly flouted its responsibility in a serious crime by terminating my employment contract in the most treacherous fashion. My abiding indignation is that my case could've been resolved in no time, if only the powerful British authorities had been willing to apply the slightest amount of pressure 'from above' on the Libyan authorities.

As soon as it became obvious to the Libyans that my case elicited little interest or commitment from the British Embassy, they relaxed their due diligence, their early efforts dwindling until they merely played a delaying game and they waited to remove me from their country. And all under the nose of a lethargic British Embassy. If international law on cross-border crimes is as profoundly inadequate as my case shows it to be by not going far enough to protect victims, then a critical overhaul is needed without delay. The British authorities held the undisputed star role in respect of overall incompetence despite their declarations of 'full consular assistance' and 'determination to pursue this case until justice was forthcoming'. As though the trauma of the rape wasn't enough, their failure to intervene meaningfully made me feel like a third-class citizen unworthy of their consideration. They held all the power to overturn an unjust situation, but chose to do nothing. Their consistently feeble stance led directly to the denial of justice in my case.

I was at the receiving end of their lack of real involvement and suffered its devastating impact. While they contend that they did all they could, the fact remains that whatever they think they did was clearly massively inadequate when compared with the steps they could have taken to bring about the redress I was entitled to. I certainly expected higher standards from such a powerful institution, and I paid the highest possible price for their refusal to stand up against the injustice meted out to one of their nationals. If constraints, or inadequacies, within the British system are such that they prevent effective assistance to nationals abroad, then, again, critical internal reviews are urgently needed there too. In place of the real assistance I should have received, I was offered plenty of sympathy, which I was initially grateful for, but sympathy alone doesn't cut it for a rape victim. The British authorities' inadequacy in dealing with my case proved so detrimental that I came to bitterly regret the non-involvement of the French Consulate. The British Embassy had waved its French counterpart aside in the early days when it decided that it would handle my case itself—and it sure did a fine job of getting me nowhere! I often wondered why the British Embassy, in view of its unwillingness to intervene, hadn't simply passed the case over to its French counterpart. I certainly believe that the French authorities would have lived up to their stalwart reputation by providing all the support my case had needed, and, who knows, maybe even closure.

While on some rare occasions some inherent elements of a crime might render it unsolvable despite the authorities' best efforts, my case had held no such impediments or challenges to place it in this category. Both the Libyan and British authorities were handed everything on a plate—the rapist's name, whereabouts, fingerprints, DNA, eye witness… They were even made aware of his admission to the crime, and yet, none of this overwhelming evidence was enough to get him arrested, let alone prosecuted. To compound the unfairness of the case even further, and if it is indeed true that SOC reinstated the rapist at work, then the spirit of justice has been intolerably trampled upon to demonstrate that rampant corruption is alive and well at the highest levels. The British authorities were aware that a major company—owned by a major government corporation of a country it paid millions in financial aid to—had a direct responsibility in a crime against a British national, and yet, they didn't feel it appropriate to intervene. There clearly were forces behind the scenes set on protecting a rapist and a state-owned company, in shameful disregard of the victim's rights.

In the face of such injustice, I had an easy choice to make: throw in the towel and let the case slowly fade into oblivion, or doggedly press ahead until someone paid attention, however long it might take. I decided that the latter was the only option left to be heard and, hopefully, make a difference, however small, for the next victim—because there will be other victims as long as rapists are allowed to get away with their crimes, and women have to continue living in fear inside a society unwilling to fully protect them. And I hope, with all my heart, that the next victim won't have to go through the shabby treatment I endured. That my rapist was allowed to escape punishment is beyond my comprehension, and is only evidence of the hypocritical lip service paid to sexual crimes globally. I often wonder how many other women were subjected to similar inadequate treatment since I couldn't possibly be the only one to whom it was meted out. There has to be systematic justice for the victims and automatic punishment through the courts for the rapists. This entails unequivocal commitment from the justice system to deal with sexual crimes from a zero tolerance perspective, and the application of the full force of the law to sentencing as the pitiful sentences often handed out are clearly insufficient to deter potential rapists.

My case is evidence that the judicial system has a long way to go before it can rightly proclaim to deliver on its obligations towards all victims of sexual violence crimes. My experience opened my eyes to the reprehensible, unacceptable manner the distribution of justice is perverted when a case is deemed unworthy of redress by the powers that be of two nations. Not a glowing, empowering conclusion to arrive at, but what other one could I realistically draw?

It hasn't been easy coming to terms with the depressing reality that justice was wilfully denied to me—first by the inaction of two governments, then by an onerous judicial system beyond my financial means to access. It's a sad fact that some of the law professionals I turned to were more interested in the monetary gains from the case than in actively defending my rights. I've had to keep my case alive by chasing after developments myself, wherever and however I could. I've had to document the case myself at great risk to my personal safety when SOC denied Selma access into the compound. I've had to track down every government minister that might assist. I've had to chase after the downright unethical lawyers that consistently failed to deliver on work they'd been paid to carry out. As a result of my experience, I shall make no apology for the deep resentment I harbour towards these parties.

For a number of years following the rape, I suffered panic attacks, flashbacks and sleepless nights, which were compounded tenfold by my frustrations at the rapist still being free, and at having sought redress both in Libya and the UK without achieving the slightest headway. My whole life had been turned upside down, and I seethed at the sneaky, deceptive manner my working days were cut short by SOC, at the hypocrisy displayed by the authorities involved, at being patronised to 'get over it' as though my rape was of no importance, at the bitter realisation that I'd been cast aside whilst the rapist walked away scot-free, at the constant fear, the sleepless nights, at the obsession with making my environment as safe as possible and never feeling it remotely was, at the systematic suspicion of any male presence around me, at my overwhelming desire to escape from everything and everyone, at the mounting indignation that, for years, something out of my control had robbed me from fully enjoying my family and my life, and at the overwhelming injustice of it all.

While nothing could erase the memory of the rape, the distress it caused me in the early years, or the frustrations I faced throughout, I'm blessed that I've been able to let go of the crushing weight that the rape and its aftermath had once placed on my shoulders. I might have forgiven the rapist for the sake of my wellbeing, but my enduring rancour remains for the dismissive, unacceptable manner I've been treated with by both the Libyan and British authorities, and the reprehensibly duplicitous way SOC ended my employment to stifle a crime within its walls. I can honestly say it was far easier to forgive the rapist than to deal with the inaction and indifference displayed by all the authorities involved, the lack of ethics of some law professionals and SOC's calculated deception. And there will be no forgiveness for all the parties that inflicted even more hardship on a rape victim it was their duty to help. But, as long as I'm able to breathe, I'll keep the flames of my quest for justice burning and, until it is forthcoming, I'll keep on fanning those flames. I'll continue pushing ahead, but I refuse to be over-burdened by my grim experience. For I know that with each passing day I succeed in tweaking my mind away from frustration and resentment towards positive thinking, I'm inching closer to the real mental freedom I aspire to.

My Spanish home, with its calming surroundings, has proved to be the perfect solution to keeping the rape and its aftermath in the past, and making me concentrate instead on all the blessings still out there. I'd been trapped for so long inside my disastrous predicament that I'd lost sight of the carefree person I was before it all happened. For a few years, I'd let uncontrolled pain and anguish gnaw at my core until I was lucky to recognise the need to disable their destructive effects. My decision to forgive the rapist before leaving England for a fresh start abroad to focus on things other than my rape experience was the catalyst to regaining the carefree spirit and joy for life that the rape had cheated me out of. My providential move to Spain, with all its wonderful challenges, proved to be the way out of the dark hole I'd been locked in for so long. I've reached a level of inner peace that I never thought possible after the rape and despite my legal case dying a slow death, I still remain optimistic that one day justice will prevail. Only then will I be able to close the Libyan chapter once and for all, and leave the past firmly behind.

I'll forever be thankful that, despite the resounding debacle that this experience has proved to be, my innate optimism never deserted me for too long, and my unwavering faith in God consistently lifted my spirits up to enable me to bounce back from the darkest moments. I'll forever be grateful that I didn't suffer a worse mental impact from the emotional journey through the rape and its aftermath. As the prospect of a resolution of my case fades with time, I find great comfort in my belief that God will one day be the supreme judge of this deliberate fiasco. But in the meantime, I'm continuing my fight through this book as it highlights the lonely, torturous journey towards *injustice* that a rape victim might be forced to travel on.

This book is my way of screaming that I shall not be silenced to all those who tried to hush my voice. After years of sustained, but vain efforts to obtain justice, with all the ensuing setbacks and disappointments, I'm thankful that there are other ways outside of the courts of fighting and exposing an injustice and, hopefully, making an impact. I've learnt the hard way that law and justice are two very different notions, and that the first doesn't guarantee the second as the justice system will be only as good—or as bad—as those operating it.

As someone who tended to see life through rose-tinted glasses, this most traumatic time of my life has given me a more realistic view of the world around me, and has even enhanced the person I once was. Yet again, life showed me just how excruciatingly painful and unjust it could be, but, as an eternal optimist, I hold on tight to the notion that since there is nothing remotely certain about my case succeeding one day, then conversely, anything and everything is still possible to make it succeed! While a civil case against SOC was filed in the London courts in June 2016, a pre-action protocol letter was forwarded in March 2020 to both SOC and NOC who, true to form, didn't see fit to respond. Since colossal amounts of funds are needed to kickstart court proceedings, the case sits on a shelf, gathering dust and dying a slow death. But the mere fact that there is a case against SOC filed in the London courts will keep my hopes forever alive that the company is not entirely off the hook and that all is not lost yet.

My rape experience opened my eyes to the potential of human beings for infinite corruption, but also for goodness and decency. It also revealed the enduring power of the human spirit to keep going against all odds for I'll keep on going despite all those who deemed my voice unworthy of being heard, who wanted me to be invisible when I desperately fought to be counted. All the naive, wide-eyed faith I had in the judicial system to protect all people indiscriminately and correct the wrongs of this world slowly disintegrated as events in my case unfolded and I experienced how dishonourable some players inside the system could be. It wasn't a swift realisation to make; it took many years to come to that stark, but only possible deduction, acknowledge it, and be grateful for the empowering challenge of penning my story down on paper to expose the deplorable treatment I received as a rape victim.

For a long time, as the denial of justice robbed me of my inner peace, I feared that all the negative emotions surrounding my case would seriously perturb my mind unless my experience could be beneficial to even just one person. Today, I'm continuing to expose my case through this book while honouring the promise made to my female Libyan colleagues that I wouldn't abandon the fight, and that my struggle would also be theirs. I've never forgotten that promise of all those years ago, and, on many occasions, it kept me pressing ahead when on the verge of capitulation. I dare hope that my story will inspire a change in attitudes towards sexual violence issues—especially in countries like Libya—as well as a review of the laws governing cross-border crimes and the handling of victims of these crimes. But I'm realistic that not one person can make a difference alone; the entire society, from ordinary citizens to the relevant professional bodies, needs to stand up for a zero tolerance of sexual crimes, and call for an eradication of this evil amongst us by the power of early education. Children will learn to respect one another, irrespective of gender, from the way we, as adults, conduct ourselves and interact with one another. If adults role model respect for themselves and others, show compassion and non-judgment towards others, then these attitudes will automatically pass on to our children to create, in time, a fairer and healthier society for all. By what we, as adults, expose our young children to, we'll either set the building blocks for a just and sound society, or seriously undermine it to create hell for the future. And no society can label itself as remotely civilised as long as its women are raped and their rapists allowed to get away with their crimes.

My rape will always be an issue I'll dislike thinking about and one I wish had been resolved to allow me to turn the page once and for all on this bleak, oppressive chapter of my life. Unless justice is served, it will hang over me like a bothersome cloud, but I am determined not to let it impact my daily life or wellbeing. For many years, I fixated so hugely on the rape and its consequences that I was blinded to the wider picture—all the good in my life that I'd set aside to focus only on the darkness of that dramatic event. For years, I felt imprisoned inside a dark, scheming world that I couldn't escape from, while all my thoughts were strictly about the rape and ways to overcome the obstacles I encountered along the road to justice.

For the sake of my own sanity, I had to reformat my thinking into a healthier mindset. By recognising the power of my own thoughts, I managed to put that traumatic event into perspective by reminding myself of the untold number of people who suffered far worse pain and grief than I would ever know. By understanding that my mental disposition towards that dark event was the key to overcoming its impact, I began focusing instead on the simple joys of being alive. By being thankful for each day that God made, I blocked all the crippling thoughts about the rape that had lived inside me for so long. I'll be forever grateful that I was able to embrace hope instead of pessimism by turning to the Higher Power to raise my spirits and keep me optimistic. From the first moment I stood at the foot of those gigantic Spanish mountains that encircled my home, I felt profoundly connected to both my vulnerability as a human being and to the all-encompassing spiritual power within my surroundings. I realised what a minuscule place each one of us occupies in the grand scheme of things, and pondered the futility of life and the dangers of clinging to worldly trappings. I feel immensely privileged to have not only recognised the wisdom of forgiving the rapist, but to have mustered the willpower and ability to do so.

My gratitude at having escaped with my life helped me accept my grief as it stirred my rage towards positivity instead, whilst the act of forgiveness saved me from holding on to untold trauma and misery. My London doctor's diagnosis that I'd live with the rape trauma for the rest of my days was spot on as I gradually noticed transformations taking place in me. I've had to make adjustments to my life and mindset in order to accommodate the inevitable changes taking place inside me, and had to accept that I'll never be the happy-go-lucky person I once was, but that it was OK not to be. I've no qualms swapping pavements if uncomfortable at a male's presence too close to me in the street, or at exiting elevators if a man walks in just as the door's about to close. The month of June is no longer just the beginning of the glorious summer months, but a yearly reminder of that harrowing event; the number 7, the year 2013, the mere mention of Libya, these are all triggers that once had the power to unlock the doors to a distressing memory that refused to bury itself permanently inside the deepest recesses of my mind. It was like an old wound that could burst open at any moment, or at the most innocuous occasions. I've accepted any over-reaction as a normal, justified consequence of a traumatic experience, turning it into a new quirk to fit into my new reality.

I believe that there's a lesson in everything significant that happens in my life, and that each person or event I come across on my journey holds a secret to bring increased insight and wisdom. I understood earlier on that the rape trauma would cause me to either shut down or, conversely, spur me into action, and that it wasn't necessarily my choice to make. I'll be forever thankful to have been guided towards the second option, but I'm still patiently waiting to discover any positives that the rape and its aftermath are supposed to teach me on a higher level! In the meantime, I'm grateful that I've been inspired into penning my story in this book and, through it, I'll hopefully achieve even greater goals.

I've lived through fear, grief, bitterness, despair and rage, but only my faith in God has kept me away from the destructive emotion of all-encompassing hate. I'm grateful to have found in my Spanish home the peace and tranquillity to soothe my once troubled mind, and rebuild myself. Despite the tragic events of my last year in Libya, I refuse to hold on to painful memories of the country that had once been my home away from home. Fate directed me to Libya when I'd yearned for a change from my life in London. I'd hoped for a new exciting chapter and, for over a decade, my time in Libya proved to be just that. I'd delved into my life there with endless joy and hope for the future, never suspecting for a second that an experience that started so full of promise would meet such a crushing end.

My time in Libya opened my eyes to human nature's most glowing facets, but to its darkest ones too. The last year I spent in Libya—2014—was a time of endless mental anguish and terror, which I felt unable to share with even my closest friends there. The world around me had moved on, my rape was nobody's preoccupation, and I didn't feel that I could burden anyone with either my fears or ongoing legal battles. I hardly slept at night for the whole of that year, keeping my feelings firmly bottled up inside. The gym opposite my house became a refuge I'd escape to daily for solace. Libya was indeed the place of one of the most harrowing events in my life, but it was also the place of untold magical and happy moments, which I'll cherish for as long as I live. All the happy memories and times I enjoyed in Libya are entangled into a bittersweet mishmash, and will live in my heart forever.

I'd made plans to visit the whole of Libya before retiring, and bitterly regret that these plans will never materialise. I've more of a chance of travelling to planet Mars one day than being granted a visa into Libya, although the incurable optimist in me still holds on to a tiny bit of hope that, just maybe, I'd get the chance to return to the country I'd loved enough to call home for over a decade. The vile actions of one criminal, of those who protected him and cast me aside, won't make me dislike a whole people, or erase the wonderful times I lived through in their beautiful country.

I still follow the current events in Libya and pray for the day that the Libyan people are able to constructively take charge of their country to solve the consequences of the chaos unleashed upon them by their 'liberators'. It is heartbreaking to observe that today, the Libyans are fighting one another in deadly power struggles. As an oil-rich country with a small population, Libya possesses all the building blocks to emerge as the next El Dorado if only it came to its senses. Its people certainly deserve that much.

I ceased thinking of myself as a rape victim the moment I forgave the rapist, but the fact remains that the system designed to render justice failed me miserably, and that I'm still the victim of unacceptable treatment at the hands of both the Libyan and British authorities. I've learnt to my detriment that justice isn't some abstract force that automatically comes into play to redress a wrong. No, it's an institution like any other run by human beings, many fully dedicated to its noble cause while others are motivated by considerations contrary to the very notion of ethics and morality, and above all, justice. Even in an open-and-shut case such as mine, my experience taught me that the justice system couldn't always be relied upon to prevail. I'd prayed for justice to be served so that I could attain that proverbial closure, but the ineptitude and corruption displayed by many whose duty it was to assist got in the way. I lived throughout my entire life with the false notion that my human rights were guaranteed under the law until I discovered, at the most critical time in my life, that I was powerless to exercise them, and that, in reality, I had none.

While my dealings with the British and Libyan authorities have shaken my trust in the justice system to the core, I still cling tightly to the idea that justice will be served one day; it is my subconscious mind's way of keeping my spirits high as I advance on my life journey. And until that day comes, I'll keep on giving thanks that my life is indeed richly blessed despite what happened. While the shoddy, dismissive treatment my case received often made me feel like the principal, wretched character of a bad movie, this time, I'm relying on myself alone to write a happy ending. I wake up each morning in awe at the glorious serenity of my Spanish surroundings, immensely thankful at being alive to witness the dawn of yet another day and all the fascinating things it might bring along with it—hopeful that, one day, it will bring justice too. Only then will I be truly liberated and ready to close the rape chapter once and for all. And until that day comes, I refuse to allow the horrid event of a glorious summer's afternoon, in a beautiful far-away country, to cast a single shadow upon my hard-earned, new-found sense of peace and contentment.

www.ingramcontent.com/pod-product-compliance
Lightning Source LLC
Chambersburg PA
CBHW031117020426
42333CB00012B/125